SANNYASI AND FAKIR RAIDERS IN BENGAL

SANNYASI AND FAKIR RAIDERS IN BENGAL

BY

RAI SAHIB JAMINI MOHAN GHOSH

GYAN

Published by

Gyan Publishing House
5, Ansari Road
Daryaganj, New Delhi-110002
Phone: 011-47034999, 9811692060
E-mail: books@gyanbooks.com

Distribution Network
gyanbooks.com
India, USA, Canada, UK, Australia

ISBN: 978-93-6433-328-3 (PB)
First Published, 1930

2nd Impression 2024

Printed at: Gyan Press, Delhi.

SANNYASI AND FAKIR RAIDERS IN BENGAL
Author: RAI SAHIB JAMINI MOHAN GHOSH

SANNYASI AND FAKIR RAIDERS IN BENGAL

[For "Sannyasi and Fakir Raiders in Bengal"]

Etched by J. A. Atkinson, from the original Drawing by Deen Allee

A Mohunt and Gossains

[See foot-note page 17]

[Reproduced from Broughton's "Letters from the Mahratta Camp during the year 1809." Published April 5, 1813, by J. Murray, Albermarle Street, London]

SANNYASI AND FAKIR RAIDERS IN BENGAL

by

RAI SAHIB JAMINI MOHAN GHOSH, B.A.

BENGAL CIVIL SERVICE

COMPILED MAINLY FROM OFFICIAL RECORDS

CALCUTTA
BENGAL SECRETARIAT BOOK DEPOT
MCMXXX

Preface

This volume traces the activities of the bands of Sannyasis and Fakirs who infested many parts of Bengal in the latter part of the Eighteenth Century. They were a feature of those unsettled times and their suppression was part of the task imposed on the British in evolving an orderly administration. This narrative has been compiled as a contribution towards the social and local history of rural Bengal and as giving a picture of a state of affairs which has happily long passed away. It is based for the most part on the documents preserved in the Bengal Historical Record Room, and the events have been mostly described in the words of the records themselves.

The material was extracted from the records by the Record Room staff under the direction of Mr. A. Cassells, I.C.S., in 1921-23 and later placed at my disposal. The work of editing and annotating these sources together with the further research involved has been possible only during the scanty leisure gained from official duties during the last few years.

I am deeply indebted to Mr. Cassells for his help and suggestions and constant encouragement and my thanks are due to Babu Suresh Chandra Roy, Keeper of Records to the Government of Bengal, and his staff for their assistance.

J. M. G.

Contents

NOTE.

Original spellings have not always been adhered to in quotations from the original.

Readers interested in finding the location of the parganas and places mentioned in the book will kindly refer to the large scale maps of Rennell issued by the Government of Bengal.

SANNYASI AND FAKIR RAIDERS IN BENGAL

CHAPTER I

Sannyasis and Fakirs

A CONSTANTLY recurring theme in the correspondence of the East India Company's officials, especially those in the northern parts of Bengal, during the latter half of the Eighteenth Century, is the incursions of the nomadic bodies known as the "Sannyasi Fakirs," who annually passed through the districts, levying contributions by violence "under the pretence of charity."[1]

"Sannyasi Fakirs."

Under the Muhammadan rule, these exactions were sometimes sanctioned by Sanads and in any case came to be tolerated by the ruling power which apparently had neither the inclination nor the means to suppress them. The apathy and fatalism of the people of the country encouraged them, as well as the awe and veneration in which these mendicants were held owing to their religious profession. Durlabhram, who was appointed Governor of Orissa by Nawab Ali Vardi Khan (1740—1756), was said to be "much addicted to the Brahmans and Sannyasis or Gentoo Fakirs who entirely governed him...."[2] In 1772, the Fakir leader, Majnu Shah, "appealed" to Maharani Bhawani, the Zamindar of Rajshahi, against what he characterised as unwarrantable persecution by the English, asking "what merit is to be gained by killing Fakirs?" Even twenty years later, the Raja of Nepal, though bound by treaty, refused to take any further steps in punishing a raiding Fakir beyond expelling him from his territories. His reasons were that "although the Fakir is full of faults and deserving of death, yet in the books containing the laws of our religion it is prescribed that except in War it is highly culpable to confine and put to death any of

---

[1] "A set of lawless banditti," wrote the Council in 1773, "known under the name of Sannyasis or Fakirs have long infested these countries and under the pretence of religious pilgrimage have been accustomed to traverse the chief part of Bengal, begging, stealing and plundering wherever they go and as it best suits their convenience to practise."

[2] *Seir Mutaquerin*, Vol. I, p. 2 (Cambray's edition).

the tribe of Zunardars or Fakeers whether Hindoos or Mussalmans."[1] Following their traditional occupation, the Fakirs "thought it strange that the English should object to their easing the richer few of the ryots of money they had not the heart to spend." Sometimes they "seemed to make a merit in not molesting those who had little or nothing to lose."[2] But none the less they were a curse to the country. Broughton in his *Letters from the Mahratta Camp* wrote in 1809:

"The numbers of Faquirs in this camp is enormous; they are of all descriptions, Muhammadans and Hindus, men and women, boys and girls. They are an intolerable nuisance; wandering among the tents throughout the day....asking or rather demanding alms with an importunity and perseverance that is equally insolent and provoking. The Muhammadans are the worst; many of them going about on horseback and asking for rupees with as much assurance as others ask for pice, and the more impertinent they are the greater is their idea of sanctity."

The circumstances favourable to brigandage described by Lord Minto in 1810 are applicable in greater degree to the Eighteenth Century:

"(1) The riches of the country (Bengal) have presented the temptation of good plunder.

"(2) The long security which the country has enjoyed from foreign enemies and the consequent loss of martial habits and character have made the people of Bengal so timid and enervated that no resistance is to be apprehended in the act nor punishment afterwards.

"(3) The best security of all, however, enjoyed by the dacoits has been the intimidation of the unhappy people who are the objects of their rapine and cruelty. It is impossible to imagine, without seeing it, the horrid ascendancy they had obtained over the inhabitants at large of the countries which have been the principal scenes of their atrocities. They had established a terrorism as perfect as that which was the foundation of the French Republican power and in truth the Sirdars or Captains of the band were esteemed and even called the Hakim or ruling power, while the Government did not possess either authority or influence enough to obtain from the people the smallest aid towards their own protection. If a whole village was destroyed not a man was found to complain."

Applications for remission of revenue were encouraged by the corrupt practices of Nawab Riza Khan, and the authorities generally viewed them with suspicion, but when they found that the security of

---

[1] Proceedings of the Governor General in Council, Political Department, dated 13th February, 1795.

[2] Extract from a letter to Mr. Y. Burges, Collector of Purnea, dated 18th January, 1795, from a Commercial Traveller in Nepal.

the agriculturists and the State revenue was threatened by the plundering Sannyasis and Fakirs, they took steps to suppress these abuses. The outcome was a conflict, for the first time in the country between these mendicants and the ruling power, from which the people—Zamindars and their tenants alike—stood aside; indeed they sometimes befriended their oppressors when in trouble. The accounts furnished by the local officials and the Proceedings of the Company's Government supply the materials for the account of the doings of these nomadic tribes in Bengal given in these pages.

The names "Sannyasi" and "Fakir."

Now, who were these "Sannyasi Fakirs"? In the official records of the period the two words are used very loosely, sometimes in juxtaposition and sometimes synonymously. Much confusion therefore exists as to their true import. Even as early as in the middle of the Seventeenth Century, Muhammed Mohsan Fani, in his *Dabistan*, "perpetually confounded Hindu Yogis, Sannyasis and Vairagis with Muhammedan Durvishes."[1] Richardson in his *Arabic-Persian Dictionary* explains the distinction between the terms. He defines "Fakyr" as "A poor man, a religious order of mendicants thus named by the Arabians; by the Persians Dervish or Sof and the Indians Senassey. In this singular class of men, who in Hindoostan despise every species of clothing, there are a number of enthusiasts, but by far a superior proportion of knaves, every vagabond of abilities who has aversion of labour, being received into a fraternity which is governed by laws of uncommon and secret nature. The Hindus view them with a wonderful respect not only on account of their sanctified reputation but for substantial dread of their powers, the Fakeer pilgrimages consisting often of many thousands of naked saints who exact, whenever they pass, a general tribute and their character is too sacred for the civil power to take cognizance of their conduct."[2] The terms are thus distinguished by Wilson: "Sannyasi is a generic term and equally applicable to any of the erratic beggars of the Hindus be they of what religious order they may. It signifies in fact nothing more than a man who has abandoned the world or has overcome his passions and therefore equally suitable to any of the religious vagrants we meet in Hindoostan; the term Fakir is of equally general application and import although of Muhammedan origin and in strictness more descriptive of the holy beggars of that faith."[3] But the words were often applied indifferently to those of either religion.[4] The confusion was helped by the fact that the Muhammadan Fakir

[1]Troyer in his *Preliminary Discourse on Dabistan.*

[2]Quoted in *A View of Hindustan* (Pennant), p. 308.

[3]*Hindu Religions*—H. H. Wilson.

[4]Even to this day the confusion exists. "Fakeer, properly an indigent person but specially 'one poor in the sight of God,' applied to a Muhammadan religious mendicant and loosely and inaccurately to Hindu devotees and naked ascetics. And this last is the most ordinary Anglo-Indian use." Yule and Burnell, *Hobson-Jobson.*

orders being organised in imitation of Hindu Sannyasis, adopted a similar dress and similar habits. It was therefore difficult to distinguish one from the other; specially in later years, hard pressed by the English, Sannyasis and Fakirs sometimes united forces. It will, however, be doing injustice to that great body of the real ascetics—Sannyasis or Fakirs, to regard them as plunderers. There were amongst them persons who were deeply religious and of great learning.

Growth of Sannyasis.

Sankaracharyya, the Hindu revivalist, who flourished in the Eighth Century, rehabilitated the worship of Hindu deities who had suffered at the hands of Buddhists and atheists. He travelled far and carried on his dialectics in different countries; he defeated the learned men of Nepal by his arguments; he compelled the Buddhists to sacrifice animals, and nuns and monks were married by his direction.[1] Sankara was helped by Saiva and Vaisnava princes in his crusades against the Buddhists. He made converts from every sect and class and established *maths* or monasteries for his disciples, e.g., the Sringeri Math on the Tungabhadra in Mysore, the Jyotir Math [Joshi Math][2] near Badrinath in the Garhwal district, the Sarada Math at Dwaraka in the Bombay Presidency and the Gobardhan Math at Puri in Orissa. Sankaracharyya had principal disciples who had again ten pupils. They were named Puri, Giri, Parvata, Sagara, Vana, Aranya, Tirtha, Asrama, Swaraswati, and Bharati. These pupils became the heads of the Dasnami or "ten-named mendicants" and anyone joining the fraternity adopts one of these names. They are ruled by an assembly called Dasnama composed of the representatives of the ten divisions, which has a complete control over all the Maths of the order.[3]

The following extract from Sister Nivedita's *Northern Tirthas* traces the military character of the Sannyasis in charge of monasteries back to the date of their establishment:

> "Ukhi Math was originally granted to the order (Kedarnath order of Sankaracharyya) subject to military service by the old kings of Garhwal of the same line as the present family and very fine reading are the copies of deed which have been made from time to time. The present Raoul [Mohanta] is said to be over hundred and twenty-fifth in succession."

As Sankaracharyya flourished in the beginning of the Eighth Century it may be conjectured that the grants were made at the time of the foundation of the various orders by him. Ukhi Math was connected with the principal Math of the North, viz., the Joshi Math.

---

[1]Wright's *Nepal*.

[2]In Jyotirdham "the dwelling of Jyotirlinga," commonly known by the name of Joshi Math, there are several Vaishnava temples.

[3]Atkinson's *The Himalayan Districts of N. W. P., Vol. II*, p. 862.

In course of time when the country came under the Pathans and the early Moghuls, their military character appears to have been gradually lost although some sects of the Sannyasis continued to bear arms. The excesses committed by them were denounced by the sober sections, and the great religious reformer Kabir, who flourished in the Fifteenth Century, delivered the following diatribe on the Naga Sannyasis: **Armed Sannyasis.**

> "Brothers, I have never seen such Yogis who forsaking their own religion go about on fruitless journeys—when did Dattyatreya demolish houses, when did Narad use muskets, when did Vyasa sound war-drums. In war one loses his religion. He who uses a bow cannot be an *Atit* (one who has relinquished worldly interest)."

The following traditional account of the revival of the armed Sannyasis is given by Rev. Dr. Farquhar:

> "In the Sixteenth Century there were thousands of Muslim Faquirs who went about armed, took part in the wars of the time and when there was no regular war fought for their own hand. One of their practices as good Muslims, was to attack and kill Sannyasis as representatives of Hinduism. As ascetics, these Faquirs held a privileged position and were thus protected from violence and also from interference on the part of the Government which was then Muhammadan. Thus when Sannyasis were killed, no one was punished while Sannyasis themselves were prevented from taking violent measures against their enemies by their vows of *Ahimsa*. Madhusudan Saraswati, a well-known Sannyasi scholar of the Saraswati sub-order, who lived in Benares in the middle of the century, at last went to Akbar to see whether anything could be done for the protection of the ancient order to which he belonged. Raja Birbal was present at the interview and suggested the way out of the difficulty. He advised Madhusudan to initiate a large number of non-Brahmans into the Sannyasi order and arm them for the protection of the Brahman Sannyasis. The Emperor agreed that armed Sannyasis should be protected by their sacred character from Government interference ....At first doubtless armed Sannyasis, used to defend Brahman Sannyasis, but soon like the Yogis, who had taken to arms long before them, large groups of them began to fight on their own account, seized lands and settled down to an easy life. Some built monasteries on their lands and tried to continue the ascetic life, but many of them married and thus became hybrids."[1]

In 1567, Akbar witnessed a fight between armed Sannyasis of "Giri" and "Puri" sub-orders at Thaneswar.[2] According to Vincent Smith, this fight was over the offerings by pilgrims who had come there to bathe during an eclipse. In 1640, there was a fight between the Sannyasis

---

[1] *Journal of the Royal Asiatic Society of Great Britain and Ireland*, July, 1925; *The Organisation of the Vedanta*, by J. N. Farquhar, M.A., D.LITT. (OXON).

[2] *Eliot's History*—Dawson, Vol. V, p. 318.

and Mundis or Vairagis in which the Sannyasis were victorious and thousands of Mundis were killed. The Nagas had similar fights with the Madari and Jelali sects of Fakirs. Writing in the middle of the Seventeenth Century, Muhammed Mahsan Fani in his *Dabistan* describes "the Sanyasis being frequently engaged in war." "Even in the pristine days of the Moghul power an army of Sannyasis led by an old woman calling herself an enchantress had at one time defeated the army of the Emperor Aurungzebe and made him tremble on his peacock-throne at Delhi."[1]

Armed Naga Sannyasis.

Regarding the Nagas, it is stated that "all the sects of Sannyasis include a division under this denomination. The Nagas in their excess of zeal carry their secession from ordinary manners so far as to leave off every kind of covering and, as their names signify, go naked. There are, however, other points in which they differ from the general character of the Hindu mendicants and they unquestionably are the most worthless and profligate members of their respective religion. A striking proof of their propensities is their use of arms. They always travel with weapons, usually a metal lock and sword and shield, and that these weapons are not carried in vain has been shown in many instances. The Saiva Nagas smear their bodies with ashes, allow their hair, beard and whiskers to grow and wear the projecting braid of hair called the Jata. Like the Vairagi Nagas, they carry arms and wander about in troops soliciting alms or levying contributions. The Saiva Nagas are very numerous in many parts of India. They were formerly in great numbers in Bundelkhand. These Nagas are the particular opponents of Vairagi Nagas and were no doubt the leading actors in the bloody fair at Haridwar which had excluded the Vaishnavs from the great fair there, from 1760 till the British acquired the country."[2] The same writer also states: "The Nagas of Dadu Panthi carry arms which they are willing to exercise for hire and amongst the Hindu princes they have been considered as good soldiers. The Dadu Panthis are said to be numerous in Marwar and Ajmere; of the Naga class alone, the Raja of Jaipur is reported to entertain as soldiers more than ten thousand."

The following account of the Naga army is given by William Irvine in his *Army of the Indian Moghuls*:—

Naga Army.

"Nagas—These bodies of so-called Hindu devotees were common in the armies of the Eighteenth Century and I believe to this day the Raja of Jaipur entertains a large number of them. There was a corps of them in the Audh service from about 1752 to the end of the century. The last leader of them was Raja Himmat Bahadur whose name appears so frequently in our own early connection with Bundelkhand. With this exception, Mohamedans do not seem to have

[1] James Grant's *History of India*, Vol. I, pp. 159-60.

[2] *Hindu Religions*—H. H. Wilson.

retained any of the Fakirs in their employ. Anquetil DuPerron (*Zend Avesta*) describes a body of these armed vagabonds numbering some 6,000 men on their way to Jagannath. The three leaders marched first, a long pike in one hand and a buckler in the other. The main body was armed with swords, bow and matchlocks. Haji Mustafa during his adventurous attempt in 1758 to reach Muslipatam *via* Western Bengal and Pachet came across five thousand of these devotees on their way to the Ganges at Sagor—'they were all of them tall, stout, well-built men in general, stark-naked, but very well armed.' (Dalrymple's *Oriental Repertory*, ii, 239). Blacker says that 'Gossys, i.e, Gossains or Nagas have always been considered good troops.' They are a Hindu caste of peculiar habits scattered over different parts of India."

Another recorded incident is the following :

Sannyasis as mercenary soldiers.

Mohan Singh, a usurper of Kumaon State, was driven away by the Raja of Garhwal who put his son Pradhan Chand (1779—86) on the throne. Mohan Singh went on a pilgrimage and at Allahabad met the leader of a fighting body of religious mendicants known as Nagas and promised him the plunder of Almora if he assisted in the invasion of Kumaon. The Naga leader consented and with 1,400 men under four Mohunts proceeded to the hills. They entered Kumaon by the Kosi and under the pretence of being pilgrims on their way to Badrinath got as far as the confluence of the Suwal and the Kosi before their real character was discovered. Harak Deb the principal officer of Pradhan Chand posted his forces at Charalekh and sending a present of money to the Nagas asked them to retire but urged by Mohan Singh they attacked the Kumaon forces and were totally defeated leaving seven hundred of their dead in the ravines of the Kosi.[1]

In Northern India.

The earliest record of these mendicant soldiers in Bengal is from a report, dated 29th December, 1761, of Capt. Martin White at Camp Battassy ka Bagh in which he writes of "an action with the combined forces of the Burdwan Raja Missery Khan, Dudar Singh, the Faquirs and a party from Beerbhoom at the pass of the river between Burdwan and Sangatgola."[2] In 1764, Sannyasis were hired by the deposed Nawab Mir Kasim of Bengal in his attempt to get back the *Masnad* of Bengal. Writing on 12th May, 1764, Sayyid Bandal Khan, Faujdar of Hooghly, reports to the Governor at Fort William as follows :

In Bengal.

"He learns that on the 3rd instant, the Nawab Suja-ud-dulah [of Oudh], Raja Beni Bahadur [Governor of Patna], Mir Qasim,

---

[1]Atkinson—*The Himalayan Districts of the N. W. P.*, Vol. II, pp. 602-3.

[2]Long's *Selections from Unpublished Records of Government*, p. 260.

Sumroo,[1] Himmat Ghir and the other commanders of the enemy marched with their whole force with canon, rockets, etc., from their camps two or three *kos* beyond Patna and attacked Major Carnac's entrenchments at Pachapahar. The two armies were engaged with artillery and small arms from 8 o'clock till sunset. The enemy were defeated wherever they made their appearance."[2]

The author of *Seir Mutaquerin* describes the battle as follows :

"Raja Beni Bahadur and Raja Balawant Singh [of Benares] took posts on the left of the Vizier's. He had in his hire three thousand Rohillas commanded by their countrymen Ynaiet Khan, the Rohilla Chief, and at the elbow of this was Ghossain [Himmat Giri] or Fakir with five thousand gentoos as naked as himself. The Ghossain with his naked soldiers advanced to the charge but being received by the English with several discharge of grapes, they soon fell into the utmost disorder after losing numbers in slain and wounded."[3]

With the break-down of the Moghul Empire, the Marhattas visualised the foundation of a Hindu Empire. The wresting of the Punjab by the Marhattas from Ahmed Shah Abdali's son and their combination with the Sikhs were regarded as a menace to the Muhammadan power in India and the Muhammadans such as the Rohillas rallied round Ahmed Shah Abdali at Panipat. The complete defeat of the Marhattas at the Third Battle of Panipat in 1761 and the consequent dissipation of the dream of a Hindu Empire is a matter of history. But the Marhattas and the Sikhs were still powerful till the complete defeat in 1766 of the combined Hindu armies of Sikhs and Marhattas, when the Sikhs were joined by the Ram Kishen Mohant, Umrao Giri Gossain and other Sardars with their respective divisions and Batta Nand Mohant with his troops of Fakirs.[4] These devotees were employed as soldiers even as late as 1809. Writing from the Marhatta camp at Doonee on April 25th, 1809, Broughton says :

In Mahratta Army.

"The army has received a considerable reinforcement since my last letter by the arrival of a body of Gossaoens under Kumpta Gir. This chief succeeded to the command of the corps, which consists of nearly 1,500 men chiefly horse upon the death of Ramgir who died about a month ago. They were both Chelas or disciples of Kunchun

[1]Walter Reinhardt, an Alsatian of Strasburg, whose swarthy look and sullen scowl earned for him the sobriquet of Sombre, corrupted into Sumroo. He joined Mir Kasim and was responsible for the cruel massacre of Patna. His wife Begum Sumroo is better known for her charity and friendship with the English.

[2]*Calendar of Persian Correspondence*, Vol. I, p. 311.

[3]*Seir Mutaquerin*, Vol. II, pp. 531-3.

[4]*Calendar of Persian Correspondence*, Vol. II, p. 5.

> Gir, the Chela of Himmat Bahadur a celebrated Gossain, in the service of Shumsheer Bahadur one of the chiefs of Bundelkhand. The Gossains are a religious order of Hindu mendicants, who attach themselves to the service of particular chiefs ; and frequently, as in the case of Himmat Bahadur, amass great wealth and raise themselves into consequence. They then adopt chelas and are themselves gooroos or teachers. Upon the death of the Gooroo the eldest chela succeeds to his honours ; and after him the others according to the dates of their adoption, before the chelas of the second gooroo. When they become numerous and wealthy, they enrol themselves as a military band in the service of some prince, their leader is termed Mohunt, they then retain but little of their original manner and appearance distinguishing themselves alone by their jutta or long matted hair folded like a turban on the head and having some portion of their dress dyed by a kind of orange colour called Geroo peculiar to their sect. As soldiers they are brave and faithful."[1]

For a time they continued to be employed in the armies of the Holkar, the Scindia, and the Raja of Jaipur, and also to join any band of rebels or insurgents who would hire them, but their organisation as regular soldiers had largely broken down and they formed into smaller groups and carried on depredations during their pilgrimages throughout the country. Rev. Dr. Farquhar wrote : " Vast numbers of ascetic warriors continued to bear arms and fight until the early years of the Nineteenth Century when the British got the upper hand. They gave up fighting though many retained their arms for a long time ; and a few monasteries may be found to-day on the walls of which swords and shields, spears and matchlocks still hang. In the autumn of 1922, when on a visit to Jaipur, a priest escorted me to a beautiful old Jain temple which stands amid the ruins of Amber. Deserted by the Jains, it is used by a group of Naga Sannyasis as a monastery, and on the walls hang many old weapons of war."[2] **In Rajput Army.**

---

[1] *Letters from the Mahratta Camp*—Broughton, p. 129. The Full title of the book, published in 1813, is interesting and gives the circumstances under which Broughton was in the Mahratta Camp. *Letters from the Mahratta Camp during the year 1809, with drawings by a native Artist, by Thomas Duer Broughton, late Commander of the Resident's Escorts in the Court of Scindia.* A picture in colour is given to face page 129 of "a Mohunt and Gossains etched by J. A. Atkinson from the original drawing by Deen Aleo, published and printed in 1813 by J. Murray, Albermarle Street." The Mohunt in white dress is on horse back and carries a lance in one hand, while there is a sword in his girdle. Two Gossains or Sannyasis are dressed in brown loin cloth with another round the body. One of them carries a matchlock, and he has a belt round his waist with powder pouches. The other carries a lance and a sword. The picture is reproduced as a frontispiece to this book.

[2] *The Organization of the Sannyasis of Vedanta*, by J. N. Farquhar, M.A., D.LITT. (OXON.), *Journal of the Royal Asiatic Society of Great Britain and Ireland*, July, 1924.

The existence of hordes of Sannyasis in the second half of the Eighteenth Century was therefore not a new feature in the life of the country.

Hastings' description of Sannyasis.

Warren Hastings as President of the Council recorded the following minute in 1773 on the Sannyasis in Bengal :—

"He cannot learn that they have any fixed abode, but that they chiefly frequent the countries lying at the foot of the chain of mountains which separate Hindustan from Tibbet, wandering continually from the Gogra river in the Domain of the Vizier (Oudh) to the Burramputter and from this line occasionaly penetrating into Euracpoor [Gorakhpur?], Butsea [Bettiah], Tirroot, Purnea, and Rungpur, he finds that except one sect among them called Hunjooghees who never mix with the hordes which infest their more civilized neighbours, they neither marry nor have families, but recruit their members by the stoutest of the children which they steal from the countries through which they pass, that some among them carry on trade in Diamonds, Coral and other articles of great price and small compass and often travel with great wealth[1]—some subsist by gratuitous alms and the others the far greater by plunder: that the various sects of them travel at fixed periods on religious pilgrimages to the Burrumpooter, Byjenath [Baidyanath] and Ganga Saugore, besides those who in all dry months of the year pass through the provinces on their way to Juggernath (Puri); that individuals of them are at all times scattered about the villages and capital towns of the provinces and where the bigotry of the inhabitants afford them an access to their homes and every right of hospitality, which they are suspected of abusing in the most treacherous manner by reuniting with the Corps whenever they enter the country and giving information of the most substantial inhabitants and of the places[2] where their wealth is deposited; that they are continually seen on the roads armed with swords, lances, matchlocks and generally loaded with heavy bundles. The castes of Ramanondo and Goorea are excepted as they are not vagabonds nor plunderers but have fixed place of abode...."

An earlier account of the *modus operandi* of Sannyasis is given in the Letter of the Supervisor at Nattore to the Resident at the Durbar,

[1]A similar description of the trade carried on by the nomadic Sannyasis is given by Bogle in his *Mission to Tibet*:—"Some Sannyasis in Tibet bring from the sea-coasts to the interior part pearls, corals, spices, and other precious articles of small bulk which they exchange for musk, gold-dust and other things of small bulk which they can conceal in their clothes."

[2]In 1763, (during Mir Kasim's time) Gurgin Khan in his expedition to Nepal was supplied with information by Cashmiris, Sannyasis and Fakirs who yearly frequented those parts. *Seir Mutaquerin*, Vol. II, p. 446.

dated 6th January, 1770. "They have their spies stationed over the country to give intelligence of those parts which will afford the richest booty and are most defenceless." And a later report notes that "these tribes seldom commence operation till the emissaries that inhabit the province join their standard and furnish information."[1]

Giri Sect of Sannyasis.

From the description of the Naga Sannyasis given above, it would appear that the caste system peculiar to the Hindu religion found a place even in the ascetic orders of the religion and the fighting castes amongst the various orders of Sannyasis bore the generic name of Naga although they kept the surname of the order. Although originally the Dasnami Sannyasis kept themselves restricted to ascetic life they were latterly forced by the circumstances given in the traditional account, to affiliate a fighting caste to their order. It is probable that the "Giri" sub-order initiated most of the fighting element, for we find marauding Sannyasis commonly bore the surname of "Giri." The nomad bands that invaded Bengal, while generally referred to by the generic name of Sannyasis, were sometimes specifically described as Naga Sannyasis. Where any Sannyasi is found to be named, he usually bears the surname of "Giri," which is one of the sects of the Dasnami Sannyasis.

Resident Sannyasis.

It is necessary to distinguish the nomadic orders from others who may be called the Resident Sannyasis living in Maths or monasteries under the Mohants. The principal monastery of the Giri sect was the Joshi Math in the Himalayas, and subordinate monasteries were scattered throughout Bengal. In these Maths, temples were erected and deities installed, principally the God Siva as most of the devotees were "Saivas" or worshippers of Siva. They were endowed with landed properties of varying extent, and were resorts of the Wandering Sannyasis in their annual travels to their various places of pilgrimage.

Though vowed to a life of abstinence and meditation, these Resident Sannyasis became in course of time avaricious and worldly and enriched themselves by usury and trade. The following account of the Dasnami sect of Sannyasis is given in a Bengali book (*Kasi Barnana*) written in the year 1800: "Many are the monasteries of the Dasnami sect of Sannyasis, who, though outwardly professing abstinence, are in their minds worldly. Every one carries on the business of merchants and money-lenders and have houses as high as hills. In the ears of some are gold ornaments with chains shining like the sun. Some wear gold chains set with diamonds; others have gold chains set with corals. Some again have gold and silver bangles—these are the favourite disciples. Every one puts on ochre-coloured garments and bears arms. Some ride on horses."[2] Besides the religious

[1]Letter from the Collector of Mymensingh to the Governor General in Council, dated 13th January, 1790.

[2]*Kasi Barnana* or a Descriptive Account of the City of Benares by Raja Joynarayan Ghosal, the founder of the Bhukailash Raj Family.

endowments, the Resident Sannyasis acquired valuable properties in the Bengal districts principally by money-lending. To this day large landed properties held by Sannyasis of the Giri sect are to be found in the districts of Bogra, Dinajpur, Malda, Rangpur and Mymensingh. Some Resident Sannyasis not only furnished shelter to the nomadic orders, but actively participated with them in their raids when opportunity occurred and helped them by furnishing information as spies. Speaking of the Resident Sannyasis of Rangpur, Glazier states that the Sannyasis settled down in hermitages, which they fortified, and where they combined the trade of money-lending with that of dacoity.[1]

Fakirs

The Muhammadan Fakirs in India were of indigenous growth. They assumed the title of Shah or King.[2] They were not orthodox followers of Islam, and according to the author of the *Dabistan* they were really Hindus. "There is a class among the Hindus who give themselves the term of Musulman—Sofies and really agree in several tenets and opinions with the Sofies. Thus, in the first place they devote themselves to celibacy. As they have heard that there are ten classes of Sannyasis and Twelve of Yogis, they also pretend to be divided into fourteen classes." But Oman gives another explanation. "Strange to relate the contagion of Sadhuism indigenous to the soil seems to have so affected the Muhammedan rulers of India that besides the peripatetic Hindu ascetics, Tavernier met a body of almost naked Darvishes wandering over the country, sometimes, as became the members of the dominant race, exceedingly haughty and over-bearing in their demeanour. One such band, consisting of about forty-seven persons, all well armed, including a few who held very high positions in the Imperial Court, is especially mentioned by the traveller. Although proceeding on foot, this band of Muslim ascetics had many fine horses led before them, their saddles and bridles adorned with gold and silver ornaments and they had also ten or twelve oxen to carry their sick. Notwithstanding their pomp and self-assertion, these wandering ascetics lived upon alms obtained by begging, for were they not Faquirs? However, in all probability, it was fear which made the people comply as did Travernier himself"[3] in vacating the camping ground when demanded by these armed Darvishes.

The Madari sect of Fakirs are frequently mentioned among the marauding gangs. *Dabistan* refers to them as follows :—

Madari sect of Fakirs.

"The Madaris, like the Sannyasi Abadhuts, wear the hair entangled and the ashes which they and the Sannyasis rub upon their body are called *bhasmas* ; besides, they carry iron chains in their heads and necks and have black flags and black turbans ; they know neither prayers nor fasts ; they are always sitting at a fire ; they drink

[1] *District of Rangpur*—Glazier.

[2] *Seir Mutaquerin*, Vol. I, p. 244, foot-note 224.

[3] *The Mystics, Ascetics, and Saints of India*—J. C. Oman, p. 96.

a great deal of *bhang* and the most perfect among them go about without any dress in severe cold in Kabul and Kashmir and such places. They say when Baditeddin Madar came to Hindustan he became a Yogi whom the Hindus held in great esteem and who had a large number of followers. Madar settled at Makhanpur in Cawnpore district. The Madaris come there as many as possible from all parts of the world once a year."

Mr. Crooke thus describes the Madaris: "Madari or Madariya is one of the Beshara or unorthodox orders of the Mahomadan Fakirs who took the name from the famous saint Zinda Shah Madar of Makhanpur or Makhampur in the Cawnpore district. But as a matter of fact the Madaris of Northern India have no connection with the genuine Sufi sects. The fact seems to be that the Indian Madaris were established in imitation of Hindu Yogis and Sannyasis and their professed division of fourteen sects is based on that of these Hindu ascetics. Like Hindu Fakirs, they apply ashes (*Bibhuti*) to their bodies, wear an iron chain round their head and neck and carry black flag and turban. They seldom pray or keep fasts and use *bhang* freely as a beverage. Some of the Madaris are family men and lead a settled life. Some have rent-free lands which they cultivate or live by daily labour or by begging ; others who are perhaps different from the true Madaris go about performing bears or monkeys or are jugglers and eaters of fire. They are a wild-looking people."[1]

The Fakir leader of whom we have the earliest reference and whose incursions are frequently mentioned in the official records is Majnu Shah, a resident of Makhanpur, where he and his successors annually went on pilgrimage to the tomb of Shah Madar after their forays in Bengal.

Buchanan Hamilton mentions the Fakirs residing in Dinajpur being suspected of complicity with the wandering Fakirs. There is a curious sect of Fakirs in Baliyadighi in Dinajpur whose religious practices are a sort of compromise between Muhammadanism and Hindu Yogism. Maulvi Abdul Ali writing in the *Journal of the Asiatic Society of Bengal* in 1903 thus describes the sect : "The beliefs and practices of these Fakirs are in many ways anti-Islamic. They grow long hair on **Burhana Fakirs.** their head, put coloured cloths, wear a small piece of cloth instead of breeches called *Kopni* and use shackles of iron and long iron tongs. They never take food touched by other persons and subsist mainly on unboiled rice, clarified butter and salt. They do not eat fish or meat and until recent years they lived a life of celibacy. In their tours they carried the fish-standard and were accompanied by a huge retinue and their title is *Burhana* or nude. Till recently they wore only one

[1]*The Tribes and Castes of the North-Western Provinces of Oudh*, by W. Crooke.

simple piece of cloth and even this was not probably worn in earlier times. The Fakirs are the members of the Basria group, Taifuria Khunwadu and Tabagati ghar. In other words, as I understand, from this—the Taifuria Khanwandu is a branch of Basria ghar and the Tabagati ghar is again a branch of Taifuria Khanwanda an order introduced by Shah Madar." Majnu Shah is referred to as a Burhana Fakir. It seems probable, therefore, that the Madari and Burhana Fakirs referred to in the old official records were of the same sect.

Sanad granted to Fakirs by Shah Suja.

The excursions throughout the provinces by Burhana Fakirs were sanctioned by the Muhammadan Government, as will appear from the following extracts from the Sanad granted to the Burhana Fakir, Janab Shah Sultan Hasan Muria Burhana in 1659 by Prince Shah Suja:

"*Clause 1.* Whenever you wish to go out for the guidance of the people or for travel into the cities, countries, divisions, and all sorts of places where you may like to go according to your free will and inclination you may take all the articles of the *Julus*, e.g., banners, standard, flags, poles, staffs, band, *mahi* and *muratil*, etc.

* * * * * *

"*Clause 4.* You will be entitled within the countries of Bengal, Behar and Orissa to confiscate as you like properties to which there is no heir or pirpal or rent-free tenures.

"*Clause 5.* When you pass through any tract of the country, the landlords and tenants will supply you with provisions.

* * * * * *

"*Clause 7.* No cess or contributions of any kind will be levied."[1]

These conditions, if ever observed, were certainly not observed in the Eighteenth Century, when bands of Fakirs roamed about the country and took what they wanted.

Fakirs levy contributions.

In a letter of 1793, Mr. Hatch, Collector of Dinajpur, informs Marquis Cornwallis, the Governor-General: "The shrine (mosque at Pandua) chiefly, together with the fairs held in the district and upon its borders, furnished pretexts for all descriptions of Fakirs and idlers to assemble and however originally the charity might have been confined to persons well disposed, these assemblies have of late years become a great nuisance to the country and Banditti composed of the refuse of mankind flock to the standard of any of the assumed followers or descendants of ancient leaders of tribes of Muslim Fakirs and among the inhabitants in whatever parts they traverse claiming arrears of contributions alleged by them to be due from the riauts and villages; it would seem that formerly the inhabitants of the

[1] Fakirs of Baliya Dighi in Dinajpur—*Journal of the Asiatic Society of Bengal*, 1903.

villages of this and of other districts voluntarily gave a small gratuity by way of charity to the Fakirs when they approached their villages—that this donation in progress of time was converted into a fixed contribution, and that separate Banditti set up claims to the right of levying it and support these self-created titles by proceeding to Acts of Hostility and bloodshed to the great annoyance of the inhabitants and subversive of the peace of the country. It further appears that the Principal Persons, residents in the villages, have taken upon themselves on the general behalf of the Riauts of their respective villages to purchase the forbearance of any hostile Acts meditated by this rabble in its progress by compounding and making a pecuniary compensation afterwards levying a tax upon their villages under the plea of re-imbursement and thereby rendering the visit of these depredators a source of benefit to themselves ; but that since the inferior class of Riauts have declined any longer being subjected to exactions of any kind, the Banditti attempt to levy contributions by committing acts of violence (sometimes attended with cruelty) on the riauts, who fall into their hands, frequently taking away in confinement the collecting officers of the Landholders...."[1]

It was against these hordes of Sannyasis and Fakirs that the British authorities on taking over the administration had to contend in a country, as yet imperfectly known and unsuitable for rapid movement owing to the innumerable water-channels. The difficulty was intensified on account of the restricted territory of the East India Company, confined only to Bengal, Bihar and Orissa beyond which the raiders found an easy asylum when pursued. Many gallant lives were lost in the first encounters, but the indomitable energy and resources of the British surmounted all difficulties and triumphed in the end. The history of this is buried in the Government records of the period, many of them still unpublished, and the following account has been compiled from the materials available.

---

[1]Revenue Department Original Consultation No. 27, dated 29th March, 1793.

CHAPTER II

Their places of Pilgrimage

PILGRIMAGE is regarded a pious duty by both Hindus and Mussalmans; so the Sannyasis and the Fakirs wandered far and wide on pilgrimage. Forbes, who served under the East India Company from 1766 to 1783, mentions in his *Oriental Memoirs* that the Sannyasis in their wanderings went "from the confines of Russia to Cape Comorin and from the borders of China to Malabar Hill in the island of Bombay." So great is the veneration of the Hindus for sacred places, that in their almanacs an auspicious time for setting out on a journey is termed "Tirtha Mrityu Joga" signifying that a person proceeding on a journey at that auspicious time will acquire merit by dying at a Tirtha or sacred place. Oman writes: "As a rule the Sadhus (Hindu Mendicants) adopt a life of easy irresponsible indolence and mendicancy. Their calendar of fairs and festivals is comprehensive and accurate. They know well how to time their devious wanderings so as to make them fit in with festal events of each locality within their annual round of pilgrimage to sacred places where on all important occasions they congregate in hosts and where they may be studied to advantage as regards the peculiarities of their costumes and external appearance generally."[1]

Hindu pilgrimages.

Kumbha Mela.

The largest gathering of Sannyasis of all sects and creeds is at the Kumbha Mela. This *mela* or fair is held successively at Hardwar, Allahabad, Nasik and Ujjain every three years, so that by this rotation the *mela* takes place at the same place every twelfth year. The first ceremony connected with the *mela* is that of bathing. The various sects of Sannyasis proceed to the bathing places in large solemn processions, displaying the paraphernalia of their respective orders. The rich Mohants or head Sannyasis lead their processions mounted on elephants and horses with richly decorated trappings of gold and silver, the armed Sannyasis carrying their arms and displaying the regalia of warfare. The procession of the Naga Sannyasis takes precedence over that of other sects, a privilege which they established by fighting. It is estimated that about two to five hundred thousand Sannyasis assemble at these fairs which usually last for a month.

---

[1] *The Mystics, Ascetics and Saints of India.*—J. C. Oman.

Having no fixed abode or earthly cares, the mendicant Sannyasis were in no hurry in their leisurely wanderings; long marches were succeeded by halts of prolonged duration depending largely on the places of pilgrimage they intended to visit and on the hospitality and wealth of the inhabitants of the country through which they passed. From the Kumbha Mela, they proceeded in various groups in different directions to attend the periodic fairs and festivals held in other places and it will be found that the Kumbha Melas were closely connected with the incursions of Sannyasis into Bengal. In 1772, the Kumbha Mela was held at Hardwar and consequently incursions of large bodies of Sannyasis took place in the latter part of 1772 and early in 1773. The next *mela* was held at Allahabad in 1775 and after the fair the large congregations of Sannyasis were not allowed to enter the East India Company's territories by the timely intervention of the military authorities stationed at Chunar.

The Sannyasis came to Bengal principally to take part in the bathing festivals. After passing through the territory of the Nawab of Oudh, they followed a route generally through the north of Bihar and the borders of the Nepal Terai. Near this route lies Janakpur in Nepal, reputed to be the birthplace of Sita where a festival is annually held on the occasion of her birthday about the end of March.

Passing either through the Nepal Terai or Purnea district, the Sannyasis usually crossed the Mahananda and made for Rangpur. From here they continued their journey by several routes. The favourite one was southward to Mahastan[1] on the ancient river Karatoya in Bogra district and thence to the river Brahmaputra; another route led east towards Chilmari and the other bathing places on the Brahmaputra.

At Mahastan, there are two bathing festivals, one in December or January on the day of the new moon and the other on the occasion of the Baruni festival in March or April. The first festival takes place only when the new moon falls on a Monday and occurs at intervals of years. Bathing on such a day in the Karatoya is very auspicious and triply so if one bathes at Siladwipa which is identified as Mahastan. This is known as the Paus Narayani festival. The Baruni festival is held on the thirteenth day of the dark half of the month of Chaitra (March-April). Mahastan.

About a week after the Baruni festival the Astami festival is held on the eighth day of the moon in Chaitra (March-April). Bathing in the Brahmaputra is regarded very sacred, as the waters of all the

---

[1]The ruins which are now known as Mahasthangarh are the relics of the town of Paundravardhana. The name Mahastan literally means the great place though some say it is a corruption of Mahasnan. According to others it is a corruption of Maha Asthan, the great place of pilgrimage.—*Bogra District Gazetteer.*

sacred places, rivers and oceans are considered to unite in the Brahmaputra water on that day. If the day falls on a Wednesday, bathing in the Brahmaputra becomes more auspicious. The notable places of pilgrimage on the Brahmaputra are Chilmari in Rangpur, Singjani (modern Jamalpore) and Begunbari in Mymensingh and Nangalbandh near Narayanganj in Dacca.

Brahmaputra River.

Sagar.

A less common route of the Sannyasis from Rangpur was direct towards the south across the Ganges to the Sagar Island. This island lies at the mouth of the Ganges, in the district of the 24-Parganas and bathing there on the last day of Paus (about the middle of January) is considered as an act of great piety.

Agradwip.

Pilgrimage was also made to Agradwip situated in the district of Burdwan about 15 miles north of Navadwip on the west bank of the Ganges. The objective was the temple of Gopinath where a festival was celebrated in April.

Puri.

The Sannyasis generally left Bengal before the beginning of the rains as in that season most parts of Northern and Eastern Bengal become submerged and travelling is difficult except by boats. On their way back from Sagar they sometimes crossed the Ganges to the district of Midnapore, and went south to Puri on a pilgrimage to the holy temple of Jagannath. Here festivals are held on the occasion of the Snana Jatra or the Bathing Ceremony in June which is followed by the Ratha Jatra or the Car festival in July. But the more common route back was the way by which they came or they took another route after visiting Assam along the Terai "from Goalpara to Benares which was covered easily in six weeks' time."

Muhammadan pilgrimages.

"Pilgrimages," writes Buchanan Hamilton (1807—1813), "are very much in fashion among the Moslems as well as among the Hindus." "The Muhammadan rulers of Gaur were greatly under the influence of men dedicated to a religious life called Pirs or Saints. In every part of the district (Dinajpur) are to be found the tombs or monuments of these personages. Many of these monuments are still resorted to by Muhammadans for purposes of worship." [1] In the Malda district, round the Muhammadan Capital of Gaur, these places are more numerous.

Makhanpur.

The headquarters of the Madari sect of the Muhammadan Fakirs, who usually came to Bengal, was at Makhanpur in the district of Cawnpore. Makhanpur is a village some 40 miles north-west of Cawnpore. "A fair is annually held there in connection with the annual pilgrimage to the tomb of Shah Madar who is said to have been a Jew. Hindus and Muhammadans alike resort to the place—the former regarding him as an incarnation of Lakhan." [2] Francisco Pelsaert in his

[1] *Dinajpur District Gazetteer.*

[2] *Imperial Gazetteer of India*, Dinajpur.

"*Remonstrantie*" writes: "In Makhanpur 70 koss (140 miles) from Agra on the eastern road is buried Pir Shah Madar who is said to possess many gifts and wield many powers. The pilgrimage to his tomb is in February when an immense number of people from all quarters gather round Sikandra beyond Agra and march thither like an army accompanied by an even greater number of mendicants than the devotees who there take various parties under their standards for protection."[1] Lord Valentia wrote in 1803: "The crowd we met going to the fair astonished me; for the first ten miles it was as great as in London streets and afterwards some party or other was always in sight. The scene amused me so much! Hindoos and Mussalmans equally hastening to the religious festivity." He added that 'at this fair were assembled all the rascals in India'.[2]

Dinajpur district.

Entering Bengal by about the same route as the Sannyasis as far as the north of the Purnea district, the Fakirs went south towards Dinajpur and Malda districts. In the former district lies the shrine of Nek Mardan, a Muhammadan Pir or saint, where a fair is held in his honour on the first day of the Bengali year. The remains of the Pir are reputed to be preserved in a thatched hut in the centre of a mango grove near the site of the fair. There are other places of pilgrimage in the Dinajpur district such as the tomb of Pir Badar-ud-din near Hemtabad, and the monument of Mullah Ala-ud-din near Damdama.[3]

Pandua in Malda district.

Near Pandua or Perua in Malda is the celebrated Adina Mosque and according to Buchanan Hamilton, at the period of his visit in 1812, "it was the most celebrated place of pilgrimage in Bengal and very few of the district of Dinajpur ever think of going to Mecca, but content themselves with Peruya." Even to this day there is a saying—"First is Medina, then is Adina." "At Pandua by the side of the Dinajpur road there is the Bari Dargah (shrine) of the saint Mukdam Shah Jalal. The endowment for the shrine is called Baishhazari because it consists of 22,000 bighas of land. The endowment is said to have been made in 1709. Strangers are fed and it is a place of resort for Fakirs from every part of India, particularly in the months of Rajab and Saban when melas are held and the fatiha (prayers for the dead) of the saint recited. Near the Baishhazari shrine are the buildings of Sheshhazari or 6,000 bighas endowment which has for one of its objects the upkeep of the Chhotti Darga or shrine of the saints, father and son, Ala-ul Huq and Hazrat Nur Kuth Alam, who lived at Pandua and died in 1384 and 1415 A.D. respectively. As at Bari Dargah, hospitality is offered to all visitors and the shrine is a place of resort of pilgrims and fakirs from

---

[1] *Jehangir's India, The Remonstrantie of Francisco Pelsaert, 1620—1627,* translated by Moreland and Geijld.

[2] *Voyages and Travels of Lord Valentia*, Vol. II, p. 204.

[3] *Dinajpur District Gazetteer.*

all parts of India. The Baishhazari *mela* is held from the 17th to 22nd of Rajab and the chief Sheshhazari *mela* from the 8th to 22nd of Saban, the last day coinciding with the festival of Shab-i-barat."[1]

Writing in 1788 of Perua, the Collector of Dinajpur reported. " Peruya is a tongue of land lying almost in a direct line north from the river Ganges. This alienation is under the management and control of a person named Sudder [....] a resident in Calcutta and I understand is a grant made for the purpose of maintaining the Madrassa at the Presidency and is a place of general resort of all Mussalman Fakeers who of late years have formed themselves into predatory bands and when opportunity favors their views lay the inhabitants under contribution."[2]

Mahastan

A favourite place of pilgrimage for the Fakirs was the Darga[3] or shrine at Mahastan in the district of Bogra which was built on the site of a Hindu temple. Fairs on the occasion of Hindu festivals mentioned before are held on the *pirpal* lands of the shrine. A Muhammadan festival or fair is also held here about April.[4]

Far to the north-east of Mahastan on the bank of the Brahmaputra in the district now called the Garo Hills is the shrine of the saint Shah Kamal and to the south-east of it on the other bank there is another shrine of the same saint. Visits to these shrines probably led to the incursions of the Fakirs in Mymensingh.

It will be seen, as has been remarked by Oman, that the Sannyasis and Fakirs had very accurate information about the dates of the festivals held at various places and timed their visits in such a way as to be present during the celebrations and to share in the gifts and offerings.

It was at these festivals that the raiding sects met, distributed arms among their members and concerted their plans of campaign by getting information from the resident Sannyasis and Fakirs. "The Darga at Mahastan," writes Rennell in 1771, "afforded a pretence to the Fakirs to assemble there and at the fair which is held in December they are furnished with arms of all kinds and commonly sally forth 2,000 strong."

[1] *Malda District Gazetteer.*

[2] Shah Sultan's Darga. "Most of the tombs are of the Muhammadan Zamindars of Silheris who are reported to have lived here."—*Bogra District Gazetteer.*

[3] *Bengal District Records*, Dinajpur, Vol. II, p. 204.

[4] *Bogra District Gazetteer.*

The Fakirs also assembled to visit the Dargas at Akkilpur and Pandua. Charles Grant, Resident at Malda, wrote as follows in 1783: "Though the professed design of each meeting of Fakirs was to commemorate the death of the Muhammadan teacher whose name the place of the congress bears, yet besides the tumult and bloodshed which sometimes happen at such meetings they by the great resort of the dealers of all kinds furnish in a considerable degree the income which keeps together the fraternities of robbers who generally make once a year excursions and extort a stated tribute under the name of charity." [1] Even in 1854, Mr. Pemberton, the Revenue Surveyor, complains of "demi-barbarous and insolent Fakeers who frequent the neighbourhood" of the Dargas near Pandua, while of the "numerous Fakeers" who resort to Adina Mosque he remarks "how they exist it would be hard to state, however it is certain they are only beggars by name, although they complain loudly of the lakhirajdars or freeholders for withholding their rights." [2]

[1] Letter to the Collector of Bhagalpur, dated 12th March, 1783; Revenue Department, dated 8th April, 1783, Original Consultation No. 17.

[2] *Geographical and Statistical Report of the District of Maldah*, by J. J Pemberton, Revenue Surveyor, 1854.

CHAPTER III

Conditions in Bengal

Administrative arrangements prior to 1765.

THE English came to Bengal as merchants. What with constant threats of expulsion by the suspicious and autocratic Nawabs instigated by the rival European Companies, and what with caution against "embroiling with country powers" emphasised in many of the Despatches from the Directors at Home, the agents of the East India Company confined their early activities to the securing of trade advantages and to the protection of their Factories at Calcutta and elsewhere. Their interests were commercial and were centred in Calcutta and in the various factories at Patna, Dacca and other places. Since the year 1760, when the districts of Midnapore, Burdwan and Chittagong were assigned to the Company and English officials became concerned with their administration to superintend the revenue collections and the maintenance of order, our knowledge of the interior of the country begins to increase, thanks to the official correspondence of that time, which has been preserved. But for the rest of Bengal, it is only when some incidents occur affecting the isolated factories that we get glimpses of the state of affairs in the rural areas. "The internal administration was left largely in the hands of the great landholders or zamindars who collected the revenue of the tracts under them and made it over to the Nawab's officers.... They were kept in check and the authority of the Nawab enforced by officers called Faujdars or military commandants, who had detachments of troops under them and were responsible for the maintenance of the public peace and the suppression of any zamindar who withheld his revenue. Practically the only civil officers in the districts were the Daroghas who tried any murderers, dacoits or other criminals who might be arrested by the zamindar but had only limited powers having to refer their proceedings to the Naib Nazim or the Deputy Governor in all but minor cases. The duties of police were in their hands and were most indifferently performed, the police and often the zamindars themselves being the patrons of dacoits who preyed on the people."[1] In this state of affairs the English traders in the interior, whether "Factors" of the Company or "Free Merchants," were left to themselves and to the feeble

[1] "*History of Bengal, Bihar and Orissa under British Rule,*" by L. S. S. O'Malley, C.I.E., pp. 85-86.

protection the Nawab's Faujdars could give.[1] Naturally, therefore, these isolated men fortified their factories and employed disciplined guards and were thus usually immune from the depredations of dacoits and nomadic mendicants who found it easier to rob the common people from whom no resistance was to be apprehended. That there are very few reports from the Company's servants of depredations by nomadic mendicants before the second half of the Eighteenth Century does not therefore prove the non-existence of the evil.

The year 1765 is a landmark in the history of British Administration of India, for in that year the East India Company obtained the Diwani and became directly connected with the revenue administration of Bengal, Bihar and Orissa. No innovation was made in the system of internal administration and there were no changes in the then existing machinery. The unscrupulous Nawab Muhammad Riza Khan as the Naib or the Deputy Dewan in Bengal "having an almost exclusive direction of all details relative to the settlement and collection of Bengal districts"[2] carried on his corrupt practices and granted large remissions of revenue on false or flimsy pretexts thereby adding to his own "Nazarana" or presents.[3] The Council at Calcutta supervised the collection of the revenues arising from the Diwani with the help of the Resident at the Durbar who was stationed at the Nawab's capital, Murshidabad. **Early British administration.**

Three brigades of troops were formed for the protection of this newly acquired territory. "The order of the formation of the brigades is dated the 5th August, 1765. The first at Monghyr was to be commanded by Brigadier-General J. Carnac, the second at Allahabad by Col. Richard Smith, and the third at Bankipur by Col. Robert Barker."[4] Speaking of these brigades Grand says: "The Army at my entrance into the service (1766) was composed of three brigades, one stationed at the Presidency, another midway at Berhampur and furthest north station extended only to Bankypur. Each brigade consisted of an European

---

[1]Writing on 14th November 1764, to Nawab Mir Jafar, the President at Fort William stated: "Has already told His Excellency that while Mr. Rose, an English gentleman, was travelling with some money and goods (the whole of the property was estimated at Rs. 13,000), the boat people having murdered him near Backergunge carried away the money and goods and took shelter in the Zemindari of Sitaram. An Englishman was sent to enquire into the affairs but the said Zemindar would not pay him attention. Requests that the Naib of Dacca (Naib Nazim Muhammad Reza Khan) may be directed to make the Zemindar refund them and to inflict due punishment on him. Requests that the Naib of Dacca may be directed to send one of the Factory Sepoys along with some of his own people to apprehend the offenders which will be very serviceable to traders."—*Calendar of Persian Correspondence*, Vol. I, No. 2464.

[2]Harrington's *Analysis*, Vol. II, p. 3.

[3]Author's *Select Chapters on Mymensingh*.

[4]Broome's *History of the Rise and Progress of the Bengal Army*.

regiment with six battalions of Sepoys and a proportion of artillery with one hundred black horse, and the highest rank enjoyed for such command was that of a Colonel."[1]

In 1769, English servants of the Company were appointed under the designation of "Supervisors" to superintend the collection of revenue in the districts and were located at various centres throughout the country. "They were to be a reporting agency and as such had to compile a history of the province, to report on the state produce and capacity of the land"[2] and various other matters. It is from this period that we get fuller information about conditions of life in rural Bengal; and the operations of the marauding bands begin to be recorded in reports and letters. This system of revenue administration proved, however, unsatisfactory and in 1771, the Court of Directors expressed "their determination to stand forth as duan and by the agency of the Company's servants to take upon themselves the entire care and management of the revenues." The Criminal and Police Administration continued to be managed as before by the Naib Nazim; the zamindars, remaining responsible for the prevention and punishment of all crimes within their parganas, maintained their own Pykes and Barkandazes for the purpose.[3] Apart from the inefficiency of this system of police, it wholly lacked in organisation and failed in concerted action against any organised band of miscreants. The Collectors employed in the districts concerned only with the administration and protection of revenue, had under them only a small body of barkandazes and pykes for the protection of the treasuries and the escort of treasure. They could, when required, call in the aid of the pargana[4] Sepoys who were stationed in small detachments in different places.

Under the Regulations of 21st August 1772, two Courts—a Dewani or Civil Court and a Faujdari or Criminal Court—were established for each provincial division or collectorship. The Collector on the part of the Company presided over the Diwani Adalat or Civil Court. The Kazi and Mufti of the district sat in the Faujdari Adalat or Criminal Court. The criminal administration continued in the hands of the Nazim, the Nawab of Murshidabad. In 1775, Muhammad Riza Khan was appointed Naib Nazim and vested with powers to superintend Faujdari Adalats. At the

---

[1] Grand—*Narrative of the life of a gentleman long resident in Bengal*—Firminger's edition, p. 18.

[2] O'Malley's *History of Bengal, Bihar and Orissa under British Rule.*

[3] Sir W. W. Hunter's *Introduction to Bengal MSS. Records*, Vol. I, p. 15.

[4] "Besides those (three brigades) there were in different cities of the three provinces (Bengal, Bihar and Orissa) Militia Sepoys under the name of Purgana. These served for the purpose of guarding the treasures where Civilians were fixed, to provide the Honourable Company's Investment and to escort the fleets of boats which conveyed goods from distant posts to the Presidency." Grand—op. cit., p. 18.

same time, Faujdars were appointed to the fourteen districts into which Bengal was divided, with an appropriate number of armed men for the protection of the inhabitants. The preservation of the peace in the interior lay with the zamindars within their jurisdictions. As this system also did not work well, the establishment of Faujdars and Thanadars or police officers acting under them was abolished in 1781 and according to a Minute of Sir John Shore of 1781, the duties of Judge, Collector and Magistrate were united. Faujdari Courts, however, continued in the several divisions subject to the control of the Naib Nazim, and the English Judges of the Court of Diwani Adalat were appointed Magistrates with power to apprehend dacoits and commit them to the nearest Faujdari Court for trial. As there was much delay in trial the Magistrates were vested with powers to try petty cases in 1787. But as defects were still not remedied, Courts of Circuit were established with English Judges for the purpose of trial of crimes as also for the supervision of criminal justice. In 1791, in conformity with an order of the Governor-General in Council the Naib Nazim ordered the Darogas of Faujdari Courts to deliver over charge of all prisoners and records to the Collectors. Under Regulation II of 1793, the duties of Judge, Collector and Magistrate were separated. The office of Judge and Magistrate was combined in one person while the duties of the Collector were limited to the collection of revenue. By Regulation I of 1793, the Governor General in Council "exonerated the proprietors of land from the charge of keeping the police" and enacted for the "appointment of officers on the part of Government to superintend the police" and a new police scheme was introduced by Regulation XXII of 1793. Section 4 of this Regulation directed "the Magistrates to divide their respective zillas including the rent-free lands into police jurisdictions, each jurisdiction to be ten kosh (20 miles) square....The boundaries are to be so fixed as to have the principal towns, bazars and Ganjes in the centre of them that the police establishments may serve for the protection of these principal places as well as the circumadjacent countries."

Although during the Muhammadan time the revenue units, such as chaklas, parganas, tappas, etc., were more or less compact, the jurisdiction of Revenue Collectors depended more upon the amount of collections than on the geographical situation of these units of revenue. Thus the term Crori indicated a Revenue Collector who collected a crore of *dams* of revenue (40 *dams*=1 rupee). Transfers of estates from the jurisdiction of one Revenue Collector to that of another were allowed on the application of the revenue payers for facility of payment; and these applications were readily acceded to owing to the insecurity of the country and the consequent risk in the transport of revenue. A notable instance of this is still found in an estate situated in the centre of the Mymensingh district for which revenue is paid in the Murshidabad Collectorate. At the time when the Supervisors took over charge of the

Revenue divisions.

various districts, these anomalies in jurisdiction existed to a very great degree. In order to follow their reports, their measures and their action against these nomadic marauders, it is necessary to have a rough idea of their jurisdictions at the time in the northern districts of Bengal and Bihar. Purnea extended on the south-east to the river Mahananda, thus including the western portion of the modern district of Malda. The eastern portion of Malda was included in Dinajpur which had the Mahananda on the south-west. Dinajpur included most of the modern district of Bogra (an Assistant to the Collector being for some time posted there), the Serajganj subdivision of Pabna and the Tangail subdivision of Mymensingh with the exception of Pargana Pukhuria on the north-west. It thus included the extensive parganas of Attia, Kagmari, Barabazu, Silberis, Pulladosy, etc. Rajshahi which was co-extensive with the huge Rajshahi zamindari or the zamindari of the Maharaja of Nattore extending over 13,000 square miles, included the present districts of Rajshahi, parts of Rangpur and Pabna. It even extended beyond the Ganges to some Parganas in the present districts of Jessore and Nadia. Pargana Pukhuria, in subdivisions Sadar, Tangail and Jamalpur of Mymensingh being included in the estate of the Maharaja of Nattore, was also under the Collector of Rajshahi whose headquarters were in those days at Nattore. The rest of the present district of Mymensingh including some portion on the north-west (pargana Karaibari of Goalpara district in Assam) was included in Dacca under its Chief. Rangpur then included the present district of Jalpaiguri, while the Murshidabad Collector stationed at Murshidabad had jurisdiction in some parganas east of the Ganges in the present district of Rajshahi. The map at the end of the book shows roughly the position of some of the places and parganas mentioned in it.

The above gives a rough outline of the revenue jurisdictions of the early British period. It was a very inconvenient arrangement from the point of view of the resident officials who had to devise measures of protection or defence when suddenly confronted with the presence of bodies of plundering Sannyasis and Fakirs within their jurisdictions. This arrangement continued till 1787 when the general re-arrangement of districts in more or less compact blocks on the plan of Sir John Shore was effected. But in following the Muhammadan system of having a Collector for collections of not less than 5 lakhs, some of the anomalies remained; an instance of which was the inclusion of Bhulua (the present district of Noakhali) in the Mymensingh Collectorate.

Physical features.

Towards the end of the Eighteenth Century certain important changes in the river systems took place. "In 1787, the Tista river which had flowed south-west into the Dinajpur district, finding its way to the Ganges met with some obstruction in its course and turned its mass of water into a small branch running south-east into the Brahmaputra forcing its way among the fields and over the country in every direction and filling the Ghagat, Manas and other rivers to overflowing."[1]

About the same time the Brahmaputra was changing its main channel. The Brahmaputra or the Jamuna, nowhere less than four miles wide in the rains, which now forms the western boundary of the Mymensingh district, dividing it from Rangpur, Bogra and Pabna districts, was not such a mighty river in the latter part of the Eighteenth Century. At that time the old channel running through the centre of the district in a south-easterly direction past Jamalpur and Mymensingh carried the main body of water, and it is this stream which is meant when the Brahmaputra is mentioned in the records of the time. It shifted its course westwards and in 1809 Buchanan Hamilton writes that the new channel between Bhawanipur and Dewangânj "was scarcely inferior to the mighty river." By 1830 the old channel was reduced to its present insignificance.

That is why in their earliest raids the Sannyasis and the Fakirs are found passing rapidly from places in the present districts of Rangpur, Bogra and Pabna to the centre of Mymensingh district and back again, which would be inexplicable, had a river of the present large dimensions been in existence at that time separating these districts. The Brahmaputra on the east and the Ganges on the south formed a sort of natural barrier to their incursions.

---

[1] *The District of Rangpur*, by Glazier (Firminger's edition), p. 22.

CHAPTER IV

The earliest incursions, 1760—1769

TRADITION has handed on a story of plunder by Sannyasis in Ali Vardi Khan's time. In 1743 when Bhaskar Pandit, the general of Raghuji Bhonsla of Satara, was carrying on his dreaded depredations known as "*Bargir Hangama*," a body of Sannyasis is said to have looted the temple of Bhawanipur[1] in Bogra district. Bhaskar Pandit hearing of the sacrilege marched against them and penetrated to Pakuria near Singra in Rajshahi district and made the Sannyasis disgorge their plunder which he restored to the temple.[2]

On examining the records and correspondence of the early British officials the earliest information found on this subject relates to Western Bengal.

West Bengal.

In 1760 "Messrs. Watt & Howitt being returned from Burdwan and Kishenghur and reporting that the Naugurs [Naga Sannyasis] and Marhattas have advanced into those countries and commenced plundering which has obliged them to retire to Calcutta and will put a stop to the collection of tuncaws [revenue] in those countries," the President was to "send such a military force to those countries as may be necessary for their defence and security."[3]

East Bengal.

In 1763 Hastings recorded the following note: "Sometime ago a large body of Fakirs infesting the country about Backergunge surrounded Mr. Kelly, my agent and put him in danger of life....The Fakirs have since quitted the country."[4] The same year, "a rabble of Fakirs," as Clive calls them, attacked the Dacca Factory and captured it. Mr. Leycester,[5] the then Chief of the Factory, justified the abandonment

---

[1]Bhawanipur, a place of pilgrimage on the Karatoya river has a temple of Bhawani, rebuilt by Maharani Bhawani of Nattore.

[2]*Rajshahi District Gazetteer.* The tradition is mentioned in a Bengali book named "*Bhabanipur Kahini.*"

[3]Proceedings, dated 21st and 25th February, 1760—Long's *Selections from unpublished records*, p. 206.

[4]*Dacca District Gazetteer*, pp. 40-42.

[5]"Ralph Leycester. Arrived 1754. Assistant in the Import Warehouse in 1756. Escaped to the ships at the siege of Calcutta. Went home 1759. Charged by Lord Clive with cowardice in abandoning Dacca to the enemy in 1763. In 1766, one of the Company's servants who quarrelled with Lord Clive and resigned." *Bengal District Records—Midnapur*, Vol. I, p. 2, foot-note.

as follows: "The gentlemen of that Factory were fully sensible of the importance of saving their treasure and tried every possible method as they did for retreating in a regular manner. In an entire absence of cooleys it was resolved to disarm some of our sepoys and employ them in that capacity, first to convey the sick and wounded, then our treasure and at last retreat with the remainder of our garrison. The sick had mostly been sent to waterside, in pursuance of this resolution, to be put on board the few boats we had been able to collect at the Gaut, when many of our sepoys left the Factory and Mr. Leycester assures the President of the Council at Fort William that while he was in the Factory expecting to hear that boats were come at the Gaut sufficient to secure the treasure and remainder of the garrison, all the sepoys in a body left the Factory without any orders and fled to the few boats that were already come, in the utmost irregularity and confusion rendering their own retreat under such circumstances very precarious and putting it out of the power of the gentlemen to conduct the affair in the manner that had been really proposed...." Quite another version is given by Clive who refers to Mr. Leycester's behaviour as unjustifiable and mentions the case of old Mr. Delaport who very quietly smoked his pipe in the Factory an hour and a half after Mr. Leycester had forsaken it and then found leisure to carry off all his own personal effects without any molestation from the enemy who proved to be no other than a rabble of Fakirs. The Factory was retaken by Capt. Grant[1] with a very small detachment without the loss of a single man. The Fakirs who were made prisoners were directed to be employed as coolies in the repair of the Factory.[2]

A letter[3] of 1773 recalls the plunder of Rampur Boalia Factory by Sannyasis when Mr. Bennett was in charge. This Mr. Bennett was a factor at Berhampore in 1763, was taken prisoner and sent to Patna where he was killed in the massacre in October of that year. A month later a Mr. Thwaite was sent to take charge of his properties at the Rampur Boalia Factory. The plunder, therefore, took place before 1763. The same letter records that in 1764 Sannyasis were encamped in a village 4 miles from Rampur Boalia and plundered it. **Rajshahi.**

In 1766, the affairs of Cooch Behar State were in great confusion. The infant Maharaja, who was under the protection of the Bhutias,[4] was **Sannyasis in Cooch Behar**

[1]Capt. H. Grant who raised "Grant-ki-pultan" (afterwards 4th Battalion of Sepoys) in September, 1758.

[2]Long's *Selections*, p. 342. Secret Department Proceedings, dated 5th December, 1763.

[3]Letter, dated 4th March, 1773, from the Collector of Laskarpur to the President of the Council.

[4]"The aggression of the Bhutias encouraged by the weak and disturbed state of the plains had been going on in increasing degree ever since the beginning of the Eighteenth Century and by 1765 Bhutan was supreme in Cooch Behar and nothing could be done without the sanction of her representative."—*Survey and Settlement Report of the Jalpaiguri District.*

assassinated at the instigation of Ramanand Gossain and a conflict arose between the Nazir Deo (the hereditary Commander-in-Chief) named Rudranarayan and the Bhutias concerning the succession, which resulted in the defeat of the Nazir Deo who was driven out of the country and appealed to the English for assistance.[1] The Sannyasis were hired by the opponents of Rudranarayan, and Lieut. Morrison was sent to help him. Rennell (the Surveyor-General) in his *Journal* describes an exciting chase of the Sannyasis by the detachment under Lieut. Morrison[2] which culminated in a fight and the defeat of the Sannyasis. '"At Mongolghat[3] we received intelligence that a detachment of English Sepoys were sent in quest of the Sanashys and that they crossed the Durla, the day before us....On coming to the western bank of the Neelcomer or Curesa river we found that the English detachment crossed this river during the night before our arrival and the rear had not crossed over many hours. The Sanashys were reported to be marching towards us and had several detachments posted in different villages to the Northward and North East....At Curesa I learnt that a party of the Sanashys' horse had been routed that morning near the town and the detachment were gone North East to meet the main body of the Enemy. I stopt at Curesa to refresh my people and during that time heard a firing of cannon and Musquetrey to the North East. We set out in the afternoon and found the detachment under the command of Lieutenant Morrison encamped at Bouterhat [Boothaut of map] having that forenoon defeated the main body of the Sanashys who retired to the S. E. towards Paradanga. Morrison had 90 Sepoys Rank and File ; and the Sanashys were 700 strong and near 150 of them armed with English Musquets. We halted with Morrison this night [the 20th February]. The next morning early Morrison set out in quest of the enemy, and my sepoys being joined with his, I acted as a volunteer under him. We marched 8 miles in the forenoon and then halted at Santoshpur to refresh the troops. About ½ past noon, we set forward again but saw no appearance of the enemy....About 4 we entered the village of Deenhatta[4] where a party of the enemy had posted themselves or rather I am inclined to think had set down to rest themselves. The sudden approach of our people however roused them and they made a desparate effort to defend themselves, at the same time that they might have run off and probably escaped. In this skirmish, I had the misfortune to be surrounded by the enemy and received several cuts from their broad swords, one of which threatened my death. Morrison pursued his course

---

[1] Hunter, *Statistical Accounts of Bengal*, Vol. X, p. 412.

[2] Lieut. Morrison had been a midshipman on board the *Medway* while Rennell was on the *America* and they had gone out to India in company.

[3] A large trading village on the Dharla, formerly the terminus of the Cooch Behar branch of the Railway.

[4] Different from Dinhata in Cooch Behar. The place is in Rangpur district.

towards the Durla the following two days....The Sanashys had separated into small parties and scattered themselves over the country, so that scarce 50 of them had crossed the Durla with their Commander who as Morrison was informed had retired towards Olyapur" [Ulipur]. In a letter, dated the 30th August, 1766, Rennell gives more details of the skirmish—" our escorte which were a few horse rode off and the enemy with drawn sabre immediately surrounded us. Morrison escaped unhurt. Richards my brother officer received only a slight wound and fought his way off, my Armenian Assistant was killed and the sepoy Adjutant much wounded. I was now in a most shocking condition indeed being deprived of the use of both my arms, a cut of a sable [sabre] had cut through my right shoulder bone and laid me open for nearly a fortnight down the back cutting through and wounding some of my ribs. I had besides a cut on the left elbow which took off the muscular part of the breadth of a hand, a stab on the arm and a large cut on the head."[1]

The Chief of Patna reported in 1767, "A body of 5000 Sinnasees entered the Sircar Saronge[2] country; the Phousdar sent two companies of sepoys after them, under the command of a sergeant who came up with them; the Sinnasees stood their ground and after the sepoys had fired away part of their ammunitions, fell on them, killed and wounded near eighty and put the rest to flight." This obliged the Chief of Patna to send Capt. Wilding "to rid the country of them as their stay strikes terror into the country people and greatly hurts the collections in that part."[3] **Bihar.**

The following year, Raja Sitab Roy, Naib Dewan of Patna, reported that the Zamindar of Halsipur (of the Hatwa Raj family) set on foot disturbances with the help of a body of wandering mendicants called Naggis (Naga Sannyasis). Capt. Wilding marching against them dispersed them and took the Fort at Halsipur [Husipur in Saran district].[4]

Northern Bengal in particular was infested by these banditti and a company of sepoys was stationed at Rangpur in 1767 under Capt. D. Mackenzie "to repel the ravages of the Fakirs and to maintain the peace of the country in general." In January, 1769, an expedition was undertaken by Capt. Mackenzie against the Sannyasis who had cut off Mr. Myrtle.[5] "At Myrgharrah one day's journey from **Rangpur.**

---

[1] *Hobson-Jobson*, second edition, p. 872.

[2] Modern Saran in Bihar.

[3] Long's *Selections*, p. 526.

[4] *Calendar of Persian Correspondence*, Vol. II, pp. 202-203.

[5] Mr. Myrtle was sent by Mr. Barwell, Resident at Malda in 1766 to procure "fir timber for the Company at easy rates from the Morung country."—Foreign Department, Select Committee Proceedings, dated 10th February, 1766, p. 13.

Sannysicottah,[1] the Hircarrahs [messengers] brought information that Sinnaysis had left Sannysicottah and marched towards the frontier of Nepal."[2]

The raiders continued their attacks during the next cold weather and several detachments of Pargana sepoys under Lieut. Keith[3] were despatched to Rangpur against them. They were cut off and Lieut. Keith was killed in action in December, 1769, on the borders of Morung.[4]

---

[1]Rennell in his *Journal* (February, 1766) notes: "The Sanashy Facquirs had once a mud Fort in this place and the remains of it are now to be seen." It is in the present Jalpaiguri district.

[2]Proceedings of Controlling Council of Revenue at Murshidabad, Vol. XI, pp. 38 and 58.

[3]Infantry Cadet, 1768. Ensign, 5th January, 1769. Lieutenant, 19th December, 1769.—Hodson, *Officers of the Bengal Army*.

[4]Morung or Murang—An old name of the Nepal Terai lying north of Purnea district. The name is an old one being mentioned more than once in the *Alamgirnamah* and in the annals of the Koch Kings.—*Purnea District Gazetteer*, p. 198.

CHAPTER V.

The raids increase, 1770—1772

SUPERVISORS were appointed for the districts in 1769 and 1770. Believing that the success of the Fakirs in their engagement with Lieut. Keith would embolden the wandering mendicants to continue their depredations, the Supervisors were on the alert to watch their movements and concert measures to check them. **1769-70.**

Rajshahi. Within a week of joining his post at Nattore, Mr. Boughton Rous, the Supervisor of Rajshahi, reported as follows in January 1770: "The Reinforcement of sepoys will be a sufficient force to deter the Sonassees from moving this way. I have advice that a party had lately advanced as far as nine coss on this side of Sheebgunge; but upon hearing of my arrival at Nattore, desisted from plundering the villages and separated into different bodies one of which went towards the Barampooter and the other consisting of about 1500 took the Rangpur route....I have dispatched letters to all the officers in the Purgannahs directing them to send immediate advice of every intelligence they may receive and have dispersed my own Hircarrahs for the same purpose. I will not fail to transmit you the most early information concerning the motions of these pernicious tribes. I have examined the state of the Raja's house here which is surrounded by two wet ditches and should my advices give me reason to apprehend that the Sonassees will make a second attempt to penetrate into this quarter, I will publish an order to the inhabitants to secure their persons and effects within the Inclosure."[1]

Early in 1770, Grand, author of the well-known *Narrative* who was at Cawnpore, "was detached with one hundred sepoys to oppose five thousand Fakeers who were reported to intend forcing a Ghaut or Ferry and crossing the Ganges to effect the usual depredation in the Nabob's [Nawab of Oudh] territories. Their intention was frustrated by timely precautions."

Rangpur and Dinajpur. On 20th April, 1770, Mr. John Grose, the Supervisor at Rangpur, applied for an additional force stating that "we should be ready to receive the Sinassees or any other vagabond plunderers that may make an inroad into this country which is not improbable considering the success the

[1] *Letter Copy Book of the Supervisor of Rajshahi at Nattore*, pp. 2-3.

Sinassees met with last year."[1] His apprehension proved to be too true as the banditti passed through the districts on their backward march. For on 24th April he reported that "Lt. Nairn has had advice from the Commander stationed at Dinajpur of the return of two bodies of Sonnasi Fakirs to that place, the first of which to the amount of one hundred have taken the road to Purnia and the other....he is now in pursuit of." Two months later Capt. Gabriel Harper, Commanding at Fyzabad, reported that some Fakirs arrived there who had "a parcel of English arms." By the Nawab's order twenty-three fire-locks, a horse, a saddle-pistol and two fowling-pieces were taken from them. These belonged to Lieut. Keith's party which had been defeated in the previous December. "The people who came to Fayzabad were a few who it seems had been sent from their main body to sell their plunder whilst they continued their route from Gurrackpore (in which province they destroyed and plundered several villages) by the range of hills to the northward until they gained the Rohillas country. The Nabob detached some troops after them from Ballarampur 30 coss North from hence but they were never able to come up with them."[2]

1770-71. Purnea. Precautionary measures were taken at the beginning of the next cold weather. Mr. Ducarel, the Supervisor at Purnea, being apprehensive of Sannyasis and Fakirs, "stationed harcaras at the Ghats and passages of the Koosy river." In October, 1770, he received news that a "body about 300 armed with Matchlocks and other offensive weapons were at Cundwah Ghat 12 coss from hence and were preparing to cross the Koosy river. He accordingly directed Lieut. Sinclair to march against them with the sepoys at Purnea. Lieut. Sinclair with his 150 men captured the entire body of 500 Fakirs besides followers, and after making them deliver their arms, brought them to Purnea. The Fakirs represented that they belonged to the Madari sect of Fakirs and were on their pilgrimage to a Darga near Maldah and another ten koss from Ghoraghat."[3] Their headmen were known to the local people and were represented as peaceful men who never committed any acts of violence. This was probably due to the awe and veneration with which these religious mendicants were held. They explained that "they had come in large numbers and with arms owing to the quarrel with the Sannysis who lately put to death a number of their people." The Supervisor allowed them to pass, keeping five or six of them as hostages and detaining their arms.[4]

---

[1] Letter from the Supervisor at Rangpur to the Resident at the Durbar, dated 20th April, 1770, and 24th April, 1770.

[2] Letter from Capt. Babriel Harper to the President and Governor at Fort William, dated 25th June, 1770.

[3] The Darga at Mahastan in Bogra district.

[4] Tetters from the Supervisor at Purnea to the Comptrolling Council of Revenue at Murshidabad, dated 25th and 26th October, 1770.

Dinajpur.

But all these protestations of good faith on the part of the Fakirs proved to be false. In November the Supervisor of Dinajpur reported the entry of "a troop of Fakirs into the province." A subadar with 10 sepoys and 100 barkandazes were sent against them but they were recalled as the Raja of Dinajpur reported that their number was 5,000 "which were too large to be routed by the small party." The Controlling Council of Revenue replied that the Fakirs may be quite peaceful people on pilgrimage as represented at Purnea in which case they are not "to be molested or provoked." Considering the small force of sepoys at the disposal of the Supervisors, the Council empowered the Supervisors of Rangpur, Dinajpur and Purnea to apply for one or two companies of sepoys from Capt. Knudson's battalion stationed at Rajmahal.[1] On 7th December Mr. Cottrell, the Supervisor of Dinajpur, again reported that the Fakirs coming from Purnea had changed their professed route to Ghoraghat on pilgrimage and were also armed with "personal arms besides 4 camels loaded with rockets. They were then 20 koss north of Rajgunj and had levied contributions as they passed along. Their number was two thousand. It was apprehended that they would make a circuit of the province."[2] Capt. Mackenzie with a party of sepoys was sent against them from Rangpur but could find no trace of them.

Attempt to enter Bihar.

Meanwhile on 30th November, Brigadier-General Sir Robert Barker reported from Patna of an assembly of ten thousand armed Sannyasi Fakirs at Benares who intended to pass through Bihar and Bengal[3] but the following month the Controlling Council of Revenue at Patna reported that they had returned towards Mirzapur.[4]

Pabna.

The Fakirs, however, had not left the province; those in Bengal "fled at the approach of sepoys" from place to place but continued their depredations in other parts. This appears from the following report in February, 1771, by Capt. Rennell (engaged in the survey of Bengal) from Belkuchy near Serajganj in the present district of Pabna. "There is now in this part of the country a large body of Fakirs who are laying all the principal towns under contribution. They were yesterday at Lutchinumpur 4 coss from this place and after receiving two hundred rupees from the Gunge Daroga marched northward to Pucharya District [Pukharia pargana in the present district of Mymensingh]....They are about a thousand in number and

[1]Letter from the Controlling Council of Revenue at Murshidabad to the Supervisor at Rajmahal, dated 28th November, 1770.

[2]Letters from the Supervisor at Dinajpur to the Controlling Council of Revenue at Murshidabad, dated 22nd November and 7th December, 1770.

[3]Letter from General Barker to the President of the Select Committee, dated 30th November, 1770.

[4]Letter from the Controlling Council of Revenue at Patna to Capt. Camac, dated December, 1770.

tolerably well-armed; they came from the western provinces about a month ago and traversed the Dinajpur and Ghoraghat districts on the way....I have met several of their detached parties which are indeed scattered over the whole province of Radshy (Rajshahi) and Ghoraghat (Dinajpur)."[1] Accordingly two companies of sepoys under the command of Lieut. Taylor were despatched from Murshidabad to join Capt. Rennell against the Fakirs. At the same time the Supervisor of Rangpur under instructions sent two companies of sepoys under the command of Lieut. Feltham to Ghoraghat to intercept them.[2]

Dacca.

About this time (February, 1771) Mr. Kelsall, the Chief of Dacca, also reported that "the Sannyasis were still levying contributions in all parts where they go; by the last advice they were at Byganbarry in the pargana of Alepsingh." But on 8th March the Supervisor of Dacca reported the Dacca province "to be quite free from any depredations of the Sinasses."[3]

Majnu the Fakir leader.

Writing on the 1st March, Capt. Rennell gives the following account of the operations against the Fakirs: "I joined Lt. Taylor's detachment the 24th ultimo and following the route of the Fakeers towards the Hoannah District, they retreating that way on hearing that they were pursued. Feltham with the Rangpur Detachment taking the route to Ghoraghat and Govindagunj surprised their camp on the morning of the 25th and after a short skirmish defeated and dispersed them, taking their camp and baggage and a few prisoners. Their chief Sheik Munjenoo fled on horseback to Mustan Gurr (a darga) where he was joined by about 150 of his followers all disarmed and many of them wounded. The rest to the number of 2,500 are dispersed in such a manner that two of them cannot be found together that it is impossible to pursue them with sepoys. They all threw away their arms in their retreat. I marched to Mustan in hopes of taking the chief prisoner but on my arrival found the place empty and was informed that he went off with a few followers on the road towards Purnia. Upon this I sent a Jemidars party after him with orders to follow this route four or five days journey and I am in hopes that the Jemidar will be successful as Munjenoo is diseased and cannot travel fast." Lieut. Taylor was directed to remain at Mahastangarh to prevent any "assemblage of Fakirs" and the Supervisors of Dinajpur and Purnea were instructed to keep watch on Majnu in his retreat to his home at Makhanpur. Lieut. Feltham was directed to return to his station at

---

[1]Letter from Capt. Rennell to the Controlling Council of Revenue at Murshidabad, dated 10th February, 1771.

[2]Proceedings of the Controlling Council of Revenue at Fort William, dated 14th February, 1771.

[3]Letter from the Supervisor of Dacca to the Chief and Council of Revenue at Murshidabad, dated 8th March, 1771.

His defeat.

Rangpur. The "Hill[1] and Dirga at Mustan Gurr was reported to be a place of natural strength; the hill being in most places extremely steep and skirted with thick wood, could be with small labour fortified which will make it tenable against a strong detachment."[2] An account of the skirmish is also given by the Supervisor of Rangpur. "Lieut. Feltham attacked and defeated Sheick Mujenoo with about 1,000 followers at a place called Cojee parrack [modern village of Cadgiparah] about 6 coss from Govin Gunge [Govindaganj] where they were encamped between two jills he killed ten took 7 prisoners and the rest run off amongst whom it is supposed many are wounded." The defeat of the Fakirs "encouraged the villagers so much that in their retreat they attacked them with bamboos and sticks and killed several so that none are now to be seen in that quarter."[3] According to Rennell's advice a party of sepoys were ordered to be stationed permanently at Mahastangarh.

Government action.

Orders for the apprehension of all travelling Fakirs were issued by the Supervisors. On the 26th March, 1771, Mr. Cottrell, Supervisor of Dinajpur, reported to the Council of Revenue:—"Mr. Peacock[4] on his way to the Morung country made a short stay here when he heard of the defeat of the Faquirs by Mr. Feltham and of the orders I issued in consequence to apprehend Shah Mudjinoo or any travelling faquirs that might be found in the country. He, having learnt that a body of about one hundred were passing close by him about 12 coss to the northward of this place, sent to their chief but as he refused to attend him, he secured the chief and some others whom he has sent to me. They do not immediately acknowledge themselves to be Shah Mudjinoo's people but they are come from Balliadiggy, a place where he has a house, have been travelling all over the country and were stripped of their arms some months ago by an English gentleman. Seeing their circumstances, I think it highly probable that they may be people whom Mr. Ducarel stript last year of their arms passing through Purnia and whom I formerly complained to you about. I have ordered them to prison till I have the honour of your commands on the subject." The Council of Revenue replied—"As it is probable that the Fakirs you have in confinement are those whom Mr. Ducarel disarmed and to whom he gave public

[1] The ruins of the ancient town of Paundravardhana known as "Khodar Pathar" consist of an oblong mound of about 15 feet in general elevation above the country and with earthen ramparts rising from 35 feet to 50 feet at the corner bastions.—*Bogra District Gazetteer.*

[2] Letter from Capt. James Rennell to the Controlling Council of Revenue, dated 1st March, 1771.

[3] Letter from the Supervisor of Rangpur, dated 28th February, and 7th March, 1771.

[4] Mr. Peacock was sent to "procure timber on account of the Hon'ble Company in that part of Morung lying to the westward of the Cossey River."

assurance that they should pass unmolested in their religious ceremonies and for the purpose of trade, it is highly improper that they should be taken or kept in custody. You will therefore be pleased to order their immediate release."[1]

In order to discourage the connivance or indifference of the local magnates, the zamindars of Pargana Silberis [Bogra District] were seized by Lieut. Taylor. The action seems to have had some effect on neighbouring zamindars for on the 15th April, the Supervisor of Rangpur reported that "some of the zamindar's servants have brought hither one of the Fakirs who accompanied the body of banditti which was lately assembled together with a camel belonging to their camp." The Fakir was directed to be sentenced to serve on the roads. Majnu appears to have lingered on in spite of these measures. On 13th April, 1771, the Supervisor of Rangpur reported to the Council of Revenue at Murshidabad: "Having received advice, while at Govindgunge, that Shaikh Mudjinoo with a party of his followers was still lurking about that part of the country Lieut. Feltham proceeded with a further re-inforcement in order to drive him from there."[2] But no report was received of Lieut. Feltham's operations.

Sannyasis attempt to enter Bengal.

On 29th April, 1771, General Barker wrote to Nawab Suja-ud-Daulah of Oudh that "six or seven thousand Naga Mendicants have crossed the Jamuna from the ghat at Kulpi and passed on towards the Ganges through the confines of Kora....The mendicants said that they had parwanah from the Nawab to cross the river Ganges and pass through his territories."[3] But no record of their entry into Bengal is traceable.

1771-72.

Sannyasis in Rangpur and Dinajpur.

The rainy season caused a lull in the depredations; but after the rains the incursions recommenced. In November, 1771, the Supervisor of Rangpur reported that he had just received information that a body of Sannyasis had entered the districts of Rangpur and Edrackpur by Bhawaniganj,[4] and the following month, the Superintendent of Sircar Saran reported to the Chief and Council of Revenue at Patna that about four thousand Nagas were encamped in Suja-ud-Dullah's [Nawab of Oudh] territory within eight or ten coss of Husseypore [Hatwa] and that it was their intention to come over crossing the Dewah. Measures were taken by the Superintendent to repel them but he apprehended that they might try a second route by crossing the Gandak

---

[1]Proceedings of the Controlling Council of Revenue at Murshidabad, Vol. V, pp. 13-14.

[2]Proceedings of the Controlling Council of Revenue at Murshidabad, dated 19th and 27th April, 1771, Vol. V, pp. 63 and 86.

[3]*Calendar of Persian Correspondence*, Vol. III, p. 197.

[4]Letter from the Supervisor of Rangpur to the Controlling Council of Revenue at Murshidabad, dated 7th November, 1771.

and pass along the borders of Betteah towards Purnea.[1] There appears to have been no further trace of them.

Fakirs in Rajshahi and Bogra.

Early in 1772, Majnu Shah returned with a large following and resenting the treatment accorded to him in the previous year sent the following petition to Maharani Bhawani of Nator, at that time the largest zamindar in Bengal[2], to win her sympathy in his favour. "We have for a long time begged and been entertained in Bengal and we have long continued to worship God at the several shrines and altars without ever once abusing or oppressing anyone. Nevertheless last year 150 Fakirs were without cause put to death. They had begged in different countries and the cloaths and victuals which they had with them were lost. The merit which is derived and the reputation which is procured from the murder of the helpless and indigent need not be declared. Formerly the Fakirs begged in separate and detached parties but now we are all collected and beg together. Displeased at this method they [the English] obstruct us in visiting the shrines and other places—this is unreasonable. You are the ruler of the country. We are Fakirs who pray always for your welfare. We are full of hopes."

In January, 1772, the Supervisor of Rajshahi at Nattore reported the appearance of 2,000 Mussalman Fakirs under Majnu Shah.[3] He enclosed a copy of a letter from the Deputy of Khatta Pargana[4] showing the depredations of the Fakirs and wrote, "Shaw Mudjendo, the Burrana Fackeer being arrived with a numerous body in the Pargana plundered all the goods and effects and carried away one of the principal men in the district under confinement. At present some of these Fackeers have taken up their residence here, they come to the village and carry off the people whom they use with the utmost severity. Owing to these, ryots and their dependants are deserting. The inhabitants are totally incapable of making any opposition. The Fackeers are very numerous and it is difficult to repel them. Some little time ago having received intelligence of them I sent a few men eastward to repel them. On Sunday a Hircarrah saw them at the village of Gheejen. Today about at 9 o'clock in the morning all the Fackeers arrived in this pargannah. There is some treasure; and what will be the result I know not."

---

[1]Proceedings of the Chief and Council of Revenue at Patna, dated 23rd December, 1771.

[2]"So extensive was this territory or zamindari (estimated in 1786 to comprise an area of 12,909 sq. miles) that it was found impossible for a single Collector, Judge and Magistrate with two assistants—one stationed at Muradbagh (near Murshidabad) and the other at Nator to administer justice."—Hunter's *Statistical Account of Bengal, Rajshahi*, Vol. VIII, p. 20.

[3]Letter from the Supervisor of Rajshahi to the Controlling Council of Revenue at Murshidabad, dated 22nd January, 1772.

[4]Khatta—Pargana in the south-western corner of Bogra district.

On receipt of the information Mr. Alexander,[1] the Chief of the Council of Revenue at Murshidabad, despatched one company of sepoys to reinforce the company at Nattore and directed the Supervisor of Dinajpur to send the two companies stationed there. The Supervisor of Rajshahi reported on the following day that the Fakirs were still at the same place, "Their number is represented to be about 1,500 besides stragglers who are continually joining them for the sake of plunder...." A letter from the officer of a village belonging to Dayaram Roy[2] in the Jeassin[3] Pargana mentions that "a party of 300 had seized 1,000 Rs. which were ready for despatch and it was apprehended they would take possession of the Purgunnah Cutchery. They are armed with swords, spears, matchlocks and rockets and some say they have a few swivals. Reports are that they will either move towards Silberis or unto this quarter" [Nattore].

It appears that the Fakirs moved on northward towards Silberis [Bogra]. On 25th January, the Supervisor at Nattore reported Majnu's further progress.[4] "This morning my Hircarrahs have brought me advice that yesterday afternoon the Fackeers moved to the northward to Kolegong where they were before encamped to a village called Kuegong in Saiburruss (Silberis) and Mudgenoon has given injunctions to his own followers to avoid all kind of oppression or severity and to take nothing but the voluntary contribution of the people by way of charity. But my letters from the Purgannahs mentioned that they have taken 500 Rs. from Noornagur a village belonging to Diaram Roy and 1690 Rs. from the Cutchery of Jyasin which had been deserted by the officers on the approach of this Banditti. It appears that they have with them two camels about 40 rockets 400 matchlock men a few swivals and altogether about 1,000 men who carry arms. Mudgenoon himself is mounted on a very good horse and several of his attendants also have Tattoo horses."

A little later he reported that the Fakirs had been in the Cosoomby[5] Pargana, where they levied small contributions in the different villages "by way of charity," and did not commit any violence, and that he intended sending a company of sepoys against Majnu Shah

---

[1]Mr. R. C. Sterndale in a popular lecture at the Dalhousie Institute in 1868 said : "A member of a family which still retains its almost hereditary connection with the Bengal Civil Service was James Alexander, Collector of Calcutta, who afterwards became Earl of Caledon."—*Bengal District Records, Midnapore,* Vol. II, p. 32, foot-note.

[2]Dayaram Roy—the principal officer of the Nator Raj. He was the founder of the Dighapatia Raj.

[3]Jaisindhu Pargana in Rajshahi district.

[4]Letter from the Supervisor of Rajshahi to the Controlling Council of Revenue at Murshidabad, dated 25th January, 1772.

[5]Kusumby Pargana in Bogra district.

who was reported to be at Mahastangarh with three or four hundred men. But later receiving news that Majnu was at Barabazu[1] and "quitting the Hon'ble Company's territories with precipitation" he did not send the sepoys.

About the same time Mr. Purling, the Supervisor of Rangpur, reported:[2] "The Fakirs are returned to Gooragaut and have been guilty of some oppressions. I have therefore thought proper to give Captain Thomas[3] orders to march with a Company of sepoys to Govingunge [Govindaganj] the Raja [of Dinajpur] having wrote me that the ryots in General are in the greatest consternation and none of the Government servants will remain at the villages. They are headed by one Shaw Mudgenow and are a body of 2,500 men most of whom are armed." The Council approved of the action but informed him that the Fakirs had left the country.

On the retreat of the Fakirs, the zamindars came with prayers for remission of revenue and the Supervisor of Rajshahi sent an "attested narration of the plunder and contribution made by the Fakirs in the different Pargannas of the province."[4] The Council of Revenue replied as follows :—"We observe the losses pretended to be sustained by the Inroads of the Fakirs amount to altogether to 8969 Rs. Losses of this kind we understand are always one of the risks to which farmers are liable ; we cannot, therefore, consent to their being borne by Government."[5]

---

[1]Barabazu Pargana in the present districts of Bogra, Pabna and Mymensingh on both sides of the Jamuna river.

[2]Letter from the Supervisor of Rangpur to the Controlling Council of Revenue at Murshidabad, dated 26th January, 1772.

[3]George Thomas—Ensign 10th July, 1763; Lieutenant 2nd February, 1766; Captain 8th July, 1766. Killed 28th December, 1772, by the Sannyasi Fakirs.—Dodwell and Miles' *Army List*.

[4] Letter from the Supervisor of Rajshahi, dated 9th March, 1772.

[5] Letter from the Controlling Council of Revenue at Murshidabad to the Supervisor of Rajshahi, dated 16th March, 1772.

CHAPTER VI

Widespread incursions and military operations, 1772—1774

1772-73. MEETING with small success in two successive years, the Fakirs under Majnu Shah appear to have abandoned for the time being the idea of further raids in Bengal and do not come to notice again till two years later, but another formidable body of raiders "who declared themselves not to be afraid of any consequence" reappeared in the form of the Sannyasis at the beginning of next season towards the close of the year 1772.

Sannyasis in North Bengal. Mr. Graham, a member of the Committee of Circuit, on his arrival at Rangpur on the 27th December, 1772, was informed by the Collector of Purnea that several bodies of Sannyasis had entered that district from the west and were scattered among the villages, plundering them and exacting contributions from the inhabitants and that they would pursue the route to the Brahmaputra through Dinajpur and Rangpur, The Assistant at Dinajpur also reported the presence of several bands of Sannyasis in that district, plundering the country as they pass along. Information was also received that another band of Sannyasis had plundered Bhawaniganj Cutchery in Rangpur. The Committee of Circuit directed the Collector of Rangpur to send the company of sepoys stationed at Dinajpur with a part of the Committee's escort, in pursuit of the Sannyasis. Early in the morning of the 29th December Captain Thomas and his company marched with these sepoys towards Zaffarganj. Before daybreak of the 30th, he attacked the Sannyasis numbering about fifteen hundred on a plain near Samgunge [west of Rangpur town] in Swaruppur Pargana. At first they gave way and

Capt. Thomas defeated and killed. the Captain "pursued them in a jungle where the sepoys expended all their ammunitions without doing the least execution ; when they perceived the ammunition spent, the Sinassies rushed in upon them in very large bodies from every quarter and surrounded them ; about 12 men are come in almost all wounded excepting those which were left with Captain Thomas' tent. Captain Thomas ordered the sepoys to charge upon them with their bayonets which they refused to do and the orderly of the Captain wanted him to mount his horse which he would not. Captain Thomas received one wound by a ball through the head which he tied, and next he was cut down. The ryots gave no assistance but joined the Sannyasis with lathies and showed the

Sinassies those whom they saw had concealed themselves in long grass and jungle and if any of the sepoys attempted to go into their villages they made a noise to bring the Sinnasies and they plundered the sepoy's firelocks."[1]

The Sannyasis pursued their usual route across the country eastward under the pretence of religious pilgrimage to perform ablutions in the Brahmaputra river. The Committee of Circuit suggested that the Sannyasis should be "opposed at their entry of the province by a respectable detachment formed from the Brigade stationed in Behar[2] as the small parties of sepoys sent against them failed." This suggestion was subsequently adopted by Warren Hastings. But a few months later the Pargana Sepoys were to meet with another reverse.

After the skirmish in which Capt. Thomas was killed at the end of 1772, a band of Sannyasis marched northward towards Cooch Behar to reinforce the Sannyasis under Durrup Deo. The old quarrel between Durrup Deo [Darpa Deb], Raja of Baikuntapur,[3] and the Nazir Deo for supremacy in the State of Cooch Behar still continued. Sannyasis numbering 5,000 were hired by Durrup Deo and they took possession of the Fort of Santoshgunj commonly known as Rahimganj.[4] The Nazir Deo naturally asked for help of the English who were his old patrons. Mr. Purling, the Collector of Rangpur, at once proceeded to Cooch Behar and in January, 1773, met the Nazir Deo and the young Raja; the Nazir Deo also had some Sannyasis in his pay. Mr. Purling made him dismiss them as "being an unnecessary expense." The Sannyasis were only too glad to disperse for they feared harm and had been under arms 1772-73. Cooch Behar.

---

[1]Extracts from letters from Mr. Charles Purling to the President, dated 29th and 31st December, 1772.

[2]Letter from Committee of Circuit, dated 2nd January, 1773.

[3]"Bycantapur, the capital of which is Sunssahcotta was originally a Jaghire annexed to the office of Rykut or umbrella bearer to Cose Behar Rajah and the post was held by the ancestors of Durrup Deo, who always attended upon the Rajah to perform the duties of that office. But Durrup Deo having for some time past separated himself from the Rajah, the post had in a manner remained vacant. When Bycantpur was conquered by Solut Jung in the time of Sujah Khawn, Durrup Deo and his brother Buckram were made prisoners and brought to Rangpore where they remained prisoners for 17 years. They were after that released by the Phougdar old Cossim Ali Cawn when he undertook an expedition to reduce Bycantpur to a more avowed subjection.... Durrup Deo nominally retains the office of Rykut but has never returned to the Court of the Rajah since the first conquest of his Jaghire by Solut Jung and is one of the petty Rajahs mentioned by Mr. Purling to be in rebellion against the Cooch Behar Raja."—The Report of the President of the Committee of Circuit on the information received from the Cooch Behar Raja's naib of Boda.—Proceedings of the Committee of Circuit at Rangpur, dated Rangpur, 23rd December, 1772 (Vol. V, p. 34).

[4]Letter from the Committee of Circuit to Capt. Stuart, dated 20th January, 1773.

for three nights before the arrival of Mr. Purling and his sepoys. As a matter of fact they themselves proposed to leave the country.[1]

Offensive against the Sannyasis.

The strong hand of Warren Hastings was now beginning to be felt in the suppression of the Sannyasis. "The Governor expressed a strong inclination to retrieve the military reputation as well as to punish as effectually as possible any set of armed men entering the districts in so riotous a manner." Accordingly on the 20th January the Collector of Rangpur directed Capt. Stuart commanding the 19th Battalion of sepoys at Rajmahal to proceed to Jalpaiguri against the Sannyasis hired by Darpa Deb so as to prevent their escape westward. The Captain was asked to be "constantly on guard against a surprise." Capt. Jones also marched from Rangpur towards Cooch Behar. The Governor directed "another battalion from Burrampore [Berhampore] to march immediately to co-operate with Captain Stuart but to act separately in order to have the better chance of falling in with them. At the same time, he ordered another battalion to march from the Dinapoor station through Tyroot [Tirhut] and by the northern frontier of the Purneah district following the track which the Senassies usually took in order to intercept them in case they marched that way. That battalion, after acting against the Senassies, if occasion offered was directed to pursue their march to Cooch Behar where they are to join Captain Jones and assist in the reduction of the country."[2]

Capt. Jones marched from Mowamari on the 24th January and reached Patgong on the 27th. He received information there that the Sannyasis were then at Bunnindanga 8 miles off and that they had two other posts within 3 miles of each other. Durrup Deo was then at Luckipore "one of the passes into the Hills of Bootan" and Rahimganj and the country westward was deserted. The strength of the enemy was five or six thousand men.[3] On the 28th, Capt. Jones reported from Sibgunj the defeat of the Sannyasis: "About eleven o'clock this morning I came up with the Sennasies with whom were joined some of Durrup Deo's people. They immediately advanced and endeavoured by their numbers to surround us at a distance. I detached parties on the flanks and rear which prevented them. They kept retiring, as I advanced, out of the reach of our firelocks, and threw their rockets pretty thick amongst us, by which I had one man killed and four dreadfully wounded. The sepoys showed great steadiness, kept their ranks and advanced without

efeat of annyasis.

---

[1]Letter from the Collector of Rangpur to the Committee of Circuit, dated 12th January, 1773.

[2]Letter, dated 31st March, 1773, to Sir George Colebrooke (Gleig's *Memoirs of Warren Hastings*, Vol. I, pp. 296-98.)

[3]Letter from Capt. J. Jones to Warren Hastings, President and Governor, dated 27th January, 1773.—Forrest's *Selections from State Papers*, Vol. I, pp. 29-30.

firing a musket. One round shot of which I had very little left, reached the enemy and did some execution; they at last broke and fled over the country. I thought it dangerous to attempt pursuing them. I hear they are all joined at Bouthaut four coss to the northward where there is a fort."[1] On 30th January, Capt. Jones wrote from Chingerabanda that "last night he was informed that the Sennassies had all crossed the Teesta and sunk the boats they used in crossing." He next proposed to take possession of the Fort of Rahimganj. "On the situation being favourable, he will next take the Fort at Jalpaiguri, the principal fort of Durrup Deo."[2]

In the meantime on the 25th January, Capt. Stuart according to directions marched against the Sannyasis. He crossed the Ganges at Rajmahal early in the morning and on the 27th arrived at Serampur thirty-six miles distant from Dinajpur. The Committee of Circuit, however, directed him from camp Dogatchey[3] on the 27th to march direct and prevent the Sannyasis (about 4,000 in number, then in possession of Rahimganj fort) from occupying Jalpaiguri.[4] He marched rapidly, not being encumbered with artillery, and reached Jalpaiguri on the morning of the 3rd February. Capt. Stuart gives the following interesting account of the engagement and capture of the Fort at Jalpaiguri: "At eight this morning I had the unexpected happiness to find myself within gunshot of the united army of the Sunassies and Durrup Dew of the Bycunpore country, which I was fortunate enough to route without firing a shot till after their flight commenced. They were strongly posted behind a bank and presented me with a very extended front imagining I suppose, that I would according to custom make an attack upon their centre, but perceiving their intention to close me in, I altered my first disposition and marched briskly up to their left flank which seemed to be their greatest dependence as their Musquetry, Jenjauls, matchlocks and Bauns played very briskly from that quarter. My resolve to attack their left proved very lucky; for there the whole Sunnassies, who were the enemies I wanted to meet and the only ones I had to fear, were posted. They confiding in their numbers and elated by their former success showed a boldness that would have done them credit had their subsequent behaviour corresponded with it. Indeed their station was very secure as it was impossible to make any

Capture of Jalpaiguri.

---

[1]Letter from Capt. Jones to the Governor, dated 28th January, 1773.—Forrest's *Selections*, Vol. I, p. 30.

[2]Letter from Capt. Jones to the Governor, dated 30th January, 1773.—Forrest's *Selections*, Vol. I, p. 30.

[3]In Thakurgaon subdivision of Dinajpur.

[4]Letter from the Committee of Circuit to Capt. Stuart, dated 27th January, 1773.

impression on them with my musquetry till I carried the bank that covered their front; perceiving this and determined not to expend a cartridge till I could present it to their breasts on the points of my bayonets, I ordered the battalion to march briskly up with shouldered arms. Till we were within a very small distance of the bank, when I gave orders to the whole to recover. This motion, together with our observed steadiness and resolution, had the desired effect and the enemy took to flight with the utmost precipitation. We pursued with the greatest briskness but they used a speed in their flight much superior to our pursuit. We killed fourteen of them on the field and had only two sepoys wounded. Ensign Marshall was slightly grazed by musket shot upon the right arm....At two in the afternoon, I made a second march and took possession in the name of the Hon'ble Company, of Jalpaiguri which the Raja had evacuated."[1]

On the 17th February, the Collector of Rangpur reported from Chicacottah that he had got information of a large body of Sannyasis in the pay of the Bhutanese; he marched with Capt. Dickson to their camp 8 coss to the south-west, but before his arrival they fled away. After this the dissensions in Cooch Behar quieted down and the Sannyasis were dispersed but not before they had plundered the Boda Pargana.[2]

Sannyasis in Bogra.

But already in early January another formidable band of Sannyasis had made their appearance in the heart of North Bengal. On 6th January, 1773, Mr. Hatch, Collector of Bogra, reported that he "had received news from Pargana Chowgong of there having arrived upwards of three thousand men and that they had confined the Chaudhury's [zamindar's] naib until he paid them a sum of money and that they had plundered the several villages which they passed through." The Sannyasis were then at Sherpur about 12 miles from Bogra.[3] On the 8th, he further reported that "the Sannyasis arrived there [Bogra] that day in number about two thousand, one hundred horses and eighty bullocks laden with ammunition. As the ryots &c deserted their houses, he thought it the most expedient method to send a vakeel on the part of Government accompanied by two Chaudhury's Naibs to know their intentions, on which they sent word they must have a sum of money paid them, otherwise they should remain in the Purgunnah until they had taken a sufficiency to pay their charges and as they compounded for twelve hundred rupees which the Chaudhuries agreed to pay....The sum was advanced out of the Treasury, on receipt of which they passed

---

[1]Letter from Capt. Stuart to the Committee of Circuit, dated 3rd February, 1773.

[2]A pargana in British territory in which the Maharaja of Cooch Behar has zamindari rights.

[3]Letter from the Collector at Silberis (Bogra) to the Committee of Circuit at Dinajpur, dated 6th January, 1773.—Secret Department Proceedings, dated 21st January, 1773.

quietly through this Pargana [Silberis] to Sibganj where there was another party of about four thousand men."[1]

Pursuit of Sannyasis by Capt. Edwards.

On receipt of this news, the Committee of Circuit then at Dinajpur directed Capt. Edwards to march at once towards Chilmary against the Sannyasis.[2] Capt. Edwards with three companies of sepoys reached Oliapore [Ulipur in Rangpur district] on the 17th and on the following day continued his march towards Chilmary. He learnt that 'on the 12th a small party of Sannyasis had entered Chilmary and carried off the zamindar with two of the principal inhabitants to their main body some 8 miles off and extorted 1,300 rupees from them.'

Rangpur.

Mymensingh.

They were traced to have passed by Dewangunge and Bosnapore to Moydapore Puckery [Madhupur in Pargana Pukharia][3] and had levied contributions from all these villages. Capt. Edwards could not trace where they went afterwards. But information regarding their depredations is obtained from the Collector of Dacca, who wrote on the 26th January: "I have this day received a letter of the 6th of Maugh [about 20th January] from Kishen Roy, the Zemindar of the Purgunnah Momensing advising that a body of 5000 Sonnasses had entered the Purgunnah of Jafferseen[4] confined the Zemindar's Naib of that Purgannah and did not release him without extorting from him to the amount of about 1600 Rs. They afterwards marched to Modepore [Madhupur], from whence they proposed to direct their course to the Purgunnah of Alephsing[5] and then to Momunsing[6], the inhabitants of which Purganna were greatly terrified at their approach in so much as to begin to desert the villages. The person who heads this body of Sonasses is named Darreangheer." The letter further announced that "another body of this race of people to the number of 6000 headed by Moitegeer are marching towards the same part of the country and it is not unlikely, with a view to join the former."[7] The Collector was apprehensive of their march to Dacca, and added that "the latest information is to the effect that the Sannyasis have entered Alapsingh pargana and are well

[1]Letter from the Collector at Silberis to the Committee of Circuit at Dinajpur, dated 8th January, 1773.—Secret Department Proceedings, dated 21st January, 1773.

[2]Letter from the Committee of Circuit at Dinajpur to the Collector at Silberis, dated 13th January, 1773. Secret Department Proceedings, dated 21st January, 1773.

[3]Madhupur about 30 miles west of Mymensingh town within what is known as the Madhupur Jungles. It contains temples belonging to resident Sannyasis of the place.

[4]Pargana Jafarshahi in Jamalpur subdivision of the Mymensingh District.

[5]Alapsingh pargana on the right bank of the Brahmaputra belonging to the well-known zamindars of Muktagacha. The town of Mymensingh is within this Pargana.

[6]Pargana Mymensingh situated on the left bank of the Brahmaputra is the largest pargana in the district. The town is named after it.

[7]Letter from the Collector of Dacca, dated 26th January, 1773.—Secret Department Proceedings, dated 10th March, 1773.

armed with matchlocks, spears and other instruments of war." On the 29th the Collector reported that he was informed by a zamindar of Alapsingh Pargana that "a body of 3500 Sonassees have plundered the house of Kinkar Sarkar, Gomastha to the other zemindar and also Ramprosad Roy's and other houses and further that the two zemindars' naibs were under the necessity of sending a vakeel to negotiate with them and in order to withhold their hands from committing further outrages paid them the sum of 3500 rupees." It was further stated that the Sannyasis would next enter Pargana Mymensingh and expected to be joined by another body of 7,000 men. The intelligence from the Sardar of Shurpur [Sherpur][1] was that "a great number of Sannyasis were about Chilmary and Jurawalgeer one of their leaders had arrived there, at the head of fifteen boats of these people, thro' dread of whom the zemindar, his family and many of the inhabitants had fled into the jungles."

Dacca.

On the 4th February, the Collector of Dacca reported that "a body of 5000 Sennasies were arrived at Cogmar [Kagmari], Attea Pargana about a day and a half distant from Dacca and that the people of Dhamrai had deserted their houses and the inhabitants of the city of Dacca were also much alarmed. Accordingly he wrote to Luckipore [in Noakhali] and Jessore for a company of sepoys. He also applied to Nawab Jessarat Khan to furnish him with 500 Burkandazes and spearmen."[2] On the 6th, he reported that the Sannyasis had marched to Patteeh Gottah [Pathar Ghata] and had crossed the Bunse [Bangsi] river near the hills [Madhupur jungles]. "Small parties of them approached within six coss of Dacca but dispersed in consequence of the preparations at Dacca. Their design was against Dacca. It is certain that their route has been the nearest road to it, and they have avoided all the large rivers that might have impeded their march....The news of their march very much alarmed the inhabitants in so much that many of them deserted their houses." By way of caution the Collector placed "a guard and some horse at the three passes by either of which it was probable they would enter the city". He received accounts of a "very large contribution that have been levied by these people in Alepsing, Chilmarry, Attea, Cogmarree &c and of very considerable sums they have plundered from merchants."

Back to Mymensingh.

On the 7th February, the Collector of Dacca further reported that the Sannyasis had recrossed the river Bangsi and were again in Attia Pargana. We get a glimpse from this report of the further progress of Capt. Edwards who was last heard of from Camp near Chilmary on the 20th January. "Some of the Hircarrahs who have come reported that two or three companies of sepoys under the command of an officer had reached

---

[1]Sherpur pargana in Jamalpur subdivision of Mymensingh district.

[2]Letters from the Collector of Dacca to the Governor in Council, dated 29th January, 1773, and 4th February, 1773.

Byganbarry when the Sonassies were at Muddapore but as it was some days since it would seem that they have not been able to come up with them which indeed I would not imagine would be possible for any single detachment, the marches of these people being so very rapid."[1]

Considering the superiority in number of these banditti to Capt. Edward's party, the Collector of Dinajpur informed Capt. Stuart at Jalpaiguri of the circumstances.[2] The Committee of Circuit also directed Capt. Stuart to act with Capt. Edwards in the suppression of the Sannyasis and the Collector of Rangpur was instructed to employ Capt. Jones for the same purpose.[3]

With Capt. Edwards in pursuit, the Sannyasis left Attia and made another attempt to reach Dacca. On the 10th February, the Collector of Dacca reported that "Onopmantageer at the head of a considerable body of Sannasis arrived at Puccoloe [Pakulla] on the 25th Magh [about 5th or 6th February] from Atteah. On the 26th they reached Chundrah [probably Andrah near Mirzapur] and seized Ramlochan Bose a Gomastah belonging to some gentlemen at Dinajpur from whom they took to the amount of 4200 Rupees. They also seized the zemindar's vakeel and insisted upon his showing them the way to Dacca. They came on the same day to Bauncehautty[4] from whence discovering they had a jungly country to pass and likewise hearing of the force at Dacca they turned back to Conchunpore [Kanchanpur in Tangail subdivision of Mymensingh district within Madhupur jungles] on their way to Pottah Gollah [Pathar Ghata on the Bangsi river] and on the 27th marched towards the hills (Madhupur jungles)." Twenty-four Sannyasis are reported as being taken by a party of sepoys 8 miles from Dacca.[5] On the 20th February, the Chief of Dacca wrote that "the Sannyasis are for the most part retired from this province. There are still about eight or nine hundred on the Bhawal[6] side and another body of like number about three or four days march from hence."[7]

Second attempt to reach Dacca.

Accounts of raids on the kutcherries of various parganas and plunder of the revenue collected there are given in several petitions sent by Zamindars to the Collector of Dinajpur. But the

---

[1]Letter from the Collector of Dacca to the Governor in Council, dated 7th February, 1773.

[2]Letter from the Collector of Dinajpur to the Committee of Circuit at Rajmahal, dated 9th February, 1773.

[3]Letter from the Committee of Circuit to the Collector of Dinajpur, dated 12th February, 1773.

[4]Probably Baemhatty on the other bank of Andra near Mirzapur Police station.

[5]Letter from the Collector of Dacca, dated 10th February, 1773.–Secret Department Proceedings, 10th March, 1773.

[6]Pargana Bhowal in Dacca District lying nearly wholly within the Madhupur jungles.

[7]Letter from the Acting Chief of Dacca to the Acting Chief of Chittagong, dated 20th February, 1773—*Bengal District Records*, Chittagong, Vol. I, pp. 74-75.

Board definitely refused "to allow any deduction on account of the incursion of Sannyassis as they considered that the depredations they have committed in Silberis &c. to have been chiefly owing to the infatuation of the Talookdars, Inhabitants &c. in not giving proper intelligence and in countenancing and abetting these plunderers."[1]

Capt. Edwards defeated and killed:

Foiled in their attempts to reach Dacca the various bands of Sannyasis retraced their steps westward, and Capt. Edwards pursued them with his detachments. Hastings had, however, recalled him as "he (Hastings) knew much confidence was not to be placed upon the discipline or steadiness of the Pargana sepoys and was apprehensive of ill consequences from the smallness of their numbers. Captain Edwards received the orders for his return but he delayed the execution of them and upon hearing the Sennassies had re-entered the district had returned in quest of them."[2] On the 1st March, 1773, he overtook the enemy who were about 3,000 in the Pargana Barabazu and he and his detachment were all cut off excepting 12 sepoys.[3] Douglas,[4] a Sergeant-Major in one of the Pargana battalions, was in the detachment. A vivid account of the skirmish is given by Capt. Williams: "He [Capt. Edwards] descried the Sannyasis about two miles in front of him. He immediately formed his detachment into a column by subdivisions from the right and marched on towards the enemy who as soon as he came near enough saluted him with a few rockets. When Captain Edwards thought himself within a proper distance for engaging he rode to the head of the column and beat to arms intending that the divisions should double upon the left of the leading division as they came up; but the men mistaking the orders wheeled to the left and formed in battalion which laid their right flank open to the enemy, he galloped to the left in order to draw them into line fronting the Sannyasis whilst Douglas exerted himself on the right for the same purpose; but it was too late; for the enemy, perceiving the confusion, rushed in upon them with their swords and spears and dispatched a few, put the rest to flight. Douglas was the first that fell but the fate of Captain Edwards was not known; his hat was found in the Nulla before mentioned, but the body has never been discovered.[5]

[1]Revenue Board consisting of the Whole Council, Original Consultation, No. 9, dated 20th July, 1773.

[2]Secret Department Proceedings, dated 10th March 1773.

[3]Letter from the Collector of Silberis (Bogra) to the Governor in Council, dated 2nd March, 1773.

[4]"Douglas was a brave soldier and was long in the service of the Honourable East India Company in Bengal." He was made a prisoner by Mir Kasim's soldiers but escaped from a boat on the way to Patna. On his joining the army at Uday Nala, he was placed in the European battalion which he served until 1766 when he was appointed Sergeant-Major to a pargana battalion.

[5]Timothy Edwards—Captain 1st September, 1769; drowned, March 1st, 1773, in a nullah at Barrypore.—Dodwell and Miles' *Army List*. Barrypore was probably a hamlet of the present town of Serajganj.

The Native Commandant[1] and adjutant were tried for their misconduct in that unfortunate action and were executed at the mouth of a cannon ; but the gallant behaviour of the jamadar deserved much praise ; for having rallied sixteen men, he made his retreat good, although attacked on every side by the Sannyasis, for which he was promoted to the rank of Subadar."[2]

After defeating Capt. Edwards, a party of the Sannyasis numbering 1,500 crossed the Ganges and on the 11th March was encamped within 8 miles of Kumarkhali factory. The spies sent to watch them reported that they were on their route to Mahmudshahi towards Jessore and that they plundered the villages they passed through.[3]

Sannyasis in West Bengal.

In this eventful year, even Western Bengal was not free from the incursions of Sannyasis. On the 3rd February, the Resident at Khirpai reported that "a party of Sannyasis amounting to six or seven thousand foot and five hundred horse were encamped within fifteen coss from Khirpai" [Ghatal subdivision in Midnapur district]. Vigorous measures were at once taken by the Governor who ordered 5 companies of Brigade Sepoys to march against them from Calcutta and also directed the Collector of Burdwan to send a sufficient force against them.[4] An officer with 3 companies of sepoys and a field-piece was despatched on the fourth night but the Sannyasis went away towards Cuttack without making any disturbance.[5] They were evidently on a pilgrimage to Puri. On the 17th March it was reported that a body of 3,000 Sannyasis had gone to Bishnupur with the intention of passing through the Midnapore jungles.[6] Two days later information was received that the Sannyasis were at Raipur [now in Bankura]. Capt. Forbes was directed to pursue them and drive them out of the Company's territory and the zamindars were directed to help Capt. Forbes. Eventually they proceeded from Raipur to Phulkusma, from there to Silda and thence to Alampur and thence to Gopiballavpur

---

1 "Immediately on the receipt of this letter you will be pleased to direct Captain Forbes to confine Jiram Subadar of the 14th battalion of sepoys who commanded the detachment of that battalion which joined Captain Edwards and was present at the defeat by the Sannyasis and you will order Jiram Subadar, immediately to be sent under a guard to the presidency to stand his trial before a sepoy general court martial for having deserted his post in the face of the enemy."—Letter from Warren Hastings to Collector of Midnapore, dated 22nd June, 1773.

2 *Historical Account of the Rise and Progress of the Bengal Native Infantry*—by Capt. Williams (published in 1817)—pp. 132-34.

3 Letter from the Collector at Kumarkhali to the Governor in Council in the Secret Department, dated 11th March, 1773.

4 Letter from the Secretary to the Council at Fort William to the Resident at Midnapore, dated 4th February, 1773.

5 Letter from the Resident at Burdwan to the President & Council at Fort William, dated 6th February, 1773.

6 Letter from the Hon. Charles Stuart to the Resident at Midnapore, dated 17th March, 1773.

bordering on the Marhatta districts beyond the reach of the Midnapore authorities.[1]

Another body of Sannyasis appeared near Agradwip in March. The Collector of Nadia reported to the Governor that "a body of Senassies consisting of about one thousand were seen near Augerdeep to which place they are going being the season of the annual pilgrimage to the Pagodas of that town—They are armed and committed great depredations in their route." The Council of Fort William entirely approved the Governor's action in sending "orders to Lt. Col. Galliez commanding the troops at Berhampur to consult with Mr. Middleton on the most effectual means of destroying or dispersing these plunderers and either to employ the whole or part of the Battalion lately ordered to reinforce Captain Stuart at Dinajpur on this service if they shall judge it expedient. The 12th Battalion ordered to replace the 9th at Berhampur will be ready to march on the 17th and may also be employed on the same service should the Sanassies still remain in this part of the province."[2]

Sannyasis in Bihar.

In this year, Bihar also was alarmed at the success of the Sannyasis in Bengal. On the 15th March the Supervisor of Tirhut, stationed at Darbhanga, informed the Chief and Council of Revenue at Patna "that in ten days they [the Sannyasis] will begin to assemble at a place called Janickpur[3] in commemoration of the birth and marriage of Sita which are on the same day of the year. They amount in number 20 to 50,000 Sunnasses. Lest they should come into Tirhut the cultivation of which is now beginning, I should be glad that a sufficient force was sent for about ten days till they are all separated to prevent their alarming the riyots."[4]

Evidently some of the Sannyasis wanted to force their way towards Bengal through Purnea and were frustrated as we find from a letter of Warren Hastings. "Several parties of the Sannyasis having entered into the Purniah province burning and destroying many villages there, the Collector applied to Captain Brook who had just arrived at Panity near Rajmahal with his newly raised battalion of light infantry. That officer immediately crossed the river and entered upon measures against the Sannyasis and had very nearly fallen in with a party of them just as they were crossing the Cosa river to escape out of the province. They arrived on the opposite bank before their rear had entirely crossed but too late to do any execution amongst them. It is apparent now that the Sannyasis were glad to escape as fast as they can out of the Company's possessions."[5]

---

[1]Letter from the Resident at Midnapore to the Hon. Charles Stuart, dated 20th March, 1773.

[2]Secret Department Proceedings, dated 15th March, 1772.

[3]Janakpur or Janikpur in Nepal, north of the Darbhanga district.

[4]Proceedings of the Controlling Council of Revenue at Patna, dated 22nd March, 1773.

[5]Hastings to Sir George Colebrooke, dated 31st March, 1773.

On their westward march they appeared in Champaran and Saran. The Superintendent of Sircar Saran reported to the Chief and Council of Revenue at Patna on the 7th April: "The Sunnassis are moving in very large bodies along the borders of Sircar Champaran and have greatly alarmed the inhabitants of that District. I have sent out all the Sepoys that could possibly be spared from this side of the country under Captain Ashe to the assistance of Captain Hardy. But both the detachments when joined will be very inadequate to the force they are to oppose and it would be of great service if three or four companies more were to march from Patna with all possible expedition by the shortest road to Betteah. The Sunnassis now take their route to the westward and must cross the Gunduck when a small party of sepoys may attack to advantage and revenge the insults which the Company's arms have recently and repeatedly suffered from them in other parts of the province."[1] Accordingly the Chief at Patna asked for four Companies of Sepoys from Col. Chapman, commanding the 2nd Brigade at Dinapur, "as a means of promoting the plan of the Hon'ble the Governor and Council for expelling the Sunnassies from these provinces." On 13th April Capt. Hay with four Companies of sepoys proceeded from Patna to join the detachment at Bettia "using the most utmost expedition on the March."[2] The result of the pursuit is not reported.

Elated at Capt. Edwards' defeat, stray bands of Sannyasis separated from the main bodies and proceeded east as far as Sylhet. On the 10th May, Mr. Thackeray, the Collector, reported that "he had reason to suspect that the Sannyasis would come that way besides the small bodies daily arriving....Accordingly he got several pieces of cannon mounted under a small Mud fort in the center of the Town.... This he thought had good effect for he had undoubted proofs of some Sanassys going to the Gentiah Raja [the Raja of Jaintia Hills north of Sylhet] and wanting him to join them and give them all the assistance in his power towards plundering Sylhet."[3] **Sannyasis in Sylhet.**

After the conclusion of the festivals at Puri, the Sannyasis retraced their steps. On the 20th October, the Collector of Cuttack reported that "1700 Gourins and 300 Fakirs were leaving for Bengal. They travel as beggars and rob in their way if they can."[4] On 28th October Lieut. Hearsay reported from Jellasore that one thousand Sannyasis were within two days' march from Batta and intended to come to Jellasore.[5] Later it was reported that the Sannyasis had taken "the route through **1773-74.** **Sannyasis march back from Puri.**

[1]Proceedings of the Controlling Council of Revenue at Patna, dated 13th April, 1773.

[2]*Ibid.*

[3]Proceedings of the Revenue Board consisting of the whole Council, dated 8th June, 1773.

[4]Letter from Henry Alleyn to Samuel Lewis, dated 20th October, 1773.

[5]Letter from Lieut. Hearsay, dated 26th October, 1773.

Singhbhoom, a Province to the westward of the Midnapore jungles at the back of the hills." On 30th November information was received from the Collector at Maidapore (Murshidabad) that two thousand armed Sannyasis with three pieces of cannon on camels appeared on the 25th in Nooney Pargana in Birbhum district but being refused a passage by the Thanadar they went towards Mooltee, but no complaints were received against them.[1] It appears from the report of the Collector of Rajshahi that they crossed the Ganges at Sady Gunge. They were three thousand in number, and well armed. Each man carried a matchlock, spear, two swords and a rocket. They had not committed any great acts of violence but levied small contributions from the zamindar's officers and their provisions and necessaries from the ryots. Capt. Thompson who was proceeding to Rangpur and was at that time at Godagary was asked to proceed against them by Mr. Middleton, the Resident at the Durbar, who happened to be at Rampur Boalia.[2] Capt. Crawford from Birbhum and Capt. Forbes from Midnapore were ordered by the Governor to operate against them. The Governor was determined to suppress the Sannyasis and directed Mr. Middleton, the Resident at the Durbar, to inform Col. Grant at Berhampur the moment the Sannyasis entered the province, and Col. Grant was to take necessary measures for sending a force to intercept and attack them.[3]

Majnu reappears in North Bengal.

After about two years, Majnu Shah, the leader of the Fakirs, appeared again in Bengal. On 18th December, the Collector of Rajshahi reported "Shaw Mudgenoo entered the Purgana Messideh [now in Dinajpur] at the head of 700 Fakirs and demanded payment of a debt of 1500 Rs. due from the deposed zamindar. On his not receiving a satisfactory answer to his demand made in writing, he detached 200 of his men to seize the zamindar who made his escape the night following and travelled with all expedition hither having been pursued by the Fakirs as far as Limboobarea about thirty miles off. The officers of the Purgunnah all left it as also many of the Riots. The Fakirs seized 1057 Rs. which was collected ready to remit here, plundered the zamindar's habitation and cutchery and collected about 1500 Rs. in different villages.... I hear that the Fakirs have joined the body of Sannyasis who were in the neighbourhood and that they are gone together through Sailburris towards the Burrumpooter River."[4]

Defeat of Sannyasis and Fakirs.

On the 23rd December, a party consisting of four companies of sepoys commanded by Lieut. Williams who was in command of a detachment of sepoys operating in Dinajpur district fell in with them and totally

[1]Letter from the Collector at Maidapur to the President and Governor, dated 30th November, 1773.

[2]Letter from the Collector of Luskerpore, dated 9th December, 1773.

[3]Secret Department Proceedings, dated 9th December, 1773.

[4]Letter from the Collector of Rajshahi to the Governor in Council, dated 18th December, 1773.

defeated and dispersed them with great slaughter.[1] On the 27th December, however, the Resident at the Durbar received information from the Collector of Purnea that a large body of Sannyasis had appeared in his district and were moving towards his residence. This disquieting news led the Resident to send six companies of sepoys under the command of Lieut. Alexander Munro against them. Lieut. Williams' detachment was also directed to proceed to Purnea.[2] Evidently the Sannyasis were in flight after the severe defeat in the hands of Lieut. Williams and they left Purnea before meeting any of the detachments sent against them.

About the middle of January, 1774, Lieut. Williams reported to the Resident at the Durbar that the Sannyasis had marched towards Cooch Behar. He added the welcome rumour of the death of Majnu, but it turned out to be false.

Writing on the 20th March, 1774, Hastings tells Laurence Sullivan.[3] "The Sannyassis threatened us with the same disturbances at the beginning of this year as we experienced from them the last. But by being....provided to oppose them and one or two severe checks which they received in their first attempts, we have the country clear of them. A party of horse which we employed in pursuit of them, has chiefly contributed to intimidate these ravagers who seem to pay little regard to our sepoys, having so much the advantage of them in speed on which they entirely rely for their safety." The party of horse is the Governor-General's Body-guard under Capt. Toone, for we find that on 6th February the Resident at the Durbar wrote to Mr. Goodlad, Collector of Purnea, to give information to Capt. Toone "respecting the manner in which he is to cross the Coorsa."

How the depredations of these raiders affected the revenues is seen from the following instance: Writing to the Court of Directors in October, 1774, the Governor-General reported a "considerable deficiency between the collections and the settlement" in the district of Rangpur. "A very considerable part of the deficiency may be attributed to the plunder, extortion and depredations occasioned by the continued incursions of the Sannyasis. It is not to be doubted that these have been productive of heavy loss to the country although we adopted it as an invariable maxim to grant no deduction to the Farmers on this account in order if possible to conquer their blind superstition in giving countenance to these religious plunderers and make it their interest to repel their incursions."[4]

---

[1]Letter, dated 27th December, 1773, from the Resident at the Durbar to Lieut. Williams, and Secret General Letter to the Court of Directors, dated 30th December, 1773.

[2]Letter, dated 27th December, 1773, from the Resident at the Durbar to the Collector of Dinajpur.

[3]Gleig's *Memoirs of Warren Hastings*, Vol. I, p. 395.

[4]Extract from Revenue General Letter to the Court, dated 18th October, 1774.

CHAPTER VII

Warren Hastings' Measures

In January, 1773, the Committee of Circuit writing from Dinajpur represented the urgent necessity for taking effective measures to prevent the annual incursions of these ravagers. They suggested that "a respectable detachment formed from the brigade stationed in Bihar should oppose the Sannyasis at their entry into the provinces" and also that "it might be an eligible expedient when they rendezvous at Saugor, their ultimate place of resort, to coop them up in that island and prevent their retreat."

In the same month Hastings took vigorous measures. He issued a circular letter on the 21st January, 1773, to the Collectors "acquainting them that from this time they were to keep a particular eye over the motions of the people known by the name of Senassies whose incursions of late had been frequent and distressing to the country and they were to spare no pains to procure the most exact intelligence of them and require the assistance of the Zamindars, Dewans, etc., for obtaining it. They were further directed to leave strict orders at every Chokey in their districts to suffer no person whatsoever to pass with arms but they be obliged to deposit them with the Chokeydars and that they also give public notice that all persons and bodies of men travelling armed through the country will be regarded as enemies of the Government and pursued accordingly."[1] Representations were, however, made by the Collectors and Residents of the various districts that the enforcement of the orders would result in unnecessary harassment to travellers and merchants. The following letter[2] from the Collector of Hooghly gives a typical account of the insecurity of rural conditions :—

> "That security and tranquillity which are the happy effects of a regular government were never to be depended upon in the interior parts of this country. Individuals have therefore been obliged to arm, for their own defence; accordingly merchants and bankers, when under the necessity of transporting treasure or goods, never fail to escort it with a party of pikes and barkandazes, and travellers singly or in company are never seen without swords or some other weapon for defending themselves."

---

[1] *Bengal District Records.* Chittagong, Vol. I, pp. 71-72.

[2] Secret Department Proceedings, 10th March, 1773.

In March the President and Council of Revenue at Fort William accordingly modified their instructions as the "orders for disarming all travellers without distinction might be dangerous to the safety of merchants and others going through the country on lawful business and consequently exposed to the attacks of the Sannyasis and dacoits" and restricted the prohibition to Sannyasis only. All merchants and others travelling on lawful business were permitted to carry arms as usual unmolested.[1]

The following notice was also issued in January, 1773, expelling all Sannyasis (with certain exceptions) from Calcutta and the provinces :—

"Notice is hereby given to all Bairagis and Sannyasis who are travellers, strangers and passengers in this country, excepting such of the caste of Ramanandi and Gauria who have for a long time been settled and receive a maintenance in land money or gundi from the Government or the zamindars of the province, likewise, such Sannyasis as are allowed charity ground for executing of religious offices, etc. to leave the town of Calcutta, its precincts, or any other place of residence in it within seven days from the publication of this advertisement, and depart from the subahs of Bengal and Bihar in two months.

"It is further declared that if any of the abovementioned sects shall be found in Bengal or Bihar at the expiration of two months they are to be seized and put on the roads for life made to work at the public buildings and have their property confiscated to the Government. If any one with a view of evading the intent of this publication shall claim donations of land and his claim be falsified, he will be punished as above directed."[2]

Two months later Collectors were required to issue positive orders to zamindars and farmers to furnish information of the movements and routes of the plunderers, failure to supply which was "to be attended with the displeasure of the Board in case of zamindars ; and in the case of farmers, they will be seriously punished for neglect of it."[3]

As the Sannyasis often found shelter in the hills from where they issued forth on the plains of Bengal, Hastings in arranging a Treaty between the Honourable East India Company and the Deva Raja or Raja of Bhutan, in 1774, secured the insertion of the following article :—

"That whatever Sannyasis are considered by the English, as an enemy, the Deva Raja will not allow them to take shelter in any part of the district now given up, nor permit them to enter into the Honourable Company's territories or through any part of his ; and if the Bhutias

[1]Secret Department Proceedings, dated 10th March, 1773.

[2]Secret Department Proceedings, dated 21st January, 1773.

[3]Secret Department Proceedings, dated 15th March, 1773.

shall not of themselves be able to drive them out, they shall give information to the Resident on the part of the English in Cooch Behar and they shall not consider the English troops pursuing the Sannyasis into these distiets as any breach of this treaty."

Most important of all, the military or other protective establishments were placed on a more effective footing. In 1766, six new corps had been raised under the name of Pargana Battalions for employment under the Revenue Department in the districts to guard treasure and for escort duties, etc. They were numbered from the 22nd to 27th and were attached two to each Brigade. Some others were added later. Their employment in small parties was found injurious to discipline and was ineffective. The defeat of Captains Thomas and Edwards and Lieut. Keith drove this lesson home. An example of the pernicious effect of employing sepoys in small parties—which Hastings complained of—is to be found in the case of the Pargana sepoys employed under Capt. Mackenzie, the predecessor of Capt. Thomas at Rangpur. The sepoys employed on this work turned blackmailers and extorted large sums of money from people, while the Captain himself lent money to zamindars at extortionate rates of interest and enforced realisation by confinement of zamindars and their agents. The Proceeding volumes of the Controlling Committee of Revenue of 1772 are replete with stories of oppression disclosed at the enquiry. Hastings accordingly organised a separate corps for the service of districts "to be officered by natives only but commanded by English officers disabled from field service. They were not to be considered as any part of the military establishment not admitted in the strength of the army but merely as burcundosses or the usual cutchery guards, to be cloathed, armed with muskets and instructed in so much discipline as may qualify them for the services they were employed in."[1] The Pargana sepoys ("a rascally corps",[2] Hastings called them) were broken up; the three regular battalions employed on Pargana duty being at the same time returned to their respective brigades and two years later being renumbered and included in the regular battalions. Detachments of the Brigade sepoys were posted on the frontiers to be employed only in the defence of the provinces.

Later in the year 1773, Hastings arranged with Raja Chait Singh of Benares to furnish 500 horse to assist the Company's troops in expelling the Sannyasis. They assisted the troop of 50 horse raised for the Governor General's own Body-guard. Hastings later wrote of this as follows: "The troop of horse appointed for my bodyguard in 1773, was raised, formed and disciplined by Major Toone but did not perform the duty assigned to it by its institution being first employed on service against the Senasses. It was eminently useful by the rapidity of its motion

[1] Secret Department Proceedings, dated 6th May, 1773.

[2] Trotter's *Warren Hastings*, pp. 103-104.

and some signal success so intimidating that order of banditti that they were entirely driven from the province."

The corps of Light Infantry commanded by Capt. Brooke, intended for hill service, was also employed against the Sannyasis in Purnea and adjoining districts.

The action taken in 1773 had a considerable effect. The problem however was to recur in future years as will be seen and in the light of the records of later years since examined, the conclusion of Vincent Smith [*History of India*, pages 5-6] requires revision, viz., "Their incursions into Bengal ceased in the second year of the administration of Hastings, and history does not mention any further depredations by them in other provinces. The bands evidently melted away when the Bengal hunting-ground was closed by the vigilance of the Governor." Bengal, or parts of it, continued to be a hunting-ground for some years to come, though Fakirs were more prominent than Sannyasis.

CHAPTER VIII

Fakir raiders reappear, 1775—1780

EVENTS outside the province of Bengal, Bihar and Orissa helped the success of the measures undertaken by Hastings within the province. The subjugation of the Rohillas in 1773, and the annexation of the Rohilla country to Oudh created a friendly buffer State in the region through which the nomadic raiders had hitherto usually passed. A strong detachment of sepoys was stationed in the then impregnable fortress of Chunar. In 1775, Benares and Ghazipur were taken over from Oudh and Raja Chait Singh of Benares became a protégé of Hastings and maintained a body of horse for the service of the Company whenever required.

The serious reverses at the Third Battle of Paniput by no means destroyed the Mahratta power. Peshwa Madhab Rao made a bold bid for the lost empire in 1769. The Rajputs and the Jats were defeated and compelled to pay tribute. The Mahrattas next captured Delhi and placed Shah Alam on the throne. They also occupied the whole of the Doab and made preparations for conquering Oudh and Rohilkhand. But the sudden death of Madhab Rao in November, 1772, was fatal to the hopes of the Mahratta Empire. Disunion broke out and the Mahrattas were divided into two rival camps with the Scindia and the Holkar on one side and the Gaekwar on the other. This necessitated the enlargement of armies of both camps and the Mahratta Army was recruited largely from the Sannyasis. The rebellion of the zamindar of Halsipur [Hatwa] in Bihar with the help of Naga Sannyasis in 1768 has already been referred to. In 1775, the zamindar, Fatch Sahi, again rebelled and took refuge in a dense jungle on the borders of Oudh and "had under him a regular battalion of trained horsemen and matchlock-men which went on increasing because of the enlistment of large bodies of lawless fakirs and banditti who came flocking in to join his standard." The bid for power in Bundelkhand about this time by Himmat Giri, the Sannyasi leader, furnished employment for a large body of armed Sannyasis. His subsequent struggle for power against the Bundelah Chiefs from 1790 to 1802 kept them on in service. A corps of the Naga Sannyasis commanded by a disciple of Himmat Bahadur was employed by Daulat Rao Scindia as late as 1809. They were also employed in the armies of the Holkar and the Raja of

Jaipur. For these reasons and also because of the opposition to be met with in the Company's territories, the Sannyasis came to Bengal at longer intervals and from this time the raiders are generally Muhammadan Fakirs.

1774-75. Sannyasis in Dinajpur.

Early in the season of 1774-75, the acting Chief of the Provincial Council of Revenue at Dinajpur informed the Board on the 28th November, 1774, of the appearance of a party of Sannyasis at Bhawanipur, about 16 coss to "the southward of Govindgunge."[1] Accordingly parwanas [orders] were issued on the naibs of the districts under the Provincial Council ; Kissen Persad, the security for Edrakpore, reported to the Provincial Council early in December that "the Hircurrah of the Chowdry of Bogra and Sherpur, etc., have informed me that one hundred unarmed Sannyasis have arrived at Bhowanypore to celebrate the Bhowani Poojah and had from thence proceeded to the Ganges to wash."[2] The information was received by the Council on the 12th December and no more was heard of these Sannyasis.

Sannyasis prevented from entering Bengal

In March, 1775, Lieut.-Col. Muir, commanding at Chunar Fort, reported to the Commander-in-Chief[3]: "I for sometime past having had information of a numerous body of armed men assembling at Allahabad and although report says they are on a religious pilgrimage yet as the annual ravages committed in the provinces in the past demands a vigilant watch over the motions of any body of men moving from the westward and particularly as when armed with matchlooks and Tulwars even let their pretentions be ever so religious I for that reason thought it prudent to station spies to bring the most speedy advice of their departure from that city....They have for some weeks past given out that their design was to bend their route directly homewards from Allahabad, whereas I have this instant received positive advice of their being now in motion to the eastward ; and in order to pass this station in the most private manner they have divided themselves into small bodies not exceeding 50, whereas report makes them out when assembled near 20,000. I beg leave to remark that upon comparing all these different circumstances you will see the propriety of my sending to their camp a message requesting immediate and positive information of their route and intention."

The parwana sent by Lieut.-Col. Muir to the encampment of Sannyasis was to the effect that "until a leader had seen the Colonel and stated all the circumstances regarding the Sannyasis, viz., whence they have come for what purpose and whither they are going, no one will

---

[1]Proceedings of the Provincial Council of Revenue at Dinajpur, dated 28th November, 1774.

[2]Proceedings of the Provincial Council of Revenue at Dinajpur, dated 12th December, 1774.

[3]Secret Department, Original Consultation, No. 4, dated 30th March, 1775.

be allowed to pass." The Secret Department of the Council approved of the measures undertaken and requested the Governor-General to write to Raja Chait Singh of Benares to use all his endeavours to compel these people to disband and return to their homes otherwise to oppose their entry in his or the Company's territories and act in concert with the Colonel to that effect.[1] This had the desired effect.[2]

1775-76.

Early in the season of 1775-76, on the 14th November, 1775, the Chief of the Provincial Council of Revenue at Dinajpur informed the Supreme Council that "having had intelligence of a body of Sinassee Fakirs being assembled at Gobindapore he wrote to Captain Fullarton for a reinforcement of the Sepoys and at the same time desired him to send a proper guard to protect the Hon'ble Company's Treasury at Rangpur. In consequence of which the two Companys of Sepoys and two officers have arrived here (Dinajpur) and one Company and an officer at Rangpur where he judged it will be proper to detain them for the present, notwithstanding he is since informed the former alarm is premature."[3]

Fakirs under Majnu in North Bengal.

Late in the season Majnu Shah again appeared. On the 19th March, 1776, the Chief of the Provincial Council at Dinajpur informed the Board that "he has received advice from Shamun Ally a religious person who resides at Mustangur that Shaw Majinah the famous Fakir who has so often been troublesome in these districts is endeavouring to collect a force in the Radshay [Rajshahi] Pergunnah where he has already committed many acts of violence."[4] The Chief on the same date placed before the Council the following letter, dated the 15th March, from Mr. Gladwin stationed at Bogra : "I have received certain information that Mejenoo has assembled a large body of Fakirs in this neighbourhood and that they intend to appear in arms at the Meelah of Mustangar, which will be on the 20th of this month, if you will instantly send me twenty or thirty sepoys I hope they will be too much alarmed to prosecute their present intention, but should these pergunnahs remain destitute of the appearance of protection, they will inevitably be plundered and I shall certainly be in a very disagreeable if not a dangerous situation."[5] The Provincial Council in reply wrote as follows on the 19th March : "The season is so far advanced that we apprehend it is not in the power of Shaw Majinah to collect a force sufficient to disturb the quiet of these districts. We however

---

[1]Secret Department Proceedings, dated 30th March, 1775.

[2]Secret Department Proceedings, dated 20th April, 1775.

[3]Proceedings of the Provincial Council of Revenue at Dinajpur, dated 14th November, 1775.

[4]Proceedings of the Provincial Council of Revenue at Dinajpur, dated 19th March, 1776.

[5]Letter from Mr. Gladwin to the Chief of the Provincial Council of Revenue at Dinajpur, dated 15th March, 1776.

are to request you will immediately despatch to Dinajpur such public treasure as you may have in readiness as we cannot spare you any force from hence for its protection having but one Comapny of Sepoys for the defence of our Treasury. Should you be under any apprehension of your personal safety you may repair to Denagepore for a few days till these disturbances have subsided when you will return to your station."[1] Mr. Gladwin wrote in reply on the 24th March as follows: "Shah Mojinoo with a body of Fakeers are now actually in possession of the Mosque at Mustangur; they have as yet levied only a small contribution from the Meelah (fair) and my hircarrahs have brought me intelligence that they intend to move tomorrow towards Maldah. I think it most prudent to remain here with the Treasure as I have no force to send with it to Denagepore, and I am not in the least apprehensive of being attacked."[2] On the 26th March he further reported to the Provincial Council that "Shaw Mojinoo with a party of Fakeers left Mustangur last night without committing any further excesses than levying small contributions at the meelah. They are now within four coss of this place in Rany Bowanny's Zemindarry where I understand they plunder who come in their way. My hircarrahs bring me the intelligence that they will move towards the Berhamputtar tomorrow."[3] But Majnu Shah returned reinforced by well-armed Rajputs during the rains. On the 14th June Mr. Gladwin reported to the Provincial Council at Dinajpur that "Shah Majenoo with a large body of Armed Fackeers arrived that morning at Mustangur and I am informed that he expects daily reinforcements. I am not under any apprehension for my own safety but as I fear he will lay the country under contribution or at least that the dread of his doing so may make the ryotts desert the Purgannah, I could wish you would send me a sufficient force to oblige him to quit this quarter."[4] The Provincial Council had no sepoys to send in aid of Mr. Gladwin and hoped that as Majnu did not commit any disturbances during the dry season at Mahastangarh he will remain quiet this time also. The Council remained content by writing to Majnu Shah "desiring him to disband the rabble who had gathered at Mustangur."[5] This inaction of the Council drew a spirited reply from Mr. Gladwin. He wrote on the 26th June as follows: "It is with concern, Gentlemen, that I perceive you think

---

[1]Proceedings of the Provincial Council of Revenue at Dinajpur, dated 19th March, 1776.

[2]Proceedings of the Provincial Council of Revenue at Dinajpur, dated 2nd April, 1776.

[3]*Ibid.*

[4]Proceedings of the Provincial Council of Revenue at Dinajpur, dated 18th June, 1776.

[5]Proceedings of the Provincial Council of Revenue at Dinajpur, dated 18th June, 1776. Letter to Mr. Gladwin from the Chief of the Provincial Council of the same date.

I entertained unnecessary apprehensions for Shaw Majinoo. Had it regarded only my own personal safety, I should never have made any application for assistance, but as the ryots are greatly alarmed and in my opinion with just cause, I thought it my duty to make you such representation. He did not come this time attended merely by a Bengal rabble but had with him a number of well-armed Rajepoots. He had begun to build a cantonment at Mustangur, publicly avowing that he intended staying there all the rainy season and was laying in a stock of provisions when a report prevailing that a force was coming against him from Denagepore he crossed the Bograh [Karatoya] with great precipitation and did not halt till he reached the Berhamputtah (Bramhaputra river). Two or three days after his arrival at Mustangur I sent the Cawzy to require from him, in my name what were his intentions he said he was come to recover some bond debts that he should remain peaceably at Mustangur provided he was not molested but that if I offered to attack him, he was not afraid but ready to oppose." The Provincial Council explained its inaction by stating that "as it was not in their power to send a sufficient number of sepoys to make head against any considerable body of Fakeers and being persuaded [?] the many accidents which have happened to the detachments formerly sent on this service have generally if not always arisen from the insufficiency of the force employed, they thought it for this reason most advisable to send you no sepoys not that they supposed the application was made hastily or without sufficient grounds."[1]

Inaction of the Provincial Council.

1776-77.

Towards the close of the rains, Majnu proceeded towards the north. The Provincial Council at Dinajpur received a report on the 1st September, 1776, from Ram Lochan Bose, Aumil of Tajpur: "Shaw Majenoo Fakeer attended by a large force is arrived at the village of Hurrampore in this pargunnah where he has committed great disturbances." The Provincial Council accordingly wrote on the 1st September to Capt. Popham at Sahebgunge to send towards Hurrampore two Companies of sepoys in order to disperse them. Accordingly Capt. Popham despatched Lieut. Boujonnar against Majnu. Lieut. Boujonnar marched with 110 men who, however, received information that Majnu had crossed the river Coosy on the west. Accordingly the Lieutenant was asked by Capt. Popham to come back[2] But the information seemed to be incorrect or in any case Majnu finding it difficult to proceed towards the west, marched back towards his usual places of shelter in Bogra district.

Operations against Majnu.

Hastings was, however, always on the alert for news of raiding mendicants and in concerting prompt measures against them. On the 22nd October, 1776, he reported to the Board "by a private letter received

[1]Proceedings of the Provincial Council of Revenue at Dinajpur, dated 2nd July, 1776.

[2]Proceedings of the Provincial Council of Revenue at Dinajpur, dated 1st September, 1776.

this morning I understand that a small party of Senassies consisting of 200 under the command of Shaik Mudgenoo, the same person who infested these provinces some years ago, made his appearance at the village of Cutta in Silberris on the 16th instant ; I beg leave to recommend that orders be immediately sent to Provincial Councils at Dinagepore and Dacca and to Mr. Gladwin (stationed at Silberris) to keep a strict look-out after these plunderers or any others that may attempt to come into the provinces and to give notice to Col. Leslie (Berhampore) and Capt. Popham (Sahebgunj) at their respective stations as occasion may require and that those officers be directed to use every precaution to intercept any party of Sunnassies that may attempt to enter the country by their stations and to march against anybody of them that shall have actually entered the country and shall be so near to them as to enable them to attack them but not to send out small detachments or to hazard an unequal engagement with them."[1] On the 30th October, Mr. Gladwin reported to the Governor-General that the Fakirs have moved off from Cutta to Ghoraghat and "it is their intention to disperse for the present and that they have fixed upon Mustan Gur in Silburris for their rendezvous in the season of heavy collections." Mr. Gladwin further reported that his harcaras had informed him that there were 25 sepoys with the banditti who were supposed to be deserters from some of the battalions.[2]

A detachment was sent from Berhampur under the command of Lieut. Robertson against Majnu Shah. On the 14th November, 1776, he had an engagement with Majnu at a place about 4 miles from Bogra which is graphically described by him in a letter to Mr. Gladwin—"I left camp last night at 9 o'clock and after marching about 9 coss arrived this morning just before daybreak at Mudgenoo's camp, as they had no intelligence of our being in their neighbourhood they were carelessly sitting round their fires to the amount of about three hundred and kept so bad a lookout that they let us advance within 20 yards of them before they took the alarm. As soon as I perceived we were discovered by their main body and seeing them stand to their arms, I ordered the sepoys to fire being so close to the Faukiers and our fire being pretty well directed they were not able to stand this shock but retired to an high grass jungle about 15 yards in their rear where they made a stand and from whence they wounded five of our sepoys, I have also received a slight wound from a ball in one of my legs. For men thus taken by surprise they made a resistance that I by no means expected, it being near half an hour before they entirely left the field and some of them stood until we were within Bayonet push of them, in the meantime Mudgenoo made his escape on horseback ; but

Retreat of Majnu.

[1]Revenue Department, Governor-General in Council, Original Consultation, No. 2, dated 22nd October, 1776. Governor-General's minute.

[2]Letter from the Collector of Silberis to the Governor-General & Council, dated 30th October, 1776. Revenue Department, Governor-General in Council, Original Consultation, No. 54, dated 10th December, 1776.

his horse being afterwards found at a small distance with two wounds in his hind parts I am from this circumstance inclined to hope that he has not escaped unhurt; we found near 20 Faukeers dead on the field and I am certain that many of those who escaped must be mortally wounded as we reserved our fire until close upon them.

"The sepoys from the long marches we have made to come up with the Faukeers are so much fatigued that it would now be a folly to think of pursuing them through an high grass jungle but if I can obtain any certain intelligence of their being collected in a body and what route they take I will resume my pursuit. We have taken a number of their large war rockets, some matchlocks, swords and shields."[1] Majnu seems to have lingered on in the Bogra district but only to have a more crushing defeat from a quite unexpected quarter in the following year.

Sannyasis *versus* Fakirs.

The old enmity between the Hindu and the Muhammadan mendicants seems to have revived. "In 1777," says the *Bogra District Gazetteer*, "a body of Nagas to the number of two hundred came to Bogra district from the northwest with what object it cannot be determined. The people say they were specially commissioned by Providence to destroy the pest of dakaits. They are said to have been well mounted on large horses and to have been armed with long swords. They and the followers of Majnu met in battle at daybreak and fought till noon, when only the infant son of the leader of the robber gang survived on the side of the dakaits. The swords of the Nagas are described as lopping off the heads

Defeat of Majnu.

of the robbers with as much ease as if they were cutting the stalks of plantain trees. A nullah near the scene of the encounter is still known as the Fakirkata khal and is about a couple of miles from the modern village of Champapur. The Nagas do not seem to have stayed for plunder and at once proceeded southward and then eastward to Mymensingh and Goalpara. In the latter place they had a fight with some semi-Portuguese settlers and were then lost sight of." The above account is on the authority of *Shetihas Bagurar Brittanta*, a brochure published in 1861 in the Bogra town; the account is not true so far as Majnu being killed, for more will be heard of his depredations in later years. Probably the news of the death of Majnu Shah was always welcome to the inhabitants and was given credence to whenever circulated. The quarrel between the Hindu and the Muhammadan mendicants broke out again at times in later years.

1777-78 Majnu reappears.

Late, however, in the season, Majnu Shah reappeared in the beginning of April, 1778. Raja Gaurnath of Dinajpur, Zamindar of nine-anna Division of Ghoraghat, petitioned to the Provincial Council of Revenue at Purnea as follows: "This day which is the 25th Chyte, I hear that Shah Mudjenoo with about 150 armed men are arrived in the village Bolwah

[1]Letter from Pat. Robertson to Francis Gladwin, dated 14th November, 1776. Revenue Department, Governor-General in Council, Original Consultation, No. 53, dated 10th December, 1776.

in the Pergunnah Masinda dependent on the seven-anna Division (of Ghoraghat). These people do not continue above a day or two at one place but traverse the country and plunder wherever they go. For which reason the ryotts are much alarmed and abscond in great numbers and as this is the season for cultivation I hope you will take some measures to remedy so great an evil." The Chief of the Council in his usual spirit of inaction replied to the Raja on the 7th April, 1778—"As the rainy season is set in, it is impossible that Shah Mudgenoo can travel much, or be attended with many people; and as I have wrote to the Phousdars to keep a look out after these robbers I hope they will soon be dispersed."[1]

In the next season, 1778-79, Majnu Shah penetrated further to the east into the present Mymensingh district. The gumashtas to the zamindars of Pargana Alapsingh reported to the Provincial Council at Dacca in 1780 that "last year an armed Fackeer Mujnoon Sha with a number of followers attacked and plundered several Mozahs under Purgunnah Alapsingh levied money from them to a considerable amount, laid waste the country and consequently prejudiced the revenues."[2] 1778-79. Majnu in Mymensingh.

Late in the season of 1779-80 Majnu Shah reappeared. "This year with a body of people, he [Majnu Shah] has attacked the house of the Zemindars of Alapsingh at a place called Shakur [Jhakar in Bogra district] and plundered it of all their effects, he has moreover seized upon the person of Chunder Seekar Acharjee, who is the son of one of the zemindars and confined him at Neemgatchy under the Zilla Dinajpur Bugwarah. A letter to the Chief at Dinajpur as also one to the Chief at Bugwarah (Bogra) may be sent that they may procure the enlargement of the aforesaid Acharjee and also apprehend and punish Mujnoon according to his deserts obliging him at the same time to restore the effects that he took from one zemindar's house that he may no longer be suffered to use such violent and oppressive practices but that the ryotts may be permitted to provide the revenue without molestation."[3] Accordingly, the Chief of the Provincial Council wrote a parwana to the Raja of Dinajpur directing him "to make the strictest search after Mujenoo and his accomplices in order that they may be apprehended and brought to punishment for the outrages they have committed as well as compelled to restore the effects they have plundered and moreover Raja Bydenaut do use every means to obtain the immediate release of Chunder Seekar Acharjee."[4] We hear no more of the steps taken. The Alapsingh zamindars, however, removed their residence about this time to Muktagacha near Mymensingh town in Pargana Alapsingh being similarly oppressed by resident sannyasis. 1779-80. Majnu in Bogra.

---

[1]Proceedings of the Provincial Council of Revenue at Purnea, dated 7th April, 1778.

[2]Proceedings of the Provincial Council of Revenue at Purnea, dated 14th March, 1780.

[3]*Ibid.*

[4]*Ibid.*

CHAPTER IX

Sannyasis in Cooch Behar

MENTION has already been made of the part played by the mercenary itinerant Sannyasis in the internal intrigues of Cooch Behar. In course of time many of these Sannyasis settled down in the neighbouring British territories especially in the Mymensingh district. Others took up their abode in the neighbouring districts of Goalpara in Assam and Rangpur in Bengal and were always available for hire as mercenary soldiers to foment intrigues; they played an important part in the internal affairs of Cooch Behar. The course of events in Cooch Behar had been like this: The minor Maharaja Devendranarayan was murdered in 1765 by one Rati Sarma at the instigation of Ramananda Gossain. Quarrels ensued over the succession and although the Nazir Deo [Commander-in-Chief] was helped by the English in 1766 in defeating the Sannyasi mercenaries of the Dewan Deo, the latter eventually gained the upper hand and his third brother, Dhairyendranarayan, was installed as Maharaja with the help of the Raja of Bhutan. In 1769 Khagendranarayan succeeded as the Nazir Deo, but the real power remained in the hands of the Dewan Deo who was supported by the Bhutias. The Dewan Deo was treacherously murdered and the Maharaja's younger brother was appointed Dewan Deo. The Raja of Bhutan, however, avenged the murder by making both the Maharaja and the new Dewan Deo prisoners in 1770. Khagendranarayan escaped and for two years the Maharaja's brother, Rajendranarayan, reigned. On his death Khagendranarayan returned and elected the imprisoned Maharaja's son, Dharendranarayan, as Maharaja. The Raja of Bhutan, however, elected another as Maharaja. Khagendranarayan removed to his residence at Balarampur the young Maharaja, his mother and the royal family. Struggles ensued between the rival Maharajas, in which Khagendranarayan was worsted and fled to Panga in Rangpur with the Maharaja and the royal family. At this time, he sought the help of Mr. Purling, the Collector of Rangpur. The Cooch Behar State became a tributary to the British Government by a treaty in 1772 and the Sannyasis employed by Khagendranarayan were dismissed and those in the pay of the other party were totally routed by the English. Peace was also concluded at the intervention of the Tashu Lama with the Raja of Bhutan who bound himself not to interfere in the internal affairs of Cooch Behar as also not to allow any Sannyasis to live

Internal dissensions in Cooch Behar.

in his territories or pass through them. By this treaty the imprisoned Maharaja Dhairyendranarayan was released and re-installed. But the administration was in the hands of the Maharani and Sarbananda, her spiritual guide. The Nazir Deo was also opposed to them. When the old Maharaja died in 1783 and the minor Maharaja Harendranarayan succeeded to the throne, he seized the opportunity of regaining his powers.

In 1784 the Nazir Deo, Khagendranarayan assumed the management of the State by setting aside the minor Raja Harendranarayan. "But Khagendra Narain met his match in the old Ranee Kanteswari, Harendra's mother, who was an able and energetic woman.... She applied with success to the Collector of Rangpur for assistance, Khagendra's claims were set aside and he was driven out for a time by the aid of sepoys. He, however, bided his time and remained in secrecy."[1] He fled to the jungles of Bijni and thence to Karaibari.

Nazir Deo breaks out in revolt with the help of Sannyasis.

In June, 1787, Sarbananda Sarma wrote to Mr. McDowall, the Collector of Rangpur: "How shall I represent the alarms created by Cogendra Narain Coor? The aunt and the son of the aforesaid Coor and Canchooah Hakim his servant, having by his means procured three thousand rupees in ready money and bullion which they have given to Gunnish Gheer Senassie. I have learnt that the said Gheer has collected between five and seven hundred men at Bulrampore with an evil intention against my principal...."[2] The details of the conspiracy and recruitment of Sannyasis are seen in the following deposition of Hari Giri Sannyasi taken by Mr. McDowall: "In the month of Chyte, Monai Hakaim, Cutchwa Hakaim, Dootea Hakaim and Kholassy Hakaim, inhabitants of the Monakusha Mahals and Sudanand Roy, Nazer Cagender Narain's vakeel and Jalee wife of aforesaid Nazir's uncle met in my presence and on consulting together agreed that Cagendra Narain could not get possession of the country unless by force of arms; having settled this they took the advice of Gunnish Gheer Sonassy whom they called upon for that purpose and promised him as bribe the Bermotter of Sherbanund Gossain, if after putting him and the Maharany to death he would take Maharaja prisoner and make Nazer Deo Rajah, they also said that they would not transact the business of the country under the English gentlemen but were resolved at all events to take it into their own hands. Having in my presence mentioned these particulars to Gunnish Gheer Sonassy, they gave him about three thousand rupees in gold and silver for the purpose of raising forces and through him, men began to be collected together at Kyder in the Pergunnah of Goorlah [Goollah in Rennell's map][3] in the zemindary of Boolchand Bhuroowah.[4] After this the aforesaid Ghunnish Gheer with five or six

[1] Glazier's *District of Rangpur*.

[2] *Rangpur District Records*, Vol. VI, p. 137.

[3] Pargana Ghurla in the district of Goalpara.

[4] The Faujdar of Rangamati and father-in-law of Khagendranarayan.

people, one of whom I was, attended on Nazir Deo at Khetabarry in Pergunnah Goorlah and having acquainted him with all the above resolutions told him that he, Gunnish Gheer, had got the troops ready and advised him immediately to make an inroad into Behar, to this proposition Nazir Deo replied that he would not accompany them but if they would first go into Behar and put the Maharanney and the Gossain to death and carry the Maharajah to Bulrampore he would then join them. Upon that Gunnish Gheer repaired to Kydar with the assistance of Achil Gheer began to get troops in readiness and sent fifty men to Rangpur to kill the Gossain. I then in the presence of the Sonnassies, Sicks [Sikhs] and sepoys who were with him asked Gunnish Gheer by whose orders he had engaged in the business to which he replied that he had in his possession the written orders of the Rajah of Behar, of Nazer Deo and of the English gentlemen. I then desired him to show these orders that I might be his friend but he could not produce them. I withdrew from his party and went to Nazer Deo who would not permit me to see him. I therefore sat opposite to his door and he sent me fifteen rupees with a message desiring me to go to Gunnish Gheer. I went to my house at Rangpur and informed Gossain Serbananda of all the foregoing particulars. I also informed the Gossain that a very intimate friendship subsisted between Gunnish Gheer and Bool Chand Burrowah in whose zemindary the former lives and has a farm of two or three thousand rupees."[1]

Hari Giri Sannyasi being examined in October, 1788, by the Commission deputed to inquire into the Cooch Behar disturbances deposed : "I went to visit Gunness Geer at Kedar at which time he gave me twelve Bhurries of silver and two rupees....Ten days after this I again went to Gunness Gur when he and Sadanund were sitting together and distributing gold and silver to the sannyasies."[2] In June, 1787, the Sannyasis raised by Ganesh Giri with Barkandazes headed by Dangur Deo, the elder brother of Khagendranarayan, entered Cooch Behar and seized the Raja, the Rani and the grand-mother in the palace. The properties in the palace were looted and the family of the Raja was subjected to personal violence. The guard of sepoys placed by the British Government was in charge of a Subadar who was bribed by Khagendranarayan's party and refused to oppose the intruders, on the pretence that the latter had shown him a parwana from the Collector of Rangpur allowing them to carry off the Raja. The atrocities were mostly committed by the Sannyasis. "Dangur Deo's troops surrounded Modun Mohun's temple[3] and the Rajah's grand-mother,

Sannyasis seize the Raja.

[1] *Rangpur District Records*, Vol. VI, pp. 189-90.

[2] *Cooch Behar Select Records*, Vol. II, p. 137.

[3] The god Madan Mohan was established by Maharaja Prannarayan (1625--1665)---*Vide* Statement showing the details of debottar grants prepared by Mr. Beveridge, Deputy Commissioner, in 1865.

the Raja and the Ranny being frightened they broke through the mat and came out on the north side with some slave women ; the Sannyasis and Burkundazes then came up and dragged the Raja and the Rany out of the place." The Raja, the Rani and the Maharani (the grandmother) were taken to Balarampur, the residence of Khagendranarayan, in charge of the Sannyasis. Here they exacted various terms from them under threats of violence. Once, "Bissen Geer Sunnyasee having drawn his Tulwar made a blow at the Maharanny with the Maharajah in her arms which providentially missed them and struck the post of the house." On their refusal to seal a paper acknowledging the Nazir Deo's proprietary interest to be nine annas ten cowries in the Cooch Behar state, "Gunness Geer gave her bad language and Mohun Geer Sunnyassy drew his Talwar to put her to death when the Maharajah and the Maharanny sealed the writing." Again in order to prevent the Collector of Rangpur from coming to the help of the Raja, the wife of Khagendranarayan asked the Rani to write a letter to the Collector not to come. On her refusing, "a Sunnyassy made a blow at her with a Talwar but she bending her head, it missed her and struck the post of the house."[1]

Measures by the Government.

The Collector of Rangpur was alarmed for the safety of the Raja when the Raja sought his help. "The time was well-chosen for this operation. Rangpur was a sheet of water and the Collector was striving might and main to make the settlement of revenue, but he nevertheless obtained reinforcements from Dinajpur across the flooded country ; still some time elapsed before the troops could march to Behar."[2] The Collector deputed a sazawal [collector] named Roy Zubberdust Sing on behalf of Government to secure the collections of revenue in Cooch Behar. As a precaution to secure the safety of the Raja, the Collector issued the following parwana to the zemindars of Bhitarbund and Baharbund : "Certain accounts having been received that the Sunnassies assisted Cagendra Narain Cooer to carry off the Rajah and the Ranny of Behar from the palace to Bulrampore, you are therefore directed on the receipt of this perwannah to place men in all their houses throughout your districts and to attach all their possessions and property and you will without delay send me a particular account of the names of the places seized upon, and of the people to whom they belong ....."[3] In July the Collector received information from Roy Zubberdust Sing of "his arrival at Nazergunge a place within 3 coss of Bulrampore where he had found a very large body of Sunnassies and Burgandassies which had been detached from Bulrampore to oppose his progress." On the same date the Collector issued a more stringent general advertisement : "Whereas as great number of Sunnassies, Burgandassies &c at the

---

[1]*Cooch Behar Select Records*, Vol. II, pp. 118-24.

[2]*District of Rangpur*, Glazier.

[3]Revenue Department, Original Consultation, No. 2, dated 13th August, 1787.

instigation of Cagender Narain Cooer having left their houses and gone to Bulrampore where they have created disturbances notice is hereby given that all the zemindars have been ordered (and engagements have been taken from them accordingly) to place peons in the house of every person who may have left their districts with intention to assist the said Cagendra Narain Cooer, and they have been further directed to take written obligations from the sunnassics who remain, purporting that all those who have gone to Bulrampore shall immediately leave the service of Cogendra Narain Cooer and return to their houses. The zemindars have also been required to deliver in a list of the names of all the absent sunnassies, and to confiscate their property if they do not return to their houses within the time stipulated by their relations, a list of all such confiscations to be sent to the Collector. And notice is hereby further given that if every person who may have left Rangpur, or its environs, for the purpose of assisting Cogendra Narain Cooer shall not return to his house within ten days from the date hereof his property will be forfeited to the Company, and whatever people may have been left behind in their houses shall be put in confinement as accessories and punished accordingly."[1] The Zamindar of Karaibari [then in Mymensingh District] was called upon to withdraw his troops sent in aid of Khagendranarayan.

Military operations in Cooch Behar.

On the 24th July, the Collector "finding that the lenient measures he had hitherto pursued for procuring the release of the Raja and the Rany of Cooch Behar have had no other effect than that of increasing the insolence of Nazir Deo's adherents," requested Lieut. Hill, commanding a detachment of sepoys, to proceed immediately to Bihar "for the purpose of establishing the authority of the Sezawal Roy Zubberdust Sing."[2] Roy Zubberdust Singh wrote the following letter on the 16th Sawan to the Collector regarding his engagement with the enemy: "Yesterday the people of the opposite party drew up in three divisions, with two stands of colours at the distance of half a coss and remained there the whole day. I wrote this circumstance to Behar when I immediately received a reinforcement of an amildar and 9 sepoys from the Rajah's company. Incharan Soubadar also, who had been detached to the Monakusha Mahals, joined me with all expedition; as on seeing that there was no occasion for his stay there, he apprehended that the enemy had moved towards Nazergunge. About an hour and a half after his arrival several lighted Mussauls [torches] appeared advancing on the north side and the enemy having drawn up against the Brigade Sepoys began to fire upon them. The Soubadar on this advanced with his men and forced the enemy to retreat and having kept the sepoys under arms till about ten o'clock p.m., he continued patrolling towards the enemy's quarters and took one of their swords and a shield.

[1]Revenue Department, Original Consultation, No. 2, dated 13th August, 1787.

[2]Revenue Department, Original Consultation, No. 6, dated 13th August, 1787.

Our men remained in readiness and stayed by the boats the whole night and in the morning about 5 or 600 Sunnassies and people from Hindostan with some swivels came and encamped at Nazergunge. On seeing the sepoys prepared for them they said they had no intention of fighting but desired that we would retire to Behar for that Nazergunge was a Jaghier belonging to them and that they would not permit us to remain in it. About 2 o'clock p.m. near two thousand men collected on the opposite side of the river and began to be very abusive they had also in the morning seized the dawk and the Hirkarrah's [mail runner] boat which they carried off. After this conduct they at last set up three shouts, and began to fire from their swivels and small arms on which having no other resource I attacked them and by the assistance of God killed and wounded about 50 men and having pursued them for two coss I had the fortune to gain a complete victory and to take their drums and colours...." [1]

On the 2nd August, the Collector informed Major Dunn that he had received information that "Danker Deo the brother of Nazir Deo and Guness Gheer the Head Sunnasis with 3,000 men have quitted Bulrampur and encamped between that place and Nazirgunge with an intention of making a second attack upon the sezwal," adding that "if this information be true Lieut. Hill must have marched to support him." [2]

Mr. McDowall, the Collector, gave the following account of the progress of events: "On the 4th I received a letter from Major Dunn informing me that he had made attempts to march with reinforcements but owing to the deluged state of the country, he had both times to return....

"On the 5th I received a letter from Lt. Hill informing me that the conduct of Nazer Deo's people having indicated an intention on their part to carry off the Raja and the Ranny he had stationed guards at all passes round Bulrampur to prevent them.

"Between 9th and 14th I received the following information from Captain Rotton communnicated to him by Lt. Hill. That the whole force at Bulrampur did not exceed 150 sunnassies and 500 Burkundazes but that 500 Burkundazes were daily expected. That Nazir Deo's people continue to threaten the Rajah and the Ranny with instant death should attempt be made on Bulrampore. That a place called Ballahaut Golah defended by a Naik and 2 Battalion sepoys, three of the Raja's household sepoys and seventy Burkundazes had been attacked by Nazir Deo's people who after a short contest were put to flight.... That the sezawals people have been driven from Toffaungunge in consequence of which Mr. Hill sent a reinforcement which took the place."[3]

---

[1]Revenue Department, Original Consultation, No. 6, dated 13th August, 1787.

[2]*Rangpur District Records*, Vol. VI, p. 223.

[3]*Rangpur District Records*, Vol. VI. p. 230.

On the 17th instant Ensign Duncanson's letter was received to the following effect: "That at a distance of about half coss from Toffaungunge to which he was proceeding with a havildar and 12 sepoys to take upon himself the command, a large body of sunnassies, who had concealed themselves in the jungles on the side of the river attacked him and fired into his boat whereupon the Dandies made their escape leaving the boat to drive down the stream until it reached the opposite bank, from whence he and his party engaged the sunnassies until he was joined by the Jemmadar and 32 sepoys from Toffangunge who immediately came to his assistance and soon enabled him to put the enemy to flight." Mr. Duncanson observed that the Sannyasis "must have lost a great number of men as 13 of them were found dead as he passed through the jungle. None of Mr. Duncanson's party suffered the smallest hurt."[1]

Release of the Raja.

When the roads between Rangpur and Cooch Behar became passable, Capt. Rotton advanced to Cooch Behar and, on the 27th August, informed the Collector that he had "got the possession of the persons of the Raja and Rani of Cooch Behar." In communicating the news to the Governor-General, Mr. McDowall observed: "The Head Sunnasie Guness Gheer who is taken prisoner and whose obstinacy has been the cause of prolonging the captivity of the Raja and the Rani ought in my humble opinion to be punished in the most examplary manner as a warning to the whole tribe of Fakeers from whom Nazeer Deo derived principal support he possessed in his late daring enterprize...."[2]

The Governor-General directed the prisoners to be tried by the Fauzdari Adalat. It appears that Gunees Giri died while under trial. Steps were also taken against other Sannyasis who had joined the Nazir Deo. In September the Collector of Rangpur wrote to the Collector of Rajshahi—"I think it proper to inform you that I lately sent a perwannah to the Sheekdar of Beeturband requiring him to apprehend and send to Rangpur the chelah of Guneess Ghir by name Kedoor Ghir who is accused of being now in possession of a considerable share of the plunder which was carried off in the late rebellion of Cooch Behar." Maharani Kanteswari having returned to power confiscated all the lands of the Nazir Deo Khagendranarayan, as also those of the Dewan Deo, while the Nazir Deo and the Dewan Deo claimed nine annas ten cowris and one anna share respectively of the Cooch Behar state. In 1788, Messrs. Mercer and Chauvet were appointed Commissioners for the investigation of the claims. The claims of the Nazir Deo and the Dewan Deo were rejected and the Raja was declared to have the full rights in the state. In 1789, Mr. Douglas was appointed Commissioner and restored peace for a time.

---

[1]Revenue Department, Original Consultation, No. 27, dated 20th September, 1787.

[2]*Rangpur District Records*, Vol. VI, p. 237.

CHAPTER X

Fakirs in Northern and Eastern Bengal, 1781—1792

IN October of the season 1781-82, the Collector of Rangpur reported of a party of Majnu's people in his district and sent the Militia sepoys posted in his district against them.[1] This probably led them to move southward, for Nandalal Roy, the farmer of Rajshahi, sent information in December that about one or two thousand Fakirs under Majnu Shah had entered the district of Bhattorea. Lieut. Kinlock, stationed at Nattore, was directed to proceed against them.[2] Mohan Babu, the son of Nandalal Roy, also represented to the Lieutenant at Nattore that Majnu Shah had entered the Pargana Siea Lund [Rajshahi district] and had plundered and robbed the inhabitants to the extent of Rs. 5,000 but had since retreated. The Company of Sepoys under Lieut. Kinlock had been detached for duties elsewhere and he had only 20 sepoys. So he asked Major Robertson at Moradbag for a complete company of sepoys.[3] The Fakirs were next reported to have gone away. But on the 23rd January Nandalal Roy informed Major Robertson of their return and stated that the Sannyasis "were close to Nattore" and a company of sepoys was wanted there. As Major Robertson was not supplied with arms, he requested the Committee of Revenue at Calcutta to send a detachment from Berhampore.[4] It appears that there were two distinct bands of nomadic raiders at work; one, a body of Fakirs under Majnu Shah, consisting of six to eight hundred, committing depredations and levying contributions in Pargana Jaysin [Rajshahi district]; and another, a body of Sannyasis "distinct from those who accompany Mudgenoo Shah" who also "entered Rajshahi and committed great depredations there."[5] The delay gave the Fakirs and Sannyasis the opportunity to disappear. This probably led to the proposal of the Revenue Committee to augment the force

1781-82.

In Rajshahi.

---

[1] *Rangpur District Records*, Vol. IV, p. 111.

[2] Revenue Department, Governor-General in Council, Original Consultation, No. 8, dated 3rd January, 1782.

[3] Revenue Department, Governor-General in Council, Original Consultation, No. 12, dated 15th January, 1782.

[4] Extract from the Proceedings of the Committee of Revenue, dated 24th January, 1782.

[5] Revenue Department, Original Consultation, No. 8, dated 29th January, 1782.

under Lieut. Kinlock by three companies and station them in Rajshahi for the protection of the district.[1]

1782-83.
Mymensingh.

In 1782, Mr. Lodge was stationed at Begunbari near the present town of Mymensingh for quelling the disturbances of resident Sannyasis in Alapsingh and Mymensingh Parganas, who extorted by violence usurious interest from the zamindars and tenants. It appears that the Mohants or the head monks of resident Sannyasis had brought to their aid nomadic band of Sannyasis belonging to the Ramayat sect. On the 11th December, 1782, Mr. Lodge reported as follows: "Ever since I was apprized of the Sannyasis assembling I have spared neither cost or pains to procure certain intelligence of their motions. To the Munts &c (Mohunts,) I sent such orders as I conceived would be most conducive to their dismissing those of the Rumtaat [Ramayat] tribe they had employed and remaining peaceably; the steps I took on the occasion have not been altogether without the desired effect. About 600 of them marched some days ago through Sharepoore [Sherpur, south of the Garo hills] pargana towards Gonasur[2] mountains. My hircarrahs in disguise accompanied them beyond the limits of the above pergannahs and returned to Bygonbarry the day before yesterday with accounts that, on the Sannyasis receiving some trifling presents rice &c they did not attempt any disturbances. A fray has, however, happened between the residue of Sannyasis and a party of others, Fackeers &c, headed by one Mudgejeenoo. In the fray he got the better of the Rumtaat Sannyasis of whom 30 or 40 were killed. The followers of Mudgejeenoo are about one thousand and it is conjectured the 600 [Sannyasis] that passed through Sharepoore will return assisted by others to revenge the death of their comrades. As plunder is the sole object of both parties I am only apprehensive of their uniting for this purpose."[3]

Sannyasis *versus* Fakirs.

Mr. Lodge was very correct in his surmise about the union of Hindu and Muhammadan mendicants for the purpose of plunder. On 10th December, Mr. Goodlad, the Collector of Rangpur, reported to the Committee of Revenue as follows: "A party of Sunnassies joined by a body of Mussalman Faqueers amounting to about 700 passed through part of this district and are assembled at Paradanga in Beterbund. As they laid several places under contribution, I have thought it necessary to detach Lieut. Macdonald against them with 180 sepoys. They came in from Dacca and crossed the Burrumputre at Dewangunge. As they will probably on the approach of sepoys make their retreat under the hills into the northern purgannahs of Purnea, I have written to Mr. Rooke [Collector of Purnea] and recommended his detaching a force to meet them."[4]

Rangpur.

Combination of Sannyasis and Fakirs.

---

[1]Revenue Department, Original Consultation, No. 4, dated 26th July, 1782.

[2]The southern portion of the Garo Hills.

[3]Revenue Department, Original Consultation, No. 26, dated 20th December, 1782.

[4]Revenue Department, Original Consultation, No. 25, dated 20th December, 1782.

It therefore, appears that the Fakirs had already fixed on the Nepal Terai as a place of safety when pursued by the Company's Sepoys. On the 15th December, Mr. Rooke informed Mr. Goodlad that he had ordered "a complete company of sepoys properly equipped to march to the north-east frontier of Surjapur Pargana [now in Dinajpur district] against the Fakirs "with positive orders by no means to commence hostilities with these people should they meet with them unless they absolutely are obliged to stand on the defensive."[1] This was the outcome of the cautious policy of the Committee of Revenue who issued orders to the Collectors of Rangpur and Purnea to the effect that "unless you should be convinced that the force you have deputed after the Senassees is fully adequate to this service, we direct the immediate recall of them and that you adopt measures rather calculated to prevent the incursions of Senassees than risque the loss of a force by attacking them, but by no means to endeavour to intercept or interrupt their retreat from the provinces."[2] The party of Sannyasis and Fakirs had horses, camels, elephants and arms of all kinds.[3] Lieut. Macdonald captured their leaders "Mohun Gyre" (Mohan Giri) and "Moosha Shaw" (Musa Shah) together with some others, but most of "the followers escaped under the hills." The prisoners were made over to the Fauzdari Court under the control of the Naib Nazim for trial. Mr. Goodlad was directed by the Committee of Revenue to "lay before the Court such evidence of their criminality as he may be able to procure both of their transactions previous to the attack of Lieutenant Macdonald as well as of the actual resistance made by them. If the sentence of the Court shall not extend to the lives of the prisoners it was directed that they may not be released till the pleasure of the Hon'ble Board is known."[4]

On 20th December, the Committee of Revenue informed the Provincial Commander-in-Chief, Major-General Stibbert, that a body of Fakirs had entered the district of Bhattorea and "occasioned some disturbances and obstructions to the revenues." Two companies of sepoys were directed by the Revenue Department to be furnished to the Collector of Rajshahi.[5]

Majnu in Mymensingh.

With the New Year of 1783 came the alarming news of Majnu's appearance in the very centre of the present district of Mymensingh. "I have this instant," writes Mr. Henry Lodge, the Resident at Begunbari, to the Committee of Revenue, "received certain intelligence of Mudgenoo's arrival in Zuffershahy Purgannah and that he has already commenced

[1] Letter from the Collector of Purnea to the Collector of Rangpur, dated 15th December, 1782. *Rangpur District Records*, Vol. II, p. 295.

[2] Letter from the Committee of Revenue to the Collector of Rangpur, dated 16th December, 1782. *Rangpur District Records*, Vol. II, p. 296.

[3] *The District of Rangpur*—Glazier.

[4] Letter from the Committee of Revenue to the Collector of Rangpur, dated 19th December, 1782. *Rangpur District Records*, Vol. II, p. 297.

[5] Revenue Department, Original Consultation, No. 30, dated 20th December, 1782.

oppressing the ryots &c confining several. He has about 800 people with him. I have, therefore, dispatched a Jematdar and 20 sepoys to the cutchery of the above Purgannah with a purwana addressed to Mudgayenoo to refrain from all acts of violence, release those he may have confined and depart from this part of the country."[1] On the 7th January there is the following report from Mr. Lodge regarding the further progress of the Fakirs: "Mudgejeenoo remained but a short time in the Zuffershahy Purgunnah, ere the sepoys I had despatched could reach the cutchery thereof.[2] Information was brought me of his being on the road to Cotgurra in Alepsing about 14 coss from hence. I therefore ordered 36 sepoys to proceed with all haste to Cotgurra directing those that had gone toward Zuffershahy to march to Cotgurra and join the party there with all expedition. To the Chowdries &c of Attyah, Cogmarry & Bowal, I also sent perwannahs directing them to use their utmost efforts and afford the sepoys every assistance to apprehend this notorious robber. A note from my European servant with the sepoys received last night gives me to understand that they have seized 3 or 4 of Mudgenoo's people, that Mudgenoo is pushing on towards Bowal that he and the sepoys have left Cotgurra and are in pursuit of Mudgenoo. If the information I have received that a large party of Burgandosses &c from the Pookareah district[3] being in search of them is a matter of fact it is not unlikely but he may attempt to reach the banks of the Burrampooter by the road of Shorajde.[4] I have therefore deputed a Sepoy and 20 Burgondosses that the zemindar of Alepsingh has assisted me with to that place to act as they may gain intelligence."[5] Pressed on all sides Majnu next pushed on through the most impenetrable portion of the Madhupur jungles and even there he was pursued and met with a reverse. Writing on the 14th January Mr. Lodge informed the Committee of Revenue — "Sixty of the sepoys commanded by the Jamadar have had a skirmish

Defeat of Majnu. with Shaw Mudgenoo at Chatter Kaite about 8 or 10 Koss from Innatpur toward Ram Bawal Purgunnah. Mudgenoo after having had 25 or 30 of his men shot dead and double the number or thereabout wounded fled into the jungles; a pursuit would have been imprudent as the sepoys

---

[1]Letter from Henry Lodge, Resident at Begunbari, to the Committee of Revenue, dated 2nd January, 1783. Committee of Revenue Proceedings, 13th January, 1783, pp. 135-37.

[2]The Cutcherry was at Singjani, present Jamalpur town in Mymensingh district.

[3]Pargana Pukharia then within the zamindari of Rajshahi of Rani Bhawani. The Barkandazes were the retainers of the zamindar In the abstract of expenditure for Pargana Pukharia of 1196 B. S. [1789-90 A. D.] we find mention of Omrao Singh Jamadar and Sibananda Ojha as being stationed in the frontier soldiers' cantonment at Chandrakona which was known as *Simanar Thana.*

[4]Probably Sagardighi within the dense jungles of Madhupur, near Innatpur.

[5]Letter from Henry Lodge to the Committee of Revenue, dated 7th January, 1783. Committee of Revenue Proceedings, dated 16th January, 1783, pp. 166-68.

had expended their ammunition. Indeed the jungles are so immensely thick and of such an extent that there was little probability of the sepoys coming up with Mudgenoo who has the advantage of having a bazar with him whilst I was under the necessity of supplying the sepoys with rice &c from hence....one sepoy was killed and four others much wounded in the action."[1] The retreat of Majnu was so hurried that he "scarcely buried those that since the action have died of their wounds."[2] Later report shows that Majnu made a detour towards the north-west of the present Mymensingh district and "continued in the environs of Dewangunge."[3]

In reviewing the Proceedings of the Committee of Revenue, the Governor-General in Council bitterly complains on 11th April in the following words: "We find from the mention of Mudgenoo Shaw's having entered the Purganna of Zuffarshahy we are weary of the annual inroads committed by Majnu and as we know he resides peaceably on the other side of the Burrumpooter and is suffered to enter the Companys' districts and lay them under contribution without any attempt being made to apprehend him." The Council accordingly wrote to the Chief of Dacca and the Collector of Silberis, "we believe it to be in their power to seize him and that we expect they will do it." The Chief of Dacca in a letter, dated 12th May, explained: " Majnu Shah has retreated to the north-west of Chilmari towards Benares and Lucknow near which he resides and this route takes about 6 weeks from Benares to Goalpara. Majnu gets his recruits from the districts in which he carries on his depredations. "[4]

On the 15th January, 1783, Mr. Rooke, Chief of Purnea, reported to the Committtee of Revenue: "A body of Sannyasis were also encamped in the north eastern portion of the Purnea district and were daily guilty of the most violent depredations." "Capt. Williams with a detachment of two companies and a half of sepoys" was sent against them.[5] On Capt. Williams' approach the Sannyasis moved off in great haste to the westward along the side of the Morung forests.

Being pursued from the borders of Mymensingh district, Majnu took a south-westerly course avoiding the Rangpur district where Mr. Goodlad was on the alert and appeared in the present Malda district. On the 8th March, Mr. Grant, Agent at the Malda Factory, reported to the Collector

Retreat of Majnu.

[1]Letter from Henry Lodge to the Committee of Revenue, dated 14th January, 1783. Committee of Revenue Proceedings, dated 23rd January, 1783, pp. 255-56.

[2]Letter from Henry Lodge to the Committee of Revenue, dated 15th January, 1783. Committee of Revenue Proceedings, dated 10th February, 1783, pp. 74-80.

[3]Letter from Henry Lodge to the Committee of Revenue, dated 1st February, 1783. Committee of Revenue Proceedings, dated 10th February, pp. 74-80.

[4]Revenue Department, Original Consultation. No. 7, dated 27th May, 1783.

[5]Letter from the Chief of Purnea to the Committee of Revenue, dated 15th January, 1783. Committee of Revenue Proceedings, dated 20th January, 1783, pp. 218-19.

of Bhagalpur: "The country in the neighbourhood of Malda was being infested by several large bodies of Fakeers (headed by Shaw Burhan) who have committed many depredations....These Fakeers seem all to belong to Mujnoo Shaw, who is himself with a greater force yet at Bydell on the borders of Purnia. A party of six or seven hundred were a few days ago at Pokua [Pokua Hat in thana Bamangola] six coss hence where they robbed the public Cutchery (taking from the Mundal 500 Rs. of Revenue money) and various individuals (taking from a grain merchant Rs. 1000), they are now near the Company's aurung[1] at Nirschindpore. Another party of 500 was on the 4th instant near Coligonj [Kaligram near Chanchal] a principal aurung of the Company's—they beat the weavers, threatened to burn their villages if they did not raise a contribution. Today I learn that there is a well armed party of six or seven hundred amongst which are 80 horse at Ookadantala within four koss of Malda. Hearing that there are some regular troops in Dinagepore or Rangpore they keep further to the south and this whole quarter is alarmed as being exposed to whatever these freebooters may think proper to attempt."[2] He asked the Collector of Bhagalpur as also Col. Ironside at Berhampore to send sepoys "by the way of Seebgunge, Curbarrin, Tulseygunge & Coligong."

Fakirs in Malda.

On 12th March Mr. Grant sent further information to the Collector of Bhagalpore: "The party which was nearest to Malda having continued at Dantola some days and advanced even within 2 coss of Nabobgunge, suddenly decamped on Saturday apprehending an early attack. They moved northward still carrying on their exactions and were yesterday at Mugdampore near Pattergotta about 18 coss from this place. Their number is about 60 including Hindu Burkandazes hired to accompany them and their leader Moosa Shah a *chela* or eleve of Mujenoo Shaw's with whom he affects to be at present at variance, though this is in all probablity a pretence. His own place of residence is at Seebpur Chouchatt which lies between Nischindpore and Buddaul, but whether he means to halt or to go to Mestingur in Goraghat or to Nekmurd near Malduar at both of which places there are soon to be meetings of Mussalman Fakirs, is at present uncertain. The other party which plundered the cutchery of Shikarpur adjoining Pokra consists also of about 600 commanded by another eleve of Mujenoos called Burhan and moved thence by Bamangola and Rajanagar towards Korry and Saddamahl probably in order to proceed to the meeting at Neckmard. Mujenoo himself was lately at Bydell with about 2,000 men has crossed the Attri at Conchon with less than half that number

[1] "During the Company's trading days the term was applied to their factories for the purchase, on advances, of native piecegoods, etc."—*Hobson-Jobson.*

[2] Letters from Charles Grant, Resident at Malda Factory, to Augustus Cleveland, Collector of Bhagalpur, and Col. Gilbert Ironside, Commanding at Berhampore, dated 6th and 8th March, 1783. Revenue Department Consultation, No. 14, dated 8th April, 1783, and Public Department, Original Consultation, Nos. 13 and 15, dated 15th March, 1783.

on the 9th in his way to Mistangur."[1] On the requisition of Mr. Clevland a detachment of six companies of sepoys under Major Buchanan started from Monghyr on the 12th March and arrived at Malda on the 22nd March and they proceeded immediately to Mahastangarh "whither the Fakirs were repairing" and Mr. Goodlad, Collector of Rangpur, was asked to co-operate with[2] the Militia sepoys at Rangpur. The detachment from Berhampur was ordered not to proceed but to be in readiness on the northern side of the Ganges as the Fakirs proposed "having a general meeting at Dinagpoor."[3] This was at the Darga of Nek Murda. On the 6th April Capt. Alexander with 4 companies of sepoys sent from Rangpur informed Mr. Goodlad from his camp at Nek Murda that a party of fakirs "is reported to have passed near this lately and said to be encamped near Jelpigory" [Jalpaiguri]. He proposed to march against them on confirmation of the report.[4] Ensign Coleby was also despatched to Apole [present Bogra district] with a large detachment to intercept Majnu "but he [Majnu] quitted the country long before the approach of the sepoys."[5] The vigorous measures taken during the 1782-83 season had evidently made the raiders beat a hasty retreat before the annual rains compelled them to retire. But back they came the following season.

1783-84.

Fakirs in Mymensingh.

In December, 1783, the Collector of Rangpur had information of "depredations committed by Musa Shah and his followers on the borders of the district at Puraungunge. The Jamadar with forty sepoys stationed at Battesson within ten coss of the place were ordered by Captain Williams, commanding the Sebundy corps at Dinajpur, to move towards Paraungunge and endeavour to seize some of these marauders and deliver them over to justice."[6] Musa Shah moved off eastward, and early next year [1784], the Vakils of the zamindars of Parganas Mymensingh, Jaffarshahy, Alapsingh and Sherpur [all within the present district of Mymensingh] complained to the Committee of Revenue that "Shaw Moosee brother of Mujnoo Shaw Fackeer with a large force attacked the

---

[1]Letter from Charles Grant, Resident at Malda, to Augustus Clevland, Collector of Bhagalpur, dated 12th March, 1783. Revenue Department, Consultation No. 17, dated 8th April, 1783.

[2]Letter from Charles Grant to Richard Goodlad, dated 22nd March, 1783, *Bengal District Records, Rangpur,* Vol. III (1783—1785), p. 33.

[3]Letter from Col. Stibbert to Governor-General in Council, dated 10th March, 1783, Public Department, Original Consultation, No. 10, dated 24th March, 1783.

[4]Letter from Capt. N. Alexander, Commanding at Camp near Neckmurd Durga, to Goodlad, Esq., dated 6th April, 1783. *Rangpur District Records,* Vol. III, p. 39.

[5]Letter from Collector of Rangpur to Charles Grant, Resident at Malda, dated 20th April, 1783. *Rangpur District Records,* Vol. IV, p. 155.

[6]Letter from Capt. Williams, Commanding Dinajpur Sebundy Battalion, dated Dinajpur, 18th December, 1783, to William Amherst, Acting Collector of Rangpur. *Rangpur District Records,* Vol. III, p. 109.

above Pergunnahs plundered the riots and carried off their effects—Ram Sing Subahdar with some sepoys went to Bygonbarry in Jaffershahi to check the depredation, a skirmish ensued in which one of the sepoys was wounded and the Fackeers retreated. It is now reported that Mujnoo Shaw is coming into Jaffershahy with 200 followers in consequence of which the ryots have all fled to other places and the Revenue of Government will of course suffer."[1]

This complaint was somewhat exaggerated. For on the 13th February, 1784, Mr. Day, the Chief of Dacca, reported that the zamindars in order to get remission of revenue exaggerated the story about plunder and flying of the ryots. "About six weeks ago a complaint was made to me by the Naibs of Mymensingh, Jaffershy, Sharepore and Alapsing respecting a body of sunasses that were about to enter their districts. I immediately sent orders to the Company of sepoys stationed at Bygunbarry to march and stop their entrance, this they accordingly did, an affray insued and the sunassees retreated, since which nothing has been heard of them ; the assertion of the Naibs respecting plunder is false ; the Sunnassees were repulsed before they entered either of the Purgunnahs and none of the ryots as I can hear of here fled from their habitations."[2]

Driven from the east and with the knowledge of sepoys stationed at Dinajpur and Rangpur, the Fakirs next appeared in Malda where there **Malda.** is the famous mosque of Pandua. On 10th June, 1784, the Collector of Bhagalpur, Mr. Chapman, reported to the Supreme Council of Revenue in Calcutta : "The renters of Rajemehal have sent me intelligence that Shaw Mudgnoo a noted Chief of Faqueers from the Morung Hills had appeared near Malda Factory, with seven hundred armed followers, several camels laden with rockets and other warlike apparatus—that some villages had already been plundered by them and that the whole district was in danger of being laid under contr ibution." The Collector accordingly directed two hundred Hill Rangers with a small party from the Sebundy corps to march immediately against them.[3] On the 22nd June the Collector further reported that as soon as the party crossed the river, Majnu and all his followers fled with the utmost precipitation.[4]

This time they carried on operations till the beginning of the rainy season and returned four months later.

---

[1]Petition of the vakeels of the zamindars of Mymensingh, Jaffarshahy, Alapsingh and Sherpur. Proceedings of the Committee of Revenue, dated 5th February, 1784, pp. 562-64.

[2]Letter from M. Day, Chief of Dacca, to the Committee of Revenue, dated 16th February, 1784, p. 149.

[3]Letter from Charles Chapman, Collector of Bhagalpur, to the Council of Revenue, dated 10th June, 1784. Revenue Department, Original Consultations, No. 20, dated 20th July, 1784.

[4]Letter from the Collector of Bhagalpur to the Council of Revenue, dated 22nd June, 1784. Revenue Department, Original Consultations, No. 21, dated 20th July, 1784.

On the 14th October, the Collector of Murshidabad reported: "Sha Mujenoo a few days since made his appearance with about two hundred and fifty armed men, a number mounted on camels and small horses and a crowd of followers. He crossed from Bettoreah about three coss from the Silberris Cutchery and began to collect immediately the assessment which he usually makes at every village. I am under some apprehension lest he should plunder the House" [the Collector's house at Silberris]. Accordingly the Collector "took two hundred Burkundazes into pay."[1] On the 17th October he further reported "Mujnoon has quitted his division and I imagine will not return before the 17th of Chyte [about the end of March] at the Mostya Mela [an annual assemblage for religious purposes] about four coss from Silberris."[2] However the Committee of Revenue announced that the "Hon'ble Board have been pleased to order a Company of Brigade Sepoys from Berhampore to be stationed at Silberris for the defence of the Company" and the Collector of Silberis was ordered to discharge the Burkandazes raised by him. **1784-85.** **Fakirs in Bogra.**

The Committee of Revenue summarised thus the reasons why the attempts to crush Majnu were failures: "Although Mujenoo has been overtaken and attacked with success in some former occasions, it has been found difficult in general to punish him for his depredations. The zemindars are apprehensive of giving information respecting his motions and as his followers are taught to disperse when pursued and unite again at appointed stations it seldom happens that they can be apprehended."[3]

The proposal of the Committee to station three different detachments of two hundred and fifty sepoys at Chilmari on the Brahmaputra, Nattore in Rajshahi and Shibganj in Rangpur[4] was not given effect to in view of Majnu's retreat and as one company of Brigade sepoys was already stationed at Silberis [Bogra].[5] Moreover, the Chief of Dacca had stationed a complete company of Sebundy corps at Mahastangarh for the protection of the eastern Parganas.[6]

---

[1]Letter from J. Champion, Collector of Murshidabad, to the Collector of Silberis, dated 14th October, 1784. Committee of Revenue Proceedings, dated 18th October, 1784, pp. 394-95.

[2]Letter from the Collector of Murshidabad to the Committee of Revenue, dated 17th October, 1784. Committee of Revenue Proceedings, dated 21st October, 1784, pp. 462-63.

[3]Letter from the Committee of Revenue to the Governor-General in Council, dated 18th October, 1784. Revenue Department, Governor-General in Council, Original Consultation, No. 1, dated 28th October, 1784.

[4]*Ibid.*

[5]Letter from the Committee of Revenue to the Governor-General in Council, dated 21st October, 1784. Revenue Department, Governor-General in Council, Original Consultation, No. 2, dated 28th October, 1784.

[6]Letter from the Chief of Dacca to the Committee of Revenue, dated 28th October, 1784. Committee of Revenue Proceedings, dated 8th November, 1784, p. 90.

It appears that Majnu Shah, Musa and Maumbly were the three leaders of the Fakirs at this time. "The two former," reported the Collecter of Silberis on the 16th February, 1785, "about two months since had a violent quarrel with the latter in which many lives were lost."[1]

Later in this cold season, Majnu Shah and his followers reappeared in one of the very districts where sepoys were stationed. In February, 1785, Mr. Champion, Collector of Silberis, reported Musa Shah to be near Jahangirpur Pargana and that "he intended to come to Jahangirpur to collect what he terms religious donations." Mr. Champion sent some peons "to direct him to return immediately and that if he did proceed to proceed alone. He accordingly came with a few followers and promised to exact nothing from the country; but as already a company of sepoys had marched against him, Moosa Shah thought proper to retire and consequently there was no depredation."[2] In March, however, the Collector of Silberis received information that Majnu Shah was coming to Mahastan and being alarmed at the account of his having made a number of rockets for his intended attack, directed Lieut. Crowe, stationed at Silberis, to proceed against him. Lieut. Crowe ascertained the strength of Majnu's followers when he was 6 miles off from Mahastan by deputing a sepoy and a Burkandaz disguised as Fakirs. The following account of the skirmish is given by Mr. Champion: "Lieutenant Crowe at three o'clock marched to his [Majnu's] ground and on his [Lieut. Crowe's] people not replying to Centries [sentries] of Mujenoo they received a severe fire and consequently returned it. A sepoy was killed and one wounded and a Barkandas very much hurt. Eighteen Burkandazes were sent as assistance but at daybreak Mujnoo fled. Lt. Crowe from want of ammunition was obliged to return to his ground. The force of Mujnoo consisted of four hundred armed men and about two hundred more with swords and clubs. On the part of Mujenoo seven men were killed and two & thirty wounded. Sixty four rockets were taken by Lieutenant Crowe by firing on the camels, who were so much wounded as to be unable to proceed." The effect was crushing and we hear no more of Majnu during the whole of the year.[3]

1786. Fakirs in Mymensingh.

He does not come to notice again till January, 1786, when the zamindars of Mymensingh district represented to the Committee of Revenue that "the sannyasis and Majnu Shah have renewed their depredations

---

[1]Letter from the Collector of Silberis to the Committee of Revenue, dated 16th February, 1785. Committee of Revenue Proceedings, dated 28th February, 1785, Vol. 51, pp. 527-29.

[2]Letter from the Collector of Silberis to the Committee of Revenue, dated 16th February, 1785. Committee of Revenue Proceedings, Vol. 51, pp. 527-29.

[3]Letter from the Collector of Silberis to the Committee of Revenue, dated 10th March, 1785. Revenue Department, Governor-General in Council, Original Consultation, No. 39, dated 9th September, 1785.

and carried off large sums of public money."[1] Accordingly on the 17th January, Mr. Day, Chief of Dacca, deputed Lieut. Field of the 4th Regiment with his company for the protection of Mymensingh.[2]

On the 18th January, the Collector of Rangpur announced the presence of three parties of raiders. The first, a large party under Musa Shah was at Kasimgunge on the borders of Baikuntapur another party entered Cazirhat [Kajirhat Pargana in Rangpur] and was at Omerkhanah; the third was a body of Sannyasis committing great oppressions in 7-anna and 9-anna divisions of Ghoraghat. The Collector was most concerned, as he had "great trouble to keep the ryots quiet and they most undoubtedly will take the first opportunity of absconding or pleading it as an excuse for not paying up their heavy kist of Pous. The cheapness of grain and tobacco, rice selling at 3 & 4 maunds the rupee and the latter at 2 Rs. per Tungee, is alone a consideration of the most curious nature and the ryots can ill bear any oppression from invaders."[3] **Rangpur.**

On the 26th January, the Committee of Revenue directed the Commanding Officer at Berhampur to despatch a force to Rangpur and in the meantime the Collector was authorised to raise a force of Burkandazes locally and Ensign Duncanson[4] was sent direct from Calcutta to take charge of the Burkandazes.[5] These forces were raised from the Burkandazes in the employ of zamindars to meet the emergency and were consequently undisciplined. They were partly armed with firelocks and partly with spears.[6] The dispersal or defeat of the Fakirs, in no way inferior in arms and discipline, by such a force was no doubt largely due to the personal qualities of the young officers commanding them. On the 16th February, the Collector of Rangpur also directed Capt. Alexander, who was quelling disturbances in Baikuntapur pargana, to march after the Sannyasis headed by Musa Shah and reported to be in Boda. Should he not meet him, he was directed to march along

---

[1]Committee of Revenue Proceedings, Original Consultation, Nos. 16-18, dated 5th January, 1786, pp. 62-64.

[2]Letter from Mr. Day, Chief of Dacca, to the Committee of Revenue, dated 17th January, 1786. Committee of Revenue Proceedings, Consultation, No. 43, dated 23rd January, 1786.

[3]Letter from the Collector of Rangpur to the Committee of Revenue, dated 18th January, 1786. *MSS. Rangpur District Records*, Vol. 23, pp. 20-22.

[4]Lieut., Infantry, Cadet, 1782; Ensign, January, 1783; Lieut., 9th February, 1788; Resigned, 8th October, 1790. (Possibly to be identified with W. M. Duncanson of Kensington Square, London, who was head of a "House of Agency to E. I. Company" (1800—1806).—Hodson—*List of Officers of the Bengal Army* 1758—1834.

[5]Letter from the Committee of Revenue to the Governor-General in Council, dated 26th January, 1786. Revenue Department, Governor-General in Council, Original Consultation, No. 15, dated 26th January, 1786.

[6]Letter from W. M. Duncanson, Commanding Rangpur Burkandazes, to Collector of Rangpur, dated 11th February, 1786. *MSS. Rangpur Records*, Vol. 32, pp. 76-83.

the borders of Dinajpur and Rangpur.[1] On 11th February Ensign Duncanson reported from camp at Senubarry [near Jalpaiguri] that about the 9th and 10th a party of 800 Fakirs had been at Bhawaniganj and carried off money and other things moving off immediately, and about two weeks before a party consisting of 500 went to a place near Nabobgunge in Boda raising money there. On arrival at Jalpaiguri on the 16th, Ensign Duncanson found "the Banditty gone; they moved off with their plunder into the Ghurka Raja's country."[2]

Bogra.

The old fight between Hindu and Muhammadan mendicants was again renewed in Bogra district. On 2nd March, 1786, Mr. Champion, Collector of Silberis, reported to the Committee of Revenue that "a few days since Hindu & Mussalman Fakirs at Champapour [in Bogra] had an engagement in which the followers of Magenoo were many of them killed and dispersed."[3] The Fakirs were not, however, completely dispersed for Mr. Champion applied for a company of sepoys to Major Dunn at Dinajpur on hearing news that "the followers of Mugennoo under one of his leaders were within four coss of Silberris" and asked for approval of his action "as the demands of Mugenoo on the zemindars are considerable."[4] On the 19th March the Collector of Rangpur informed Major Dunn that a large body of Sannyasis numbering 1,500 were at Dewangunge where they were levying contributions on the zamindars and ryots and would take the western route to Ghoraghat and Dinajpur.[5] "They crossed the Brahmaputra at Dewangunge; they had rockets, jinjal pieces and 110 horses."[6] Evidently the raiders were on their return journey. Lieut. Ainslie who was then north of Mahastan was directed to proceed to Dewangunge with his 80 men and 50 more were sent as reinforcement.[7] On the 26th March the Collector of Silberis informed the Committee of Revenue that the Sannyasis had crossed the Brahmaputra with a view to plunder the Mela at Mahastan, which was to begin 3 days hence and last about 8 or 9 days, Lieut. Ainslie who was under

Sannyasis *versus* Fakirs.

---

[1] Letter from the Collector of Rangpur to Capt. Alexander, dated 16th February, 1786. *MSS. Rangpur Records*, Vol. 23, p. 31.

[2] Letter from W. M. Duncanson, Commanding Rangpur Barkandazes, to the Collector of Rangpur, dated Sanubary, 11th February, 1786. *MSS. Rangpur Records*, Vol. 32, pp. 76-83.

[3] Letter from the Collector of Silberis to the Committee of Revenue, dated 2nd March, 1786. Committee of Revenue Proceedings, Consultation, No. 3, dated 6th March, 1786.

[4] *Ibid.*

[5] Letter from D. H. McDowall, Collector of Rangpur, to Major Dunn, dated 19th March, 1786. *MSS. Rangpur Records*, Vol. 23, p. 75.

[6] Glazier's *District of Rangpur*.

[7] Letter from Major Dunn to the Collector of Rangpur, dated 20th March, 1786. *MSS. Rangpur Records*, Vol. 33, pp. 37-38.

orders to proceed to Dewangunge left at Silberis (Bogra) a guard of a Jamadar and 18 sepoys. The latest account received by the Collector was that the Sannyasis numbering twelve hundred were near Islamabad, a pargana then under Bogra.[1] On the 1st April, the Collector of Rangpur told Major Buchanan then negotiating with Nepal, of "several parties of Sannyasis being within Rangpur extorting money from the inhabitants, one of those parties consisting of about 7 or 800 armed men and 40 horse, rockets, jinjal pieces etc. were within 8 or 10 coss of Rangpur on their return to the Gurkha country." Major Buchanan was requested to attack them should they pass through Kasimgunge and also in his negotiations with Nepal to obtain a stipulation from the Nepal Raja "to refuse this tribe of Sannyasis protection in the Goorkha country."[2] It appears from a report of Capt. Alexander that "Moosha Saw Faquer has a Fuckeer [Jageer] in their [Goorkha] country about a mile from Cassimgunj consisting of nine Goteh of land, five of which was given to him by Secumpully and four latterly by Gunga Ram,"[3] who were Subas [local governors] of Nepal. It is therefore clearly proved that the raiding Fakirs had definitely established their headquarters within the Nepal Territory. As a check to their inroads, the Governor-General accepted the recommendations of the Committee of Revenue of a plan from Mr. Pagan for cultivating the country lying on the frontiers between Purnea and Morung and for maintaining a force to preserve the tranquillity of that part of the borders. As the orders of the Court of Directors forbade the farming of lands to Europeans, the matter was referred to the Court for approval in July, 1786.[4]

Fakirs in Dinajpur.

Early in August, the naib of Gilabari Pargana represented to the Collector of Dinajpur that Majnu Shah with a large body of followers had entered the Pargana and encamped in village Chackool, 4 miles south of Gilabari, and that some of the followers had been to the cutcherry and taken away the Head Tahsildar or collector and several inhabitants and demanded money. A company of sepoys under Lieut. John Ainslie was deputed from Dinajpur on the 2nd August. On the 6th the Collector received information that Majnu was proceeding to the borders of Goraghat bearing about 40 miles south-south-west from Rangpur and was encamped at Recavie and informed Mr. McDowall, the Rangpur Collector accordingly.[5]

---

[1] Letter from the Collector of Silberis to the Committee of Revenue, dated 26th March, 1786. Revenue Department, Governor-General in Council, Original Consultation, No. 73, dated 30th March, 1786.

[2] Letter from the Collector of Rangpur to Major James Buchanan, dated 1st April, 1786. *MSS. Rangpur Records*, Vol. 23, p. 85.

[3] Letter from Capt. Alexander to the Collector of Rangpur, dated 25th March, 1786. *MSS. Rangpur Records*, Vol. 33, p. 45.

[4] Extract from Revenue General letter to the Court, dated 3rd July, 1786.

[5] *Bengal District Records*, Dinajpur, Vol. II, pp. 10-13.

On the 9th August Lieut. Ainslie reported to the Collector of Dinajpur from "Cockna Ghur about three coss from Serratty. On receipt of your letter of the morning of the 17th, I marched after Mujenoo six coss, gave my sepoys a little rest and same night made a forced march of nine coss in order that I might attack him in the night time, when I arrived at the ground where I expected to have found him, I was informed he had moved five coss towards Silberris. In the morning of the 8th I marched and attacked him about 10 coss from Silberris and after an engagement of two hours and a half, the day went in my favour. I have the pleasure to inform you that I have not lost any of my sepoys and have but very few wounded. I dispatched a Hircurrah to Lt. Brennan who commands a detachment at Silberris informed him of the circumstances that Majinoo had moved that way. I shall remain here this day in order to prepare Doolies for my wounded men and tomorrow shall move towards Dinagepore."[1] Majnu's party consisted of two and three thousand and Lt. Ainslie commanded only one company of sepoys. The gallant and spirited behaviour of the Lieutenant was highly commended.[2] The victory was decisive and further activity on Majnu's part was considered improbable for some time to come. Majnu fled towards Silberis (Bogra) and was within four coss of Bogra on the 12th August, a circumstance "which was unusual for that period of the year."

Defeat of Majnu.

On the 25th September, 1786, the Collector of Dinajpur instructed Lieut. H. M. D'Esterre to proceed to Tellun in the Pargana of Bejanagar as "Moosa Shah had confined many of the principal riauts in the Pargana and been guilty of other enormities such as beating and extorting money from them." On the 26th Lieut. D'Esterre was at Brool (Birol) and on the same date moved on to Jagannathpur in pursuit of the Fakirs. The instruction of the Collector of Dinajpur was to pursue Musa Shah to the boundaries of his district and not beyond and in case he should escape out of the district to inform the Collector of the district into which he may fly.[3] Evidently the Fakirs moved south towards Bogra district for on the 28th October, the Collector of Silberis informed the Collectors of Rangpur, Dinajpur and other neighbouring districts of "Mudgenoo Shaw, the travelling Fakeer being in the neighbourhood" of Bogra.[4] On the 29th he again informed the Collector of Dinajpur that "Mudgenoo Shaw was at Munjurah near Coltal" (Kollal in Bogra) and that "he will proceed to Appole which is the way of his general route."[5] Lieut. Brennan with 59 sepoys marched from Bogra in pursuit of Majnu Shah to

[1] Revenue Department, Original Consultation, No. 15, dated 7th September, 1786.

[2] *Bengal District Records*, Dinajpur, Vol. II, p. 15.

[3] *Bengal District Records*, Dinajpur, Vol. II, pp. 21-22.

[4] *Bengal District Records*, Dinajpur, Vol. I, p. 17.

[5] Letter from the Collector of Silberis to the Collector of Dinajpur, dated 29th October, 1786. *Bengal District Records*, Dinajpur, Vol. I, p. 17.

"Calleswar where he found him attended by about five hundred armed men, attacked and dispersed them, the sepoys behaving with great spirit. The country is so much under water and the river so deep that it was then impossible to pursue the advantage any further against so large a body."[1] As regards the loss on the Fakir's side a letter of the Lieutenant, dated December, states: "I now learn from people who were dispatched after him yesterday that he buried several of his men before he reached the first Nullah (S. W. of this place)[2] where the people of the ferry boats which had been in waiting informed my Hircarra that they crossed over five of his principal men dangerously wounded. And as they particularised the places where they were shot I cannot doubt the truth of the intelligence. The ferry men added that Majenoo in his flight had been thrown by his horse that when he crossed at the ferry before mentioned he was very ill and covered over with mud and water. My Hircarrahs likewise received information that he had boats in readiness at the Jobuna river which he must have crossed yesterday, as I learnt it was his intention not to halt until he reached Saapore [in Rajshahi district] from whence I can only suppose that he will either lurk about the vicinity of Malda or cross the Ganges."[3] This was the last raid of Majnu, for he died next year at Makhanpur. **Flight of Majnu.**

But a few months later, other parties of raiders had to be dealt with. **1787.** In February, 1787, a detachment from the Regiment stationed at Dinajpur marched against and drove a party of Fakirs headed by a chela of Majnu named Madar Bux into the jungles of Perua and captured their ammunition, etc. The Collector entertained spies for the purpose of ascertaining the "routes of the Fakirs."[4]

On 5th March, 1787, the Collector of Dinajpur informed Major Dunn, Commanding at Dinajpur, of the depredations committed by a body of Fakirs numbering three to four hundred in Pargana Sikarpur about 50 miles south-west of Dinajpur and asked him to disperse them.[5]

The following rainy season brought a renewal of the campaign In July, 1787, a petition from Cassinaut, Naib of the Pargana Musidah to the Collector of Murshidabad ran as follows: "Musa Shaw Fackeer with near six hundred armed men have assembled at the village of Soorhutty in the Pargunnah Bayeshhazzarree in the district of Panduah **Musa Shah in Northern Bengal.**

[1]Letter from the Collector of Silberis to the Board of Revenue, dated 2nd December, 1786. Board of Revenue Proceedings, dated 26th December, 1786, pp. 182-85.

[2]Probably the Tulsiganga river.

[3]Letter from Lieut. A. Brennan to the Collector of Silberis from camp near Calleswar, dated 8th December, 1786.

[4]Letter from the Collector of Dinajpur to the Secretary to the Governor-General, dated 19th December, 1787. *Bengal District Records*, Dinajpur, Vol. II, p. 160.

[5]Letter from the Collector of Dinajpur to Major Dunn, dated 5th March, 1787. *Bengal District Records*, Dinajpur, Vol. II, p. 65.

and is continually sending men to the naib of the Pergunnah Musscedah, your petitioner's constituent's zemindaree to make a settlement: he has beat the ryotts of many villages and collects money from them. He has summoned the Gomastahs and headmen of the villages and illtreats them; the ryotts and inhabitants in consequence fly in fear of him and the cultivation of the country is stopped."[1] In consequence of the above representation, Mohan Singh and Darap Singh, Harcarrahs, were ordered by the Collector "to go to the aforesaid Pergunnah, keep good guard assisted by the zemindary Amlah and seize and confine the said Fackeer and send the Fakir to him." When the Dastak or order was shown to the Fakir he took it away and "paid no attention to it. He committed great outrages plundering the Company's Revenue and the ryotts. On pretence of asking charity he plundered. On hearing of the orders of Govermnent he was enraged and spoke very disrespectfully."[2] The defiant nature of Musa Shah will be apparent from the following letter he sent to Dulal Chaudhuri, Naib of Pargana Musidah: "You have complained against me at the cutchery of the zillah of Moorshidabad. Hircarrahs are sent. What is to be gained by complaining and sending Hircarrahs? The sum I have required of you must be prepared for. I will most certainly take it, I inform those of it to whom you complain. You must not be negligent on the Hircarra's Security."[3] Being thus defied Mr. Dawson, Collector of Murshidabad, complained on 12th July to the Board of Revenue "of the depredations committed in Pargana Mussida by Musa Shah with followers numbering about 500 many of whom being dismissed sepoys from different brigades and are armed and dressed in the same manner as the English troops." Mr. Dawson asked that the Collectors of the neighbouring districts should act in co-operation and concerted action should be taken.[4] The Board of Revenue accordingly directed the Collectors of Dinajpur, Rangpur, Purnea, Bhagalpur and Rajshahi to act in concert with the neighbouring zamindars of Pargana Musidah for apprehending Musa Shah; should this fail the Board assured them that a regular Force would be sent.[5] According to these orders Mr. Dawson, requested Mr. Hatch, Collector of Dinajpur, "to send some troops against Musa Shaw."[6] But Musa Shah had already moved on. On the 17th August, the Collector of Dinajpur reported to the Board of Revenue "the depredations of Musa Shah with a number of armed men in Pargana Appole" and called upon the Commanding Officer at Dinajpur to detach a party of sepoys against

---

[1]Board of Revenue, Original Consultation, No. 3, dated 20th July, 1787.

[2]Board of Revenue, Original Consultation, No. 2, dated 20th July, 1787.

[3]Board of Revenue, Original Consultation, No. 4, dated 20th July, 1787.

[4]Board of Revenue, Original Consultation, No. 1, dated 20th July, 1787.

[5]Board of Revenue, Original Consultation, No. 5, dated 20th July, 1787.

[6]Letter from the Collector of Murshidabad to the Collector of Dinajpur, dated 13th August, 1787. *Bengal District Records*, Dinajpur, Vol. 1, p. 64.

him.[1] A guide was directed to conduct them to Musa Shah's encampment but on the 3rd September, the Collector reported that "upon intelligence being obtained by him of the steps taken he removed before the party could possibly reach the spot." The Jamadar of sepoys with his party, however, continued the pursuit.[2] This was against the express orders prohibiting employment of small parties and the party met with defeat. On 9th September, Mr. Dawson thanked Mr. Hatch for sending sepoys against Musa and wrote that he had also sent a "force consisting of one Jamadar and 30 sepoys with a number of Burgandosses against him to finish this trade of plundering under the pretence of charity by making an example of Shaw Musa and his followers."[3] On the 10th September, Mr. Dawson informed the Board of Revenue that Musa Shah had an engagement with the party sent from Dinajpur. "The Black Officer commanding the said party acquainted him that having received two wounds he is obliged to retreat."[4]

Defeat of Sepoys.

In November, Mr. Dawson reported to the Board of Revenue that "a body of people belonging to Shaw Moosoonoo have entered the zemindary of Chandly and are plundering the same" and asked Col. Mattocks, Commander of the Invalids at Moradbaugh, "to take or destroy them."[5] Mr. Hatch was infuriated at the news of the defeat of the Jamadar's party sent from Dinajpur, so when he next received news of Musa Shah preparing to renew his depredations he asked on 1st December Major Maitland, Commanding at Tajpur, "to send a force against Musa Shah, who was proscribed, and was believed to be at a place five coss north-east of Taujepur,"[6] with the instructions that "the officer commanding the detachment be authorised to cause a summary examination of the persons taken in actual arms and make an example by hanging upon the spot every tenth man and if a lesser number be captured the officer to use his discretion as to the number to be made examples of and send the rest to the nearest Fauzedarry Court to take their trial. If Moosa Shaw be taken and his person identified to the officer, the same fate should attend him without any ceremony." The

[1] Letter from the Collector of Dinajpur to the Board of Revenue, dated 17th August, 1787. *District Records*, Dinajpur, Vol. II, p. 117.

[2] Letter from the Collector of Dinajpur to the Collector of Murshidabad, dated 3rd September, 1787. *District Records*, Dinajpur, Vol. II, p. 120.

[3] Letter from the Collector of Murshidabad to the Collector of Dinajpur. *District Records*, Dinajpur, Vol. I, p. 71.

[4] Board of Revenue, Original Consultation, No. 16, dated 18th September, 1787.

[5] Letter from the Collector of Murshidabad to the Board of Revenue, dated 17th Novmeber, 1787. Board of Revenue, Original Consultation, No. 47, dated 23rd November, 1787.

[6] Letter from the Collector of Dinajpur to Major Maitland, dated 1st December, 1787. Revenue Department, Governor-General in Council, Original Consultation, No. 13, dated 18th January, 1788.

Board approved of the measures taken but "disapproved of the instructions for summary punishment and resolved that the Collector of Dinajpur be directed to instruct Major Maitland to deliver all prisoners taken to the Magistrate in order to their being tried before the Faujdary Court" remarking that "prisoners can suffer the punishment of death upon due conviction only after a regular trial."[1] The detachment sent against Musa Shah was reported by the Commanding Officer at Tajpur to "have succeeded in obliging that freebooter to quit the Company's districts."

1787-88. Sannyasis in Rangpur.

About this time the Sannyasis also reappeared after a long interval in the district of Rangpur. On the 18th December, the Collector of Rangpur, reported to the Board of Revenue that "a body of Nagurs [naked religious mendicants] to the number of between three and four hundred men have assembled at the cutchery of Pergunnah of Dehutt" and the Commanding Officer of Tajpur was called upon to detach a party against them.[2]

It was found that the employment of spies by the Collector of Dinajpur to ascertain the movements of the Fakirs had worked well. The Governor-General in Council "being of opinion that some other measures more effectual than those hitherto taken should be adopted for securing the country against the inroads and depredations of Mujenoo Shaw and his adherents," the Collectors of Rangpur and Dinajpur were directed by the Secretary to the Government in the Revenue Department on 7th December "to employ spies at a monthly sum not exceeding sixty rupees in the most private and disguised manner to follow him, ascertain his haunts, his routes and the mode in which he lives with a view to ascertain the possibility of apprehending him and his principal attendants.... The expense incurred in this service is to be defrayed by the Civil Paymaster and the bills to be drawn out of Secret Service. The correspondence on the subject of these orders is to be with the Secretary only, for the information of the Governor-General in Council."[3]

In December, Major Maitland reported to the Collector of Rangpur that the detachment sent against Musa Shah had succeeded in obliging the freebooter to quit the Company's districts and that he has asked it to operate in Pargana Dehutt against the Sannyasis and Lieut. Cuthbert deputed to Cooch Behar was asked to march to Bojunpur to operate in

---

[1]Revenue Department, Body Sheet, Order and Resolution, Nos. 12 and 13, dated 18th January, 1788.

[2]Letter from the Collector of Dinajpur to the Board of Revenue, dated 18th December, 1787. *District Records*, Dinajpur, Vol. II, p. 159.

[3]Letter from the Revenue Department to the Collector of Dinajpur, dated 7th December, 1787. *District Records*, Dinajpur, Vol. I, p. 82.

Bodah Pargana.[1] Another party was sent on 26th January, 1788, by Major Maitland Commanding at Tajpur to "proceed by the route to Gubinagar to Burabary, or as it is commonly called Bojunpur, in the purgunnah of Bodah."[2] On the same date the Collector of Rangpur made representations to the Subas of the Goorkha Raja requiring them as friends of the English Company to prevent Musa Shah from taking refuge within their jurisdiction,[3] and about the same time the Board of Revenue instructed the Collectors of Dinajpur, Dacca, Mymensingh, Murshidabad, Rajmahal, Purnea and Rangamati to co-operate with the Collector of Rangpur against Musa Shah.[4]

Action taken by Government.

The remonstrance made to the Goorkha Subas had some effect, for on the 28th February, Mr. McDowall, the Collector of Rangpur, wrote to Major Maitland that he had received letters from the Goorkha Suba informing him that Musa Shah "had come into his district after quitting Pargunnah Bodah but in consequence of his perwannah he has refused him protection and he (Musa Shaw) had therefore entered into Beejurpore lying to the north of the Purnea district." Mr. McDowall thereupon asked the Major to recall the sepoys.[5] It appears that the Collector of Rangpur was misinformed about the movements of the Fakirs or they had stealthily taken a south-eastern course and appeared in Rajshahi district. "On the 9th of Choit" [corresponding to about 20th March], says a letter from the Collector of Dinajpur to the Collector of Rajshahi, dated 24th March, "an engagement happened between a party of Burcandosses belonging to the Ranee of Radshye and Moosa Sah and his adherents at a place called Paulla near Orjoonpoockre in Purgunnah Jeah Sing. The Burcundosses were worsted and three of them made captives, some villages were plundered after the defeat of the Burcundosses. On the 10th of Choit, a detachment of a Jemautdur and thirty sepoys drove this Marauder before him but the Jemautdur as well as the spies represent that the spectators from the surrounding villages peaceably looked on and offered no assistance either to join the Jemautdar of the party or intercept Moosa in his flight."[6] The Collector of Rajshahi was asked to take action against the villagers. This skirmish took place at Neamatpur in the Pargana of Jeasingh in Rajshahi. Musa and his

Skirmishes with Musa Shah.

[1]Letter from Major Maitland to Collector of Rangpur, dated 22nd December, 1787. *District Records*, Rangpur, Vol. I, pp. 51-52.

[2]Letter from Major Maitland to the Collector of Rangpur, dated 20th January, 1788. *MSS. Rangpur Records*, Vol. 10, pp. 13-14.

[3]Letter from the Collector of Rangpur to the Secretary to the Government, dated 26th January, 1788.

[4]Letter from the Board of Revenue to the Collector of Rangpur, dated 12th February, 1788.

[5]Letter from the Collector of Rangpur to Major Maitland, dated 28th February, 1788.

[6]Letter from the Collector of Dinajpur to the Collector of Rajshahi, dated 24th March, 1788. *Dinajpur MSS. Records*, Vol. 67B, pp. 242-43.

adherents fled towards Silberis.[1] But they lingered on for on the 22nd June, the Collector of Dinajpur wrote to the Collector of Murshidabad as follows: "On the 28th ultimo early in the morning Lt. Christie surprised and put to flight Moosa Saw who together with his adherents was encamped near to two villages named Jehangueerpore and Chumpore belonging to Purgunna Jehangueepore....." During the pursuit by the detachment, "the inhabitants of these villages made away with the baggage which Moosa Saw had abandoned...." It was represented that Musa Shah could have been captured if the villagers had given assistance. The next remark in the letter is significant and shows the general attitude of the people. "The alertness of the villagers to seize upon what did not belong to them manifestly shows that mere timidity is not solely the cause of their flying or remaining inactive, as is their custom, upon these occasions." It was suspected "that the villagers on these events became partisans of the Fakirs and restore to them in the hour of safety what they took charge of at the moment of their danger."[2]

1788-89. Fakirs in Dinajpur.

In September, the Collector of Dinajpur informed Major Maitland that "he had received news to the effect that Parighul Saw and Cheragh Ally Saw, chellahs of late Mudgenoo are encamped at a place named Tetulea [Purganna Mussida] about ½ a coss to the eastward of Poorsa a village situated in the high road south from this [Dinajpur] to the Ganges and where the Dawk Hoda is stationed. One of the Dowrahs [mail runners] of that station has been confined in their camp for six days and bears the marks of having been very ill-treated by them and three of the dawks have been opened and searched. The Dowrah was released this day seven night and says that according to his calculation while under confinement the Banditti consisted of about three hundred men carrying matchlocks and that they were employed in seizing the riauts of the neighbouring villages and making collections from them." It was requested that a force might be sent against them, another party under the Subadar stationed at Bogra being already directed to march direct west and join the detachment from Tajpur.[3] Hemmed in on all sides some of the Fakirs were captured. The Collector of Dinajpur informed the Magistrate of Murshidabad: "Twentyone of the Fakirs who were late assembled in arms upon the borders of this district have been captured and seventeen of the number delivered over to the Foujdarry Court to take their trial.... The inhabitants of the villages of Porsa in Pergunnah Jehangueerpore and of its environs have been plundered and carried about prisoners from one village to another. If it were practicable to send

Capture of Fakirs.

[1] Letter from the Collector of Dinajpur to the Collector of Rangpur, dated 24th March, 1788.

[2] Letter from the Collector of Dinajpur to the Collector of Murshidabad, dated 22nd June, 1788.

[3] Letter from the Collector of Dinajpur to Major Maitland, dated 27th September, 1788.

some of the sufferers to Dinagepore their evidence would most probably tend to a speedy conviction of the parties. From the deposition of Burkutulla the Hircarrah sent in search of the Fakirs it would appear that Pharagul Saw, the leader of their banditti was lying ill in the house of Kinoo Dewan an inhabitant of the village of Ghedusah in Pergunnah Canchun Musseeda at the time the detachment was in pursuit and that Kinoo Dewan assisted in carrying Faraggul to and secreting him in the jungle." Accordingly, the Collector of Murshidabad ordered an enquiry. Kinoo Dewan was summoned and the Collector of Dinajpur was asked to send witnesses to depose against him.[1]

Nothing further is recorded till April, 1789, when the Fakirs appeared again presumably on the occasion of some religious festival at Perua (Pandua) and the Collector of Dinajpur informed Capt. Lambert, the Officer Commanding at Tajpur, that "Shaw Cherragh Ally, Pier Ackool Ally and Shaw Zhumuru with about 500 followers and that Moosa Shaw with about 400 followers were encamped at Deotella about 9 coss east from Purruah armed with matchlocks &c committing depredations" and he asked for a force to be sent against them.[2] On the 20th, the Subadar surprised and dispersed the Fakirs.[3] But about a month later, on the 13th May, the Collector of Dinajpur again informed Capt. Lambert that Musa Shah and his followers had returned to the borders of Dinajpur District and threatened to plunder the Parganna of Baishhazari.[4]

Malda.

In the following cold weather the trouble reappeared. In January, 1790, Mr. Wroughton, the Collector of Mymensingh, forwarded to the Board of Revenue a petition from the zamindars containing the following account of the depredations of Sannyasis and Fakirs who it appears were acting in concert: "Cherag Ally &c Fakeers belonging to the tribe of Mudgnu Shaw together with Mongeer and other Sanassies heading a very large party have arrived at Jaffershahy where they have commenced depredations, are laying waste the country and plundering the revenues of Government, causing the utmost terror to the Aumlahs and Ryotts who are running away to prevent the danger they apprehend."[5] Simultaneously with this report, Mr. Wroughton asked for help from Capt. McKenzie commanding at Dacca and informed him that the

1789-90.

Sannyasis and Fakirs in Mymensingh.

[1]Letter from the Collector of Dinajpur to Collector of Murshidabad, dated 20th October, 1788. *Bengal District Records*, Dinajpur, Vol. I, page 161.

[2]Letter from the Collector of Dinajpur to Captain Lambert, dated 17th April, 1789. Board of Revenue, Original Consultation, No. 193, dated 23rd April, 1789.

[3]Letter from Capt. Lambert to Mr. Hatch, dated 11th May, 1789. *Bengal District Records*, Dinajpur, Vol. I, pp. 216-17.

[4]Letter from the Collector of Dinajpur to Capt. Lambert, dated 13th May, 1789. Board of Revenue, Original Consultation, No. 7, dated 18th May, 1789.

[5]Revenue Department, Original Consultation, No. 60, dated 20th January, 1790.

raiders were at least 2,000, of which 500 may be reckoned fighting men, armed with matchlocks, spears and tulwars,[1] and that they had come through an unfrequented path from Mahastangarh to Jaffarshahy where they have erected their standard and are increasing their force by various emissaries who have been in the province for some time. Capt. Clayton, who was stationed at Goalpara, was directed to assist Mr. Wroughton, who informed the Collector of Goalpara on the 20th January that "the report of the detachment under Captain Clayton has so far operated on the fears of Shaw Mujnu's party that they have retired from Jaffershahy." Mr. Wroughton, however, was not without fears of further trouble for he added—"Whether they have entirely given up their intentions or only hid themselves in jungles and unfrequented parts of the country until a more favourable period offers, it is impossible to devise, knowing that they do not easily relinquish an object when once undertaken."[2]

Rangpur. In May, 1790, Capt. Thomas Cust, Commanding at Tajpur, informed the Collector of Rangpur that "Mussa Shaw had made his appearance in the neighbourhood of Sannyasikotta with an armed force consisting of above 250 Matchlocks and Rocket men....On the information of the Havildar at Sannyasikotta it appeared that Musa Shaw was within three coss from there and threatened to plunder some neighbouring villages."[3] Capt. Ridley with a detachment was sent from Tajpur. On the 8th June, Capt. Ridley informed the Collector of Rangpur from Sannyasikotta that Musa Shah had fled into the territory of Nepal with a large force some days before his arrival there.[4] The detachment was therefore recalled.

There is no record of further troubles from the nomadic marauders
1791-92. till December of next year. In that month, the Collector of Rangpur
Fakirs in reported to the Board of Revenue that "a large body of armed
Rangpur. Fakeers amounting to seven or eight hundred men under the conduct of either Cherag Ali or Rowshan Ali have entered Cageerhaut with a view to exacting contributions from the ryots many of whom have fled. They entered the district by the way of Bykuntpore where they committed no depredations having received from the zemindar, according to report, a supply of 200 Rs. either in cash or provisions to purchase their forbearance." It was further reported that "Cheragali was the adopted son of the late notorious Mujenoo Saw and he and Rowshun Ali are said to have established a sort

[1]Letter from the Collector of Mymensingh to Capt. McKenzie, dated 13th January, 1790; Revenue Department, Original Consultation, No. 61, dated 20th January, 1790.

[2]Letter from the Collector of Mymensingh to Hugh Baillie, Esq., at Goalpara, dated 20th January, 1790.

[3]Letter from Capt. Cust to the Collector of Rangpur, dated 29th May, 1790. *MSS. Rangpur Records*, Vol. 16, p. 71.

[4]Letter from Capt. Ridley to the Collector of Rangpur, dated 8th June, 1790.

of partnership in plunder under the Firm of Cherag Rowshan Ali the name which is cut on their seals."[1] The Collector on further information corrected his report on the 21st December, when he reported that the Fakirs under Roshun Ali had sent an application to him stating that the reason for his [Roshun Ali's] keeping an armed following is owing to his enmity with Cherag Ali and Musa Shah. Intimation was at the same time sent of Musa Shah having entered Pargana Saruppur. But before any Government force was sent, the farmer of Saruppur drove off the Fakir and his followers with his own Burkandazes; and Musa Shah retreated to Delalpur, "the property of the zamindar of Bhitarband appertaining to Rajshahi district."[2]

A few weeks later, an atrocious attack was committed on the Factory of the Company at Birtara subordinate to Hurrial.[3] On the 30th Magh [about 15th January], a large body of Fakirs to the number of five or six hundred arrived in the neighbourhood of Birtara, from whence a party of fifty or sixty armed men proceeded to the Factory and demanded from the Gomasta one thousand Rupees.[4] The attack was made by "Shaw Moosah, Peraugh Ali and other Fakirs who extorted from Ramsunder Roy the Gomasta of the Factory Rupees 375. The Fakirs not only beat the Gomasta but applied lighted matches of their guns to his body to force him into a compliance with their demands." It transpired during enquiry that "certain Burkandauzes, inhabitants of Pargana Cagmarry in the district of Mymensingh were very active in assisting the Fakirs to seize the people belonging to the Cooty and to collect the tribute claimed." The Magistrate of Rajshahi at the request of the Commercial Resident at Hurrial "to take action"[5] deputed as many sepoys as he could spare but they returned without success, "the Fakirs having retired" previous to the approach of the sepoys "being too rapid in their motions to be overtaken by a pursuit."[6] Although the Magistrate had no chance of apprehending the Fakirs, he hoped to discover some of the accomplices and the Governor-General in Council was requested by the

Mymensingh.

[1]Letter from J. Lumsden, Collector of Rangpur, to the Board of Revenue, dated 15th December, 1791. Revenue Department, Original Consultation, No. 7, dated 30th December, 1791.

[2]Letter from J. Lumsden, Collector of Rangpur, to the Board of Revenue, dated 21st December, 1791. Revenue Department, Original Consultation, No. 11, dated 30th December, 1791.

[3]Hurrial in Rajshahi district but Birtara is in Mymensingh district near Sarisabari Railway station.

[4]Letter from Samuel Beachcroft, Resident at Hurrial, to the Board of Revenue, Revenue Department, Original Consultation, No. 28, dated 17th February, 1792.

[5]Letter from the Magistrate of Nattore to the Resident at Hurrial, dated 5th March, 1792. Revenue (Judicial) Department, Original Consultation, No. 41, dated 13th April, 1792.

[6]Letter from the Magistrate of Nattore to Governor-General in Council, dated 27th February, 1792. Revenue (Judicial) Department, Original Consultation, No. 5, dated 2nd March, 1792.

Revenue (Judicial) Department to realise the amount plundered, from the zamindar "agreeable to the law of the country."

In February, the Magistrate of Mymensingh reported to the Governor-General in Council that "Parragullah Shaw had entered Pergunnah Jaffershahy with a number of followers amounting to 200 men armed with matchlocks and other offensive weapons. Parragullah Shaw was the natural son of the late Mugnoo Shaw.... The son having shown his inclination and ability to pursue the steps of his father, is plundering several villages and carrying off many ryots therefrom, at the complaint and remonstrance of the Landholders, a Jematdar and 20 sepoys were deputed against them. Upon their arrival at Jaffershahy the Jemadar informed the Sezawal that he did not think his parties sufficiently strong to cope with or follow Paragulla Shaw whose number was increased to 300 men formidably armed with matchlocks, spears, Tulwars &c." The Magistrate thereupon instructed the Jamadar to try to seize Paragulla and his gang by stratagem and the Subedar was ordered to pursue them to the confines of the Rajshahi district as they had taken refuge in Pratabbazu Pargana on the banks of the river Jhenai, "the boundary between Rajshahi and Mymensingh districts, and the Fakirs came over when there was no danger of their being opposed."[1]

On the 27th February, Mr. Harrington, Magistrate of Rajshahi, stationed at Nattore, wrote to the Governor-General in Council submitting the expediency of ordering a "Soobadaur and fifty men from Berhampore to be stationed at Mustangarh during the ensuing month in which the annual religious meeting of the Sunnassies at Mustangarh will take place [on the 10th Chyte or about 28th March] and to remain there till the Sannyasis who were then traversing different parts of Dinajpur, Rangpur, Mymensingh, Murshidabad and Rajshahi under their leader Cheraug Ally and Shaw Moosa shall have dispersed or retired from lower country which they will probably do after the festival. He also hoped that the sepoys may surprise and capture the Fakir leaders."[2] The sepoys remained at Mahastangarh during the Baruni festival but "no information of Peraug Ally or Cherag Ally was received, so they returned to Nattore." In a letter, dated the 4th April, to Lord Cornwallis, Mr. Harrington wrote that "Shaw Moosa was killed in the beginning of the past month in a skirmish with Peraugally."[3]

---

[1]Letter from the Magistrate of Mymensingh to the Governor-General in Council, dated 13th February, 1792. Revenue (Judicial) Department, Original Consultation, No. 8, dated 24th February, 1792.

[2]Letter from the Magistrate of Rajshahi at Nattore to the Governor-General in Council, dated 27th February, 1792. Revenue (Judicial) Department, Original Consultation, No. 5, dated 2nd March, 1792.

[3]Letter from the Magistrate of Rajshahi at Nattore to the Governor-General in Council, dated 4th April, 1792. Revenue (Judicial) Department, Original Consultation, No. 11, dated 13th April, 1792.

CHAPTER XI

The Fakir leaders

THE most notorious of the Fakir leaders who raided Bengal was Majnu Shah Fakir. He belonged to the Burhana sect of the Madari order of Fakirs whose headquarters was at Makhanpur where he usually withdrew when the rainy season stopped marauding operations.[1] According to the *Shetihash Bagurar Brittanta* (a narrative of the Bogra district) published in 1861, one of his local headquarters in Bengal was at Madargunge near Goail, 12 miles to the south of Bogra town. Another was Mahastan where he built a fort in 1776;[2] he also "annually visited the famous darga at Pandua."[3] "The no-man's land lying south of the stations of Dinajpur and Rangpur and west of present Bogra towards the Ganges far removed from any local authority was a favourite haunt of the banditti."[4] **Majnu Shah.**

About his depredations the *Shetihash* states: "At that time, the people of these parts did not even see fire-arms. Majnu's *modus operandi* was to fire some shots on entering a village which frightened the villagers so much that they all fled leaving their cash and valuables; in this way Majnu collected a large booty without resistance. He had a machine called 'Bhela' which when revolved vomitted forth fire all round."

His oppression obliged some of the powerful zamindars living within the zone of his activity to leave their original homes and build residences elsewhere. "It is said that the ancestors of the present Raja of Gauripur in Assam had to leave Karaibari, their original home on account of the depredations of Majnu."[5] Srikrishna Chaudhuri, zamindar of a small pargana named Karai in Bogra district, acquired the large parganas of Mymensingh and Jaffarshahi in the Mymensingh district about the middle of the Eighteenth Century. His son Chand Ray was the Ray Rayan of Bengal during Nawab Ali Vardi Khan's time. Majnu announced his intention of plundering Karai unless a sum of Rs. 50,000

---

[1]Letter from the Collector of Rangpur to Government, dated 26th January, 1788.

[2]Letter from Mr. Franci Gladwin at Silberis (Bogra) to the Provincial Council of Revenue at Dinajpur, dated 26th June, 1776.

[3]Letter from the Collector of Bhagalpur to the Council of Revenue at Fort William, dated 22nd June, 1784.

[4]*The District of Rangpur* by Glazier.

[5]*Bogra District Gazetteer*, pp. 126-27.

was paid to him on a certain date. There were difficulties of transport in those days. It is said that the zamindars in order to escape the depredation had a small khal excavated within one night to connect their residence with the river Nagar, removed their family and valuables in boats and fled to their cutcherries in Jaffarshahi pargana of Mymensingh district.[1] The ruins of their houses at Malancha and Krishnapur within Jaffarshahi pargana in the Jamalpur subdivision of Mymensingh district are still in existence. From Jaffarshahi the oppression of the resident Sannyasis caused the zamindars to move north of the Brahmaputra to pargana Mymensingh where they built their present homes at Gauripur, Ramgopalpur, Kalipur, etc.

Srikrishna Acharyya, a contemporary of Srikrishna Chaudhuri and zamindar of Tappa Jhakar in Bogra district acquired the extensive zamindari of Alapsingh pargana. As stated before owing to Majnu's oppression in 1780 the heirs of Srikrishna Acharyya removed to their present residence at Muktagacha within pargana Alapsingh in Mymensingh district.

Bhawani Pathak the dacoit.

Majnu had his adherents amongst the local dacoits. He was in league with Bhawani Pathak a leader of dacoits,[2] whose sphere of operations was in parganas Pratabbazu and Patiladaha. The former is now in Bogra and Mymensingh districts and the latter in Rangpur and Mymensingh districts, being separated by the river Jamuna. In 1787, some merchants carrying on business in tobacco and other goods between Rangpur and Dacca complained to Mr. Williams, Superintendent of Government Customs at Dacca, of "Bowanny Pathuck a desperate man having taken and plundered their boats in their passage." Mr. Williams "gave the merchants some sepoys and a perwanna to take Puttuck in custody. Puttuck refused to obey the sepoys or the Perwannah and the sepoys having complained to Mr. Fendall, Judge of the Nattore Adalat, they brought an order to the naibs of Pargana Pratabbaza and Pargana Puttah Deh [Patiladaha]. Puttuck having received intelligence of this retired to the village of Cheriah Candy [Seriakandi now in Bogra] in the district of Gour Ghaut where having collected a number of people he plundered the boats of merchants and actually seized on one and the property that was in it."[3] In June, 1787, the merchants complained to Lieut. Brennan, Commanding a detachment at Silberis, who was informed that Pathak was within 10 coss of Govindagunge in Rangpur district with fifty Burkandazes. "He despatched a Havildar with twenty-four sepoys in search of the robbers and they surprised Pathak with sixty of his followers in their boats.

[1] *Barendra Brahman in Mymensingh*, Vol. I, by Kumar Sourindra Kishore Roy Chaudhury, pp. 58-59.

[2] *District of Rangpur*, Glazier.

[3] Letter from Lieut. Brennan, Commanding a detachment of the 29th Battalion, to the Collector of Rangpur, dated 28th June, 1787.

Pathak's chief man, a Pathan, headed a desperate resistance during which the Pathan, the Pathak himself and two other headmen were killed and eight were wounded besides forty-two taken prisoners. Of the attacking party, two sepoys only were wounded. Seven boats with arms, accoutrement and ammunition were taken. Pattak's force consisted wholly of upcountrymen; he himself was a native of Budgepore and he was in league with another noted dacoit Majnoo Shah who made yearly raids from the southern side of the Ganges. We just catch a glimpse from the Lieutenant's report of a female dacoit by name Devi Chaudhuranee also in league with Pattak who lived in boats; had a large force of burkundazes in her pay and committed dacoities on her own account besides getting a share of the booty obtained by Pattak."[1] On receipt of Lieut. Brennan's report regarding the capture of the dacoits, the Collector of Rangpur asked him on 12th July, 1787, to send the prisoners under proper escort for trial in the Faujdari Adawlat. He added "I cannot at present give you any orders with respect to the female Dackoite mentioned in your letter. If on examination of Bengal [Bengali] papers which you have sent it shall appear that there are sufficient grounds for apprehending her and if one shall be found within the limits of my jurisdiction I shall hereafter send you such orders as may be necessary."[2] It may be noted that Bhawani Pathak and Debi Chaudhurani have been immortalised by the great Bengali novelist Bankim Chandra Chatterjee in his novel *Debi Chaudhurani*.

Majnu and his followers.

With the opposition met from the English, Majnu Shah organised his followers as will appear from the following extract of a petition in 1772 by Majnu Shah to Maharani Bhawani of Nattore: "Formerly the Fakirs begged in separate and detached parties but now we are all collected and beg together." In June, 1776, Mr. Gladwin stationed at Bogra reported to the Chief of the Provincial Council at Dinajpur that "Majnu did not come this time attended merely by a Bengal rabble but had with him a number of well armed Rajepoots." In October, Mr. Gladwin again reported to the Governor-General that Majnu had 25 disbanded sepoys in his party.[3]

"Majnur Kabita."

A vivid account of his oppressions and the terror created by him is given by a local poetaster named Panchanan Das in a Bengali poem named *Majnur Kabita* or a poem on Majnu. The poem, in the Appendix, was written in 1813, twenty-five years after Majnu's death. A translation is given below :—

"Listen, all of you, to a new poem. Majnu the Burhana is the ruin of Bengal. A fakir is he? The monster is as destructive as Yama.

---

[1] *The District of Rangpur*, by Glazier.

[2] Letter from the Collector of Rangpur to Lieut. Brennan, dated 12th July, 1787.

[3] Letters from Mr. Gladwin at Silberis to the Provincial Council of Revenue at Dinajpur, dated 26th June, 1776.

the god of death. In fear of him, the ruler trembles and the people have no peace. His march is well ordered like a king's. See how the standards and banners precede him. Behold his retinue of camels, horses and elephants with sturdy Telingas[1] armed to the teeth. Majnu himself is mounted like a warrior on an Arab steed, with his escort of mounted archers. The powerful array strikes terror everywhere and even at the distance of a day's march. At every halting place, a hundred guns are fired. Everyone laments and thinks of flight. Such is the state of the country. What can the Bengalis do but flee? The villages echo with the cry 'The Fakir has come' as he seeks the fugitives in every hamlet. The peasant leaves his plough and cattle in the field and his pot of juice on the palm tree. Women with hair and garments dishevelled rush from their houses. Mothers flee without their babes and the rich ladies with their maids. The Sannyasi runs off hiding his money in his matted hair. The Fakir scorns pots of brass. In his greed he breaks boxes, digs the loose earth and even rips open the pillows, seeking for coins. He empties the merchant's chests. House after house, the hamlet is looted. The lady of gentle birth seeks the woods but the Fakirs quit their thieving to chase her. Like hawks on a pigeon they pounce on her and seek embraces. She entreats and implores 'You are holy fakirs: deal not thus with me. God will call you to account.' The good Fakir stops his ears in shame but the vile one works his will and strips jewels and raiment from his victim. Of such shameful deeds the women are dumb but invoke the god of justice to bring a curse on Majnu, and pray for the monster's death. Whence has this plague come? The death god has brought him to India and has forgotten him."

Majnu Shah died in March or May, 1787 (according to different reports), at Makhanpur and his bones were carried to a famous burial place in the country of Mewaat lying to the southward of Dholly.[2]

Successors of Majnu.

The successors of Majnu Shah were Musa Shah, said to be his brother or cousin, Cherag Ali Shah, his son Pharagul Shah, Subhan Shah, Madar Bux, Jori Shah, Karim Shah and others—all claiming to be his followers. So great indeed was the terror of Majnu's name that any other Fakir claiming to be his follower was sure to strike terror in the country and could levy contributions unopposed. The latter Fakirs had their permanent encampments in the Nepal Terai and only occasionally went to Makhanpur on pilgrimage.

In 1794, an enquiry regarding these Fakirs was ordered by the Governor-General and carried out by Mr. Bruce, the Commissioner at

[1]Native soldiers dressed in quasi-European fashion, so called because the first soldiers of the type came to Bengal from Telinga or Madras. *Hobson-Jobson.*

[2]Letter from the Collector of Rangpur to the Secretary to the Government, dated 26th January, 1788.

Cooch Behar, who deputed an Ameen and messengers. The letter from the Ameen and the deposition of one of the Sannyasis employed by the Fakirs give an interesting description of the Fakirs' encampments and their *modus operandi*. These were sent by Mr. Bruce in a letter, dated 27th August, 1794, to the Sub-Secretary to the Government, and are as follows :— **Fakir camps in Nepal.**

Letter from Busunt Lall Ameen, 18 Assar, 1201 (about 3rd July, 1794).

"I have the honour to send you all the accounts I have as yet been able to collect concerning the Fakeers who live in Goorka formerly belonging to Morung but long since annexed to the Nepaul Government. Hurrcundergury is the residence of the Goorka Soubah on the part of Nepaul and about three coss to the westward of it is Rungaelly, a place which is cultivated and where there is a Tesseldar's Cutchery. Not far from this on the north and south side of the river is the Chowny [camp] of Cheraugally, the chela of Modjous Saw [Majnu Shah] and of Jory Saw the nephew of Cheraugally both of them Fakeers of the Mandaro [Madari] tribe. At three coss distance from this, which is all the way cultivated land is Kwaliah where there is also a Tessildar Cutcherry and Chowny of Sobanny Saw and Sumsheer Saw. These persons were chellas of Moosy Saw who was the slave of Modjous Saw and when their masters died Cheraug Ally and Sobanny Saw set up for themselves. They have no commerce or lands or Revenues. They are supported by the Haukum of the place. They live in jungles hard of access and supply men whether Hindoos or of the Sonassy caste who are willing to serve and who come by the road of Mogullan or by Napaul. They reside in Kadar Phause Sakoo and Hissargurry jungles which are full of elephants, rhinocerasses, tigers and other wild beasts and where near to Nidantarra or near to Condo Haut in Bootan about four coss to the eastward of Nidantarra or near Demy Jar and Pauny Saulah in the Goorka district. In these and similar other places they have encampments in the woods. They plunder at Corbjeswar [Cooch Behar] in Bodah [a pargana in Rangpur] in Purniah in Rangpore to the great injury and oppression of the inhabitants of the Company's provinces. From the accounts of the Burkundazes who took the letters to Nidantara it appears that without the protection of the Nepaul Soubahs it would be difficult for the Fakeers to remain there. It is also known that Hurchundargurry Kowleah and Rungailly are situated in the lowlands that the hills are two or three days' journey distant and that the jungles are penetrable about one coss to the northward of Rungailly and Kwaliah...."

Deposition of one of the Fakeers.

My name is Govind Gior [Giri]. I came from Surat and attended Shumsheer Saw and Jory Saw who live at Rungailly and Kwaliah in

Napaul. These people are now at Nedantarrah where they come on business and will soon return back to their dwelling. They have between them above one thousand people, of which number there are four hundred Mussulman Fakeers and one hundred Hindoo Sonassies, four hundred sepoys, twenty Byragies and the rest are people of different descriptions. They lead these people into Bengal to plunder the country and they live upon the booty which they can take there for they have no landed property at their residences. There is a soubah on the part of the Napaul Rajah at Gur Nidantarrah and when the Fakeers brought home any plunder they present him with the wratich (?) impliments they had taken also with money. They generally went there and staid some time. Shumsheer Saw and Jory Saw generally take all the booty to themselves and pay to their adherents wages. The party I was enrolled with consisted of 100 Sonassis and they paid 1500 rupees per mensem. They paid us when we took property and they then divided the spoils equally between them. Sonassygottah, the Soubah will not allow this place to be touched. The Napaul Rajah residence is a month's journey distant from Nedantara. There are thirty Napaul sepoys at Nedantarrah and twenty at Hurchunder. One place we attacked in Bodah and conducted them to Nidantarrah on purpose that by flogging them we might make them deliver as much money as they would give to us. Rungailly is four or five coss distant from Kwaleah and is distant three munsils from Nidantarrah. Kwaleah is about the same distance from Nidantarrah. When Jory Saw and Shamsheer Saw after a plundering excursion return home they dismiss most of the Fakeers and Sanassies. They retain, however, about 100 or 150 always in their employ and those who are discharged have no habitation at Rangaily or at Kauliah but live elsewhere. Jory Saw and Chiragally are cousins. It has in another place been said they were uncle and nephew and live at Rungaily. They are both chilahs of Modjous Saw [Majnu Shah] Shumsheer Saw and Sabanny are brothers and live at Kwaliah. They were slaves of Modjous Saw but now had set up for themselves and pillage Bengal. These proceedings are not known to the Napaul Rajah but the Soubah of Hurchundgurry knows them and receives a present of horses and camels or money from the spoils of the fakeers.

A letter to Mr. Burges, Collector of Purnea, in 1795, from a Commercial Resident near Morung, gives a vivid description of the Fakirs' camp: "About two years ago, I was in Morung and encamped at Cherag Ali's Chownee at Quilah. He drew out his people about four hundred, half Sonassies dressed in orange and half Molungs in blue jackets. They made a good appearance went thro' their platoon firings better than I could have expected and gave an excellent volley....Shortly after I passed Sooban Alli's Chawnee near the Mudgeruck a horseman came out and delivered a very insolent message from him. I told the man as I was in Morung, I could take no other notice of his master's behaviour but report it to the Soubah and had not a doubt he would be punished. He leaped his horse into a Nulla swam over and joined his companions. I was soon overtaken by a party of six horsemen." They stopped him, and asked for forgiveness showing the fear they had of the Subah.

The following method of recruitment was adopted by a Fakir leader in 1791 in the district of Bhagalpur: "The Fakir named Shah Karim attended by fifteen cavalry and near three hundred burkandazes and men with a camel and a horse furnished with military ensigns arrived from the westward daily collecting more followers to which such as Barkandazes he gives Rs. 5 per mensem and to such as are mounted he gives Rs. 15. Indeed by these many persons enlist with him from Pharkiya Baliya and other parganas. He pays them for one month in advance and he takes rupee one as a salami from each village he passes through."[1] In 1795 the Collector of Purnea reported "that they are no longer that despicable rabble that used formerly to maraud these districts and fly on the report of a sepoy being after them but now consist of Pathans, Rajputs and disbanded sepoys."[2] **Recruitment.**

---

[1]*Hunter's Statistical Account of Bengal*, Bhagalpur, p. 90.

[2]Letter, dated 9th January, 1795, from the Collector of Purnea to the President and Members of the Board of Revenue.

CHAPTER XII

Their final suppression, 1793—1800

In 1793, series of Regulations consolidating and amending the previous rules and Regulations were passed which gave a complete code for the administration of the province. The zamindars were exonerated from their duty of keeping the peace and police-stations or thanas were established. The nomadic raiders were driven away from most of their haunts within the provinces; the only place of safety for them being, outside the British Territories, within Nepal. There, in spite of the profession of friendship, the local Governors or Subahs afforded them shelter, and shared in their spoils. In 1792, the Raja of Nepal entered into a commercial treaty with the British and the Fakirs were repudiated by the Nepal Subahs in public although they were helped in secret. The raids of the Fakirs during this period were confined to the northern districts.

1792-1793. Mr. Heatley, Collector of Purnea, informed the Board of Revenue, in January, 1793, that "Soobhun Alley Shah [Chela of the late Mooshah Shah] with a party of Fakirs had plundered several places on the frontier and carried off a principal ryot whom he did not release until by torture he had extorted a considerable sum of money. The Fakirs also made an attempt on one of the frontier posts but were repulsed." Mr. Heatley further stated that "Soobhunally had a fixed residence in Morung and that the Officers of the Goorka do not attempt to restrain or discourage his depredations."[1] He had therefore written to Jay Mangal Upadhyaya [naib of Dinanath Upadhyaya, the Subah of Morung] remonstrating with him against the behaviour of Sobhan Ali, pointing out that "he seized one Seiries, a raiot of Pergana Salbari in Dinajpore on a demand of alms. He put him to torture: Upon Gurjeet Sing Havildar of Sepoys writing several letters for his release and offers being made of alms to the amount of four or five hundred rupees, the Shah instead of releasing him began torturing him the more, until his relations borrowing 4,500—rupees paid that sum to him and then only he was released. One day the Shah plundered the Haut of Sannassythan and another time on being opposed attempted to give battle to the sepoys of the Company. The Collector requested the Naib to direct his amla on the spot where Subhan Ally Shah has fixed a Tannah to restrain the Shah and not allow him to abide there."[2]

Fakirs in Purnea.

[1]Revenue Department Proceedings, No. 13, dated 25th January, 1793, pp. 254-61.

[2]Revenue Department, Original Consultation, No. 55, dated 22nd February, 1793.

Lord Cornwallis directed a copy of Mr. Heatley's letter to be sent to Capt. Kirkpatrick then on deputation in Nepal with directions "to state the circumstances to the Nepal Government and to obtain the release of the person carried off by Sobhan Ally Shah and also urge the propriety of their punishing the offender and causing him to restore the plundered property." The Governor General, however, did not approve of Mr. Heatley's further proposal to pursue and capture the Fakirs within the Nepal Territory.[1]

A fortnight later, Mr. Heatley informed the Board of Revenue that some followers of Sobhan Ali Shah had been apprehended in his district and committed for trial before the Court of Circuit. He reported the depredations of another party of Fakirs headed by one Kalum Ullah who had attacked and plundered a village about 12 coss north of Purnea and measures were taken to intercept him in his flight back to Morung.[2]

Mr. Harrington, Magistrate of Murshidabad, reported to Lord Cornwallis in March: "The Mahals to the north east of the Pudda dependant upon this jurisdiction have been infested by a large body of plundering Fakirs. On the 13th Falgun (about 28th February) Subhan Ally and Budjeer Buttoo at the head of their gang attacked the cutcherry Rajshahi
of Purgunah Musseedah and having fired upon and overpowered the peons broke open the treasure chest carried off the money it contained and plundered the cutcherry of everything they could find, proceeding to a Gunge in the neighbourhood where they committed similar outrages upon the houses of the Mahajans and others, plundering likewise the inhabitants of adjacent Perganahs of Musrool, Sunkerpore, Gokrah etc. One person of the name of Jeatah Khelaut they murdered and have wounded many and were in the neighbourhood of Jehangeerpur practising their depredations." It was suspected that 'they were concerned in the robbery lately committed between Malda and its subordinate aurangs of Nichundpur and Buddaul'. A company of Native Infantry under a European Officer was sent from Berhampur on Mr. Harrington's requisition "for encouragement of rayats to return to their houses and for making the chiefs of the gangs prisoners if possible or at least to drive them from the country adjacent to Poostole in Pergana Jahangirpore." His suggestion to issue instructions to Magistrates not to allow any Fakir to travel with talwars, spears, firearms or other offensive weapons or to travel in large bodies did not meet with the approval of Lord Cornwallis.[3]

At the suggestion of the Collector of Dinajpur, a detachment of the corps of Hill Rangers was stationed at Deotolla near Malda for the

---

[1]Revenue Department Proceedings, dated 25th January, 1793, pp. 254-56.

[2]Revenue Department, Original Consultation, No. 55, dated 22nd February, 1793.

[3]Letter from the Collector of Murshidabad to the Governor-General in Council, dated 11th March, 1793. Proceedings of Revenue (Judicial) Department, dated 15th March, 1793, Vol. 27, pp. 381-86.

suppression of the Fakirs.[1] On 30th March Mr. Colebrooke, Officiating Magistrate of Purnea, informed Major Lewis Smith, Commanding at Tajpur: "Soobhan Ally Shah with a party of Fakirs said to amount to 4 to 500 is committing depredations in Pergunah Bhownra. This party being distinct from that which lately committed depradations in Moorshidabad District." He asked for a detachment of Sepoys for the expulsion of the Fakirs adding that "as these Fakirs are at enmity with Shah Roshan Ally it is not improbable that on their return towards Morung they may make an attack in the Nek Merda fair which will be held on the 11th April and following days."[2]

Dinajpur and Malda.

Two months later, Mr. Eliot, Acting Magistrate of Dinajpur, reported: "I have this day received a letter from Balject Singh Jamadar commanding a party of sepoys stationed at Silbaries acquainting me of his having surprised Ramzanny Shaw and Jowharry Shaw, the Chelas of late Shaw Murdgenno at Nowgong in Burbucpur where they and their Banditti had been plundering the ryots and defeated them in a pitched battle. The Jamadar informs me that Ramzany Shaw and Jowhurry Shaw's party of Fakirs consisted of about 300 people, that they had sixty men killed after a battle of some duration and three horses taken from them besides some arms. None of the sepoys have been hurt."[3] About a week later, Mr. Eliot reported another reverse of the Fakirs to Major Smith, commanding at Tajpur: "The party stationed at Chinchura on the border of the Purnabubah under the command of Ramzawan Khan came up with the Fakirs and pursued them for some time without much success. They were actually engaged with Cheraug Ally at Dumduma whose force is said to have been seven hundred strong, seven of the Fakirs were wounded and one taken whose wound is said to be dangerous."[4] The Major was requested to send a party to Bydell towards which the Fakirs would march to fly to the Hills, and a few days later Mr. Eliot intimated that "on a junction being effected between Jamadar Ramzan Khan and Subadar Juggernath Singh they marched after the Fakirs who fled precipitously to Malda being prevented from retiring to the hills this time by intelligence that a party from Taujipur were coming that way." Further information was received from Mohamed Jutor Subadar commanding at Poorsa that "in consequence of a Perwana to him he had marched from thence and attacked a gang of Fakirs at Mahagunge belonging to Cheraug Ally who returned into the jungle where these daring vagabonds fought him for a considerable time. Having lost some of their men they fled to the

---

[1]Revenue Department, Body Sheet, No. 5, dated 29th March, 1793.

[2]Board of Revenue, Miscellanoous, Original Consultation, No. 12, dated 10th May, 1793.

[3]Judicial (Criminal), Original Consultation, No. 3, dated 31st May, 1793.

[4]Judicial Department (Criminal). Original Consultation, No. 16, dated 14th June, 1793. Judicial Department (Criminal), Original Consultation, No. 13, dated 31st May, 1793.

inner parts of the jungles where they could not with propriety be pursued by the Sepoys."[1]

About the same time the Collector of Purnea informed the Board of Revenue that a party of Fakirs reported to exceed four hundred and headed by Sobhan Ali Shah, Chela of late Musa Shah were committing depredations in the northern Tuppa of pargana Suryapur and had extorted considerable sum of money from several inhabitants of pargana Suryapur and other adjoining parganas of Dinajpur. He accordingly asked for a detachment to be sent against the Fakirs.[2] "A small detachment accordingly marched but Sobhan Shah with his followers had taken flight a day or two preceding the arrival of the Sepoys which precluded the possibility of a pursuit. A slight skirmish took place between the Fakirs and the Guard stationed at Tanah Mundamela[3] in which it was reported several of Subah Saha's party was killed and wounded. Of the guard at Mundamala one sepoy and three men belonging to the Tanah were wounded."[4] Purnea.

With the coming of the dry season the raiders reappeared and in October, Mr. Harrington, Magistrate of Dinajpur, informed Major Smith, Commanding Officer at Tajpur, that Sobhany Fakir had been committing his usual depredations in the neighbourhood of Thakurgaon in Pargana Salbari and asked the Major to detach a Jamadar with 25 or 30 Sepoys to co-operate with the Daroga there.[5] Accordingly Asaram Subedar was deputed who pursued the Fakirs southward of Salbari which they had passed. On receiving further information that a large body of Fakirs was about mid-way between Tajpur and Dinajpur, Mr. Harrington 'despatched Jagannath Subedar with 22 men from his own and the Collector's guards and 8 men of the guard for treasure to form a junction with the Jamadar and Sepoys stationed at Chinchera and endeavour to fall in with the Fakirs.'[6] The Subedar went in pursuit of the Fakirs but did not venture to attack them owing to the inadequacy of his force.[7] On the 31st October, Mr. Harrington informed Major Smith that he had received intelligence of a strong party of Fakirs (computed to be 700 in number) committing depredations in the neighbourhood of Malda under Cherag Ali in addition to the party of 300 under Sobhany Shah

1793-1794.

Fakirs in Dinajpur.

[1] Judicial Department (Criminal), Original Consultation, No. 18, dated 14th June, 1793.

[2] Board of Revenue, Miscellaneous, Original Consultation, No. 41, dated 9th July, 1793.

[3] In Araria Subdivision of Purnea district.

[4] Board of Revenue, Miscellaneous, Original Consultation, No. 12, dated 6th August, 1793.

[5] Judicial Department (Criminal), Original Consultation. No. 5, dated 15th November, 1793.

[6] *Ibid.*

[7] *Ibid.*

pursued by Asaram Subedar. He added that he had already requested Col. White commanding at Berhampore to replace a strong guard at Porsa for the protection of the southern part of the district, and asked Major Smith whether the four detachments already sent, consisting of altogether 90 men were considered sufficient.[1] It was reported by Mr. Harrington to Col. White that the party under Cherag Ali "have bid defiance to the established Police officers as well as detachment of Sepoys and Burkandazes of near 20 each."[2]

Further news of the depredation of Fakirs is contained in the report from Jagannath Singh Subedar to Mr. Harrington: "On the 17th Kartick on my arrival at Koksan, I was informed by the Hircarrahs that Cheraug Ally Fakir had encamped at Deotaullah in Perganah Balleshazary [Baishazary] and on the 18th I found they had proceeded to Haut Hurrerampore in Purnea. I accordingly pursued them to this place with my own sepoys and those of the Jamadar and Havildar stationed at Chinchera and Bamingola and had an action with them in which many of the Fakirs were killed but the whole of my ammunition being expended I was obliged to retreat and am now at Zillah Okra, three coss distant from Hareerampore. One of the Sepoys is killed and four wounded. The Fakirs threaten to attack me and I have no ammunition I therefore request you will immediately send me a supply and also give additional men." Ninety sepoys besides Barkandazes were in the Subedar's party. Another report from the Subedar showed that "twenty Fakirs were killed and thirty five wounded. The number of Fakirs and Sannyasis amounted to about 1300 men though a small proportion of these have fire arms." The Magistrate sent off 14 Burkandazes with a small supply of ammunition and asked Major Smith "to depute an European Officer to command a very considerable party of sepoys now employed against the Fakirs in this District."[3]

Rajshahi. On the 4th November Mr. James Grant, Magistrate of Rajshahi at Nattore, reported to Col. White commanding at Berhampore that two parties of Fakirs headed by Cherag Ali and Sobhany Shah had assembled in the Dinajpur district, and were then committing depredations on the borders of the Rajshahi district. The Colonel was requested to send a detachment, especially as the detachment at Silbiris (then annexed to Rajshahi from Dinajpore) was withdrawn by the Magistrate of Dinajpur[4] and the sepoys at Nattore were barely adequate for their duties there. It was further stated that the Fakirs were well armed "and are a formidable body and cannot be effectually opposed by any

[1]Judicial Department (Criminal), Original Consultation, No. 5, dated 15th November, 1793.

[2]*Ibid.*

[3]*Ibid.*

[4]Judicial Department (Criminal), Original Consultation, No. 2, dated 15th November, 1793.

other than a disciplined corps."[1] The depredation committed by the Fakirs during this raid as also the oppression of the prisoners are brought out vividly by the deposition of one of the captives: "In Augrahan, 1200 [1793 A. D.], Cheraug Ally Saw and Sobhan Ally Saw plundered the house of Momin Mundal at Sutua and took away the property. Cheragally was accompanied by one thousand people and Soban Ally had about seven hundred and they seized me as a coolie to carry their things with them. They proceeded to pillage Jumaulgunge and afterwards destroyed the house of Cannoo mondol which is situated in Dinajpur but I did not recollect the name of the place. The house was built pucca and we left it to proceed to Gar Nidantorrah. There we stopt a night and the next day waited on the Subah when we presented him with various articles of plunder and with some money. We then took leave and Sobanny Shaw went to Rangelly I was taken to Rangelly by which accident I saw the place. Ten days after his arrival Cheraug Ally went on a pilgrimage to Mokanpore and left me in custody of Fakir Bux Jamadar while he was absent the Jamadar put handcuffs on me. Some time after this Jory Saw went to Nidantorrah and took me along with him. He went to meet Shamsher Shaw. Jory Shaw and Shamsher Shaw set out from Nidantorrah and plundered a Paramanick's house at Burbary[2] at Bodah and also another which I do not remember they gave me a red turban and a lootah and tussar and a white Dooty and that evening I ran away."[3]

Rangpur and Rajshahi.

Later in November, Mr. Harrington reported that on receiving information of the presence of bands of Fakirs in Rajshahi and Rangpur from the Magistrates of those districts, he deputed Lieut. Ainslie who in spite of "good information and expedition" had been unable to come up with them. Mr. Harrington further stated: "The two large bodies of Fakirs under Cheragali and Shoobhany after plundering the inhabitants as usual and in one instance to the alleged amount of nineteen thousand rupees are now gone northwards and from information given to Lt. Ainslie appear to be pursuing each other in the route to Jalpegorry but will again return to the southward unless aware that a complete force is prepared to oppose them and I have also received intelligence of two large bodies one computed to be about a thousand, the other thirteen hundred who were lately seen in Purnea advancing eastward towards this district; though they must have since altered their course and I apprehend will soon be heard of in the neighbourhood of Malda which has induced me to request Lt. Ainslie if he sees no possibility of overtaking the Fakirs gone northwards to proceed to Poorsa."[4]

---

[1]Judicial Department (Criminal), Original Consultation, No. 2, dated 15th November, 1793.

[2]This incident happened in June 1794 and is narrated at page 123.

[3]Judicial Department (Criminal), Original Consultation, No. 7, dated 19th September, 1794.

[4]Judicial Department (Criminal), Original Consultation, No. 4, dated 20th December, 1793.

No further report of the Fakirs was heard of either in Purnea or at Malda and on 30th November, the Collector of Purnea reported the withdrawal of the Sepoys stationed at Udryal in pargana Suryapur.[1]

The Charter Act of 1793 laid down that the pursuit of schemes of conquest and extension of dominion in India were repugnant to the wish, honour and policy of the British nation. Sir John Shore succeeded Lord Cornwallis as Governor-General in November, 1793, and his accession marked a distinct change in the policy of the Government of India. Non-interference and non-intervention were the key-note of his administration. As a result the profession of friendship by the Raja of Nepal was accepted and cordial relation maintained with him, in spite of definite reports from the Magistrates showing the complicity of the local officers of Nepal with the marauding Fakirs. The same policy dictated the peremptory withdrawal in July, 1794, of the forces sent to Assam under Capt. Welsh.

Sannyasis in Assam.

Even when nomadic Sannyasis came at longer intervals for raids in Bengal, they did not cease to hire themselves as soldiers although ostensibly coming on pilgrimage. In the latter part of 1792 the Raja of Assam sought the help of the Governor-General against Krishna Narayan, Raja of Darrang, who had defeated the Raja's forces and occupied Gauhati, his capital. Capt. Welsh was sent to restore order. In January, 1793, Krishna Narayan was defeated near Gauhati by Lieut. Williams in a "fierce engagement which caused many of the barkandajes to desert Krishna Narain but a large number of Sannyasis still remained with him. These Sannyasis were most probably men from the North-west who had come to Assam to visit different Shrines and several places."[2] Krishna Narayan also had his recruits from the ranks of the disbanded Barkandazes of Rangpur who had been discharged by the zamindars and had settled in that district. To put a stop to this, the properties of the Barkandazes who had joined Krishna Narayan were attached in 1792 at the instance of Capt. Welsh. The chief of these Barkandazes was one Harry Singh Hazary, who resided at Ulipur in Pargana Bhiterbanda [Rangpur]. In 1793 Krishna Narayan, being induced by Capt. Welsh agreed to disband his mercenaries from Bengal. Capt. Welsh also purged the Court of Assam of the intriguing and undesirable elements along with the mercenary recruits from Bengal. But the more daring of them were not conciliated and early in 1794, they collected north of Cooch Behar and threatened to plunder in co-operation with the Fakirs. The withdrawal of Capt. Welsh and the policy of non-intervention left them without any impediment. The recall of Capt. Welsh also favoured the malcontents in Assam. On his return to Bengal in July, 1794, they gained the mastery over the weak-minded Raja of Assam and at Gauhati the Bengali mercenary Hajary Singh held the post of Bara Phukan [chief

[1] Board of Revenue, Original Consultation, No. 11, dated 6th December, 1793.

[2] *Captain Welsh's Expedition to Assam*, by Col. J. Johnstone, p. 20.

minister] at his disposal which he sold to aspirants. "Hajary Singh was at length defeated—killed by some mercenaries brought up from Bengal."[1]

Sannyasis and Fakirs in Cooch Behar.

Towards the end of February, 1794, the Raja of Cooch Behar informed Mr. Leslie, Magistrate of Rangpur, that "a number of Fakirs and others to the amount of two or three thousand men who had been for some time collecting near his country had publicly avowed their intention of attacking his treasury and town on a certain day."[2] Accordingly, Lieut. Sloane, commanding a detachment at Gobindnagar, advanced towards Cooch Behar to overawe the Fakirs from attacking that State. On the 2nd March he reported from camp near Mulla Baugah that the Fakirs numbering three thousand were "not more than six coss from Behar" and that he proposed to move towards Cooch Behar to join the detachment there if Rangpur was not in danger from Fakirs.[3] Mr. Leslie thereupon ordered Lieut. Sloane to take up a position in or near Behar (Cooch Behar) till "re-inforced or relieved or the Fakirs move off towards Assam which is their avowed route." A week later Mr. Bruce, Commissioner at Cooch Behar, reported to the Governor-General in Council: "A body of Fackeers are in the low countries of Bootan bordering on Cooch Behar from whence small parties make occasional excursions and plunder the houses of ryots which are near them. They are very numerous but not in one place and are commanded by Hazary Singh, Futtick Burwah, Jungal Geer and Cheragali Fakir the two first of whom in the employ of the Chiefs of Assam. They appear to have been assembled from Morung and the Company's provinces to the westward of Cooch Behar that they might enter Assam by the low countries of Bootan, they cannot go through the Company's provinces and unless the Bootan Soubahs act with energy in preventing them to pass their country, a passage will always be open for them. I have addressed the Buxadowar, Luckydowar and Cheraugdowar Soubahs of Bootan requesting they would stop them ...." Mr. Bruce added: "These constant incursions of a body of men from a country so little known as that they come from induces me to request permission to proceed to the frontiers of their country, remonstrate against their proceedings and demand satisfaction as they appear to be an independent nation or a resolute Banditti of plunderers."[4] The Governor-General in Council probably did not want to have complication with Nepal before ascertaining the exact state of affairs and accordingly directed Mr. Bruce to depute some trustworthy person to ascertain from whence the Fakirs had come and the object of their

---

[1]Gait's *History of Assam.*

[2]Judicial (Criminal), Original Consultation, No. 4, dated 14th March, 1794.

[3]Judicial (Criminal), Original Consultation, No. 5, dated 14th March, 1794.

[4]Judicial Department (Criminal), Original Consultation, No. 3, dated 14th March, 1794.

expedition.[1] On the 21st March Mr. Leslie informed the Government that "the banditti have quitted Cooch Behar."[2]

Fakirs in Purnea and Dinajpur.

Meanwhile on the 19th April, Capt. Witherstone, Commanding at Tajpur, informed Mr. Bird, Magistrate of Purnea, that Golam Hyder who commanded the guard at Udrayl had reported to Lieut. Sloane that a party of Fakirs numbering over 1,000 passed near Kissènganj, but no action could be taken as the Daroga of Kissenganj did not give any information.[3] The Daroga was accordingly dismissed. Golam Hyder further complained that "the Phousdarry and Dewanny servants have positively refused to give him any assistance and Captain Witherstone supposed that they had been privy to the operations and schemes of Fakeers."[4] In the same month a large body of Cherag Ali's followers passed within a mile or two of the town of Purnea after being pursued from Dinajpur by Lieut. Ainslie, but no information was received of them by the Magistrate "till they made a halt near the Thanna of Arareah whose daroga informed the Magistrate but it was too late as the Fakirs fled by long marches."[5]

In May, Mr. Wilkinson, Magistrate of Dinajpur, reported that "Lt. Sloane had lately apprehended and sent in 29 of the followers of Roshun ally Shaw who not having been hitherto considered as one of predatory Fakeers had been allowed to travel about begging alms unmolested."[6] The Governor-General in Council, however, in a Resolution asked the Magistrate to direct Roshan Ali to dismiss his followers and to warn him not to appear in future with any armed persons in which case he would be apprehended and committed to take his trial.[7] Mr. Bird, Magistrate of Purnea, was directed "to represent to the Raja of Nepal against the Fakirs who plunder the inhabitants and convey hostages as they are inhabitants of Rengelly, Kwaliah and Nidantara in Nepal" as he "had addressed the Subahs of Bissapore and Hurchundgerry"[8] without success.

Rangpur.

In June, Mr. Leslie, Magistrate of Rangpur, reported "the depredations of the Fakirs in Karguhaut [Kajirhat] and Bykontpore Chaklahs causing great alarm and ryots daily absconding with their families leaving the effects in charge of the Tannadars and the Bykantpore Rajah has had a demand of Rs. 2,000 from him with the threat of enforcing

[1]Judicial Department (Criminal), Body Sheet, dated 14th March, 1794, Resolution.

[2]Judicial (Criminal), Original Consultation, No. 3, dated 25th April, 1794.

[3]Judicial (Criminal), Original Consultation, No. 1, dated 12th May, 1794.

[4]Judicial Department (Criminal), Original Consultation, No. 2, dated 12th May, 1794.

[5]Judicial (Criminal), Original Consultation, No. 9, dated 25th July, 1794.

[6]Judicial Department (Criminal), Original Consultation, No. 2, dated 23rd May, 1794.

[7]Judicial Department (Criminal), Body Sheet, dated 23rd May 1794, orders on No. 2.

[8]Judicial (Criminal), Original Consultation, No. 10, dated 25th July, 1794.

it if not speedily complied with."[1] He enclosed two petitions from the Thanadars of Dimla and Fakirgunge which clearly describe the nature of the oppression. Gauriprasad, thanadar of Dimla, reported: "The Fakirs at night attacked and plundered the houses of Bunderam Peramanick and Sam Churn Peramanick at Burabarry in the Chuckla of Boda and carried off the two nephews of the said Peramanicks, one Burkandauze and three ryots making in all six. Two of the Fakeers were apprehended by the above mentioned Peramanicks and sent to Behar."[2] Govindaram Dutt, Daroga of Fakirgunge, reported: "I was honoured by the receipt of your Perwanah dated the 17th May 1794 informing me that Ramkant Roy, Gomosta of Srimant Choudry had represented to you that Soban Shaw Fakeer with a number of armed followers had come to the Talook of Aumeer Kharak where they seized Bugwan Sahoo, Alim Chand, Tuleram and other ryots of that Talook and having beat and bound them carried them off and therefore directing that I should collect all the Burkandauzes of the Tannah and likewise the inhabitants about Aumeer Kharak in order to release the above mentioned ryots from the hands of the Fakeers and that I should endeavour to apprehend two or three of the Fakeers. Sometime previous to the arrival of the perwanah, the Fakeers had carried Bugwan Sahoo and the other men to Nidantarrah in Goorka which is three days' journey from Patchghur. Shortly afterwards one of the above mentioned men escaped to his own house. Another man having entered into a settlement and given a sum of money to the Fakeers was released. Bugwan Sahoo was likewise set at liberty but his son was detained as prisoner. There has lately been a large body of Fakirs and Sannyasis to the amount of 400 or 500 men come from the north and from the Botan countries to this part of the country and have plundered several of the houses belonging to the ryots of Bykuntpore and have also plundered Needyram Gomostah inhabitant of Bodah besides this carrying off five or six men bound from the same Gomasta's house."[3]

These outrages stirred the authorities to action and the Governor-General in Council resolved on 20th June to request the Commander-in-Chief to station the detachment under Captain Welsh in Rangpur or Dinajpur district as may seem suitable.

Sobhan Ali Shah, however, was still active and plundered the Company's commercial settlement at Ramgunge in Purnea district on his way back from Dinajpur to Morung and carried off Rupees 6,000; the Fakirs killed two sepoys and took four away.[4] The letter from Radhanath Das, Gumashta of Malduar aurang to Mr. G. Udny, Resident Purnea.

[1] Judicial (Criminal), Original Consultation, No. 7, dated 20th June, 1794.

[2] Judicial Department (Criminal), Original Consultation, No. 8, dated 20th June, 1794.

[3] Judicial (Criminal), Original Consultation, No. 9, dated 20th June, 1794.

[4] Judicial Department, (Criminal), Original Consultation, No. 7, dated 19th September, 1794. Deposition of Basantalall Amin.

at Malda, gives a vivid description of the atrocities of Sobhan Ali: "On the 8th Ashar [19th June, 1794] Thursday at 2½ Par of night about 3 or 400 Fakeers all armed with two or three horses came and surrounded the Cootie of Ramgunge with drawn swords—advancing to the doorway they shot with a ball the Burkandaze Krishnaram who was upon guard and then rushed into the Cootie seized all the amlah and bound them; the cash which was on hand in the large chest and escritoire in the treasure house, they took away, breaking open the chest and taking thence the bags and carrying off the escritoire with its contents all the clothes which had come in and were deposited in the cloth godown they carried off and undoing all the papers they took away the pieces of cloth in which they were tied up. The money and effects belonging to the Gomasta, cash-keepers, writers and other servants of the cootie they carried off and with only the cloths we had on we escaped with our lives. The Burkandaz aforesaid is very ill of the wound he received from the ball. The ball is not extracted. The arms belonging to the Burkandazes stationed here, guns, bayonets &c were all carried away.... After they had plundered the cootie and were going away, they bound me, a Burkandaze and one of my servants all three of us together and at a little distance from the cootie on the north side they beat us and left us bound. We took to a poor man's house and saved our lives. Rananund Ray Suzawal, Ram Konhoy Roy, Cash Keeper, his brother Kebelram Sircar writer, all these they bound and taking them about ¼ of a coss west of Ramgunge they beat them and let them go." The property plundered including cash, cloths, guns and cartouche boxes was worth Rs. 2100.[1] A zamindar who resided near Ramgunge 'furnished the whole of the Fakir party, which was between two and three hundred, with provisions and secreted them during the day preceding the night of the robbery' while he refused food to the small party of sepoys.[2] The Jamadar, Golam Hyder and his party with the assistance of the Daroga, Meer Ebbas Ali "immediately on the receipt of the news of the robbery made every exertion to overtake and apprehend these plunderers, yet they made their escape in the Morung country, and one man only of the party was taken with three pieces of cloth in his possession."[3]

Plunder of Ramgunge Factory.

Information was also received regarding the depredations of Sannyasis and Fakirs in other part of the district "the Sirdars or leaders of whom are Cherragh Ally, Souban Shah, Hazarry Sing, Currem Shah and Zahoor Shah; some of these men have but of late shown a turbulent disposition. Curreem Shah has been it is reported a resident for many years in Tirhoot in the zemindari of Rajah Madoo Sing and usually received one rupee from each village throughout his zemindari of which Pargunnah Dharampur

[1] Judicial Department (Criminal), Original Consultation, No. 11, dated 25th July, 1794.

[2] Judicial (Criminal), Original Consultation, No. 13, dated 18th July, 1794.

[3] Judicial (Criminal), Original Consultation, No. 9, dated 25th July, 1794.

in this Zillah forms a part, he also collected the like Russum [fee] from Pargunnah Dhappa and Nautpur the zemindaries of Cummollani Chowdry and Rani Inderoutty. This man has of late however thought proper to assemble with the other marauders on the borders of this zillah and sent two threatening letters to the mother of Khya Keram demanding from her as a loan the sum of 4000 Rupees and observing that in case of refusal God knows what may happen. The merchants and other inhabitants of Nautpore are also under continued apprehension from similar threats....I have received accounts also that Shumsher Shah and Zahhoor Shah have lately assembled with about 700 armed men in the borders of Morung near Powercolley and threaten to plunder the adjacent villages. However few depradations have been committed owing to the watchful attention of Lieutenants Sloane and Ainslie, who were constantly in pursuit of them whenever information could be obtained of their route....Shumshur Shaw and Zahhoor Shaw's party plundered the houses of Tuppyram and Munsyram Mundals who reside close to the borders of Morung, but the followers of Cheraug Ally did not in the least molest anyone in the Purnia district in their route."[1] In July, "the sepoys on the frontier stations made an attack upon Curreem Shaw and his followers in which affray thirteen Fakeers were killed, several of them wounded. The sepoys took from them 1 camel Semeniana [canopy] and a chintz carpet with some horses and tulwars &c."[2]

The Government was impressed by the constant complaints from the Magistrates and recorded a resolution that in case the Raja of Nepal failed to accede to a further representation for preventing the Fakirs from finding a retreat in the Nepal territory, the Governor-General in Council would "take into consideration the propriety of pursuing the Fakirs beyond the Company's limits."[3] Mr. Bruce reported to the Government in August that Cherag Ali was killed[4] under the following circumstances as gathered from the deposition of Barkandazes sent to Nepal with his letter to the subah at Harchandgury—"Cherag Ally who lived at Rangelly had some transactions with Mooty Singh a Sonassay who lived in Tirhoot. The Sonnessy sent people to recover the money which Cherag Ally owed to him but without success for the latter treated them rudely and refused an answer ; when they returned and complained to Mooty Sing he was greatly enraged and set about collecting people to take his revenge. He marched by night till he waylaid him and then cut him off."[5] Moti Giri was apprehended for murder and suffered

Cherag Ali killed by Moti Giri.

[1]Judicial (Criminal), Original Consultation No. 9, dated 25th July, 1794.

[2]Judicial (Criminal), Original Consultation, No. 12, dated 19th September, 1794.

[3]Revenue Department, Body Sheet, No. 2, dated 22nd August, 1794.

[4]Judicial Department (Criminal), Original Consultation, No. 7, dated 10th September, 1794.

[5]*Ibid.*

capital punishment, thus "the country was relieved of two freebooters."[1] Mr. Bruce stated that "since Cherag Ally's death and since the arrival of a company of sepoys from the 16th Battalion the country was quiet."[2] His optimism was too premature as events happening before the close of the year proved. Government was, however, under no illusion and took effective measures. Lieut.-Col. Stuart was directed to take command of the troops in the districts of Rangpur, Dinajpur and Purnea with the observation. "On the appearance of a force they (Fakirs) are unable to cope with, they either retire rapidly to their fastnesses in the hills or separate to elude observation and again assemble and ravage a more defenceless quarter of the country. The Battalion stationed at Taugepore has been found by experience insufficient to protect so extensive a country. It has neither been able effectually to prevent their incursions nor intercept their return. For these purposes, the Rajas of Nepal and Bootan have been desired to withhold all shelter and protection from them and the Command has been augmented and placed under your orders...."[3]

Government action.

In October, Mr. Burges, Collector of Purnea came in possession of some intercepted correspondence from Deo Singh Upadhaya [the vakil or representative of the Subah of Morung at the Collector's Court at Purnea] to Karim Shah, Sobhan Ali Shah and the Subah. The correspondence shows how the Fakirs were kept informed of the operations against them.

1794-1795.

Complicity of Nepal officers with Fakirs.

The letter to Sobhan Ali Shah ran as follows: "To the noble friend Sree Shoobhanee Sajee, Deo Sing Oppadeah writes with his Salam Health that you may enjoy content. The Gentlemen [the British officers] here treat me with great severity by saying all the Fakeers live in your country and plunder our district, therefore seize those Fakeers and deliver them up. I answer that the Fakirs do live in my country but they subsist on charity what character shall I gain by seizing them. The gentleman replied I am sending troops to seize them wherever they are found and to bring them here. If you all feel a desire to fight advance and engage with all your strength, if not and you prefer the care of your bellies you would do well to nourish them in some other country. Otherwise the ryots of the Maharaja will experience much distress the gentleman will certainly proceed." He wrote to Karim Shah: "To the noble friend Sree Karim Shahjee Deo Sing Oupadeah Vakil sends Salam. I am well and form daily wishes for your health that you may be happy. The Burra Sahib [the Collector] having sent for me the following conversation ensued—Seize Kerim Shah and deliver him up—strong and pointed language took place on both sides. The gentleman then desired I would

---

[1]Extract from Judicial General letter to the Court, dated 8th March, 1795.

[2]*Ibid.*

[3]Judicial Department (Criminal), Original Consultation, No. 14, dated 31st October, 1794.

secure the person of Kerim Shah otherwise he would send troops to seize him whenever they should find him.

"I likewise inform you that Mr. Smith has taken powder and ball with him and has sent to Bhopla for sepoys, you must therefore be on your guard. Consult the Maharaja if he advises opposition and you are equal to the contest you must prepare to fight, while I shall preserve an intercourse with the people here. But if your bellies be your chief concern, you would do well to seek their gratification in some other country. The people here rule by the influence of their name (Hauk) not by their actual strength (Dhak). The ryots of the Maharaja will suffer distress for troops will certainly proceed."[1]

Deo Sing was made a prisoner by the Collector who reported the matter to the Governor-General. Sir John Shore, however, on a perusal of the original letters put a more liberal interpretation. Although he held Deo Sing's correspondence to be improper he suggested that instead of punishing Deo Sing himself, the Collector should represent the facts to the Raja of Nepal to whom Deo Sing should be sent under custody.[2] The policy of non-intervention of Sir John Shore thus saved a complication with Nepal.

Capture of Fakirs in Rangpur.

In October, Mr. Bruce, the Commissioner at Cooch Behar, reported the capture by a clever ruse, of 59 Fakirs (of whom 3 were sirdars employed in a plundering expedition) by Mozaffer Hosain, the Police Daroga of Bodah, Patgram and Purubbhag. "The prisoners prove to be Burkundauzes in the service of Shum Shur Saw and most of them inhabitants of Lucknow and Benares. They undertook to levy money on one of the hostages the Fakeers had taken away from Bodah and entered the Company's provinces with that intention; the family of the hostage gave notice to the Police Darogah and applied for his assistance against them and it occurred to the Daroga that the hostage's life might be in danger if the Fakeers were attacked when they held him their prisoner. He therefore endeavoured by the aid of the family to get the Fakeers to send the hostage to a particular place by way of ascertaining whether he was the real person or not and when they complied with the preliminary (which they readily did, as soon as the family gave them 70 Rupees as an earnest of their proceeding) the Darogah with 28 men fell upon them so precipitously that none of them had time to escape. He took them all prisoners, disarmed them and sent here [Cooch Behar] for an escort to conduct them to Cooch Behar. He has taken upon them part of the property stolen at Raingunge in Purnea and part of the property stolen in Bodah—101 swords, matchlocks, lances, weapons and after an examination I have sent the prisoners to the Rangpur Jail to be tried by the Court of Circuit."[3]

---

[1]Judicial (Criminal), Original Consultation, No. 4, dated 24th October, 1794.

[2]Judicial (Criminal), Original Consultation, No. 5, dated 24th October, 1794.

[3]Judicial Department (Criminal), Governor-General in Council, Original Consultation, No. 1, dated 21st November, 1794.

Fakirs in Dinajpur and Rangpur.

Baffled in their attempts with small parties, the Fakirs came in larger number towards the end of the year. Mr. Eliot, Collector of Dinajpur, reported in November "that the sanassees, having in the two last years, been severely beaten and harrassed by the sepoys when only in parties of two or three hundred, have entered the zillah this year a thousand strong and that Soobanny Shaw who heads them was at Piergunge near this place two days ago[1]". A month later, Mr. Mathew Leslie, Magistrate of Rangpur, informed the Governor-General in Council that "a large body of Fakeers numbering by report to be 1800 had entered the district and plundered several talooks in Soroopore within 12 coss of this place. Having no force to oppose them, he sent off an express to the Commanding Officer at Consamagunge." Mr. Leslie remarked that "the audacity of these people seemed to increase in proportion to the military force sent against them" and added that "on consultation with the Gumashtas of several zamindars, it seemed to be a pretty general opinion that if a positive order was given to the landholders of every description to assemble their people on the first notice of the Fakirs having entered their pargana and drive them back by force of arms, that they would willingly undertake it; but at present they are fearful of attacking them lest in the skirmish any of the Fakeers should be killed and the landholders or their followers become liable to be tried for murder." Mr. Leslie also suggested the propriety of publishing an advertisement subjecting "all armed Fakirs who may be found in the district to be seized and put to work on the roads for a certain time unless they can give security for their peaceable conduct."[2]

Dinajpur.

About the same time Mr. Wilkinson, Magistrate of Dinajpur, reported that "Shaikh Attah Oollah Daroga of Thana Nababgunge was murdered on the 9th instant by a party of Fakiers while in the discharge of his duties in expostulating with these banditti and admonishing them peaceably to retire and desist from their depredations. A Burkundauz of the Tannah is also reported to be mortally wounded and most of the records of the Tannah destroyed and the officers and Burkandazes pillaged of their clothes and several of their matchlocks....This party plundered and carried off about 5000 Rupees of Treasure from the cutchery of Navaubgunj the Jaghier of Rajah Rauj Bullub."[3]

Purnea.

A few days later in a letter to the Persian Translator to Government Mr. Burges related a tale of depredation committed by Fakirs in Purnea district. "I have for these ten days past been wearied with

---

[1]Extract from Original Consultation, No. 2 of the Revenue Department, dated 19th December, 1794.

[2]Judicial (Criminal), Original Consultation, No. 12, dated 19th December, 1794.

[3]Extract from the Judicial Department (Criminal), Original Consultation, No. 11, dated 19th December, 1794. Raja Raj Ballav was the Ray Rayan [Chief Indian Revenue officer] and enjoyed Jaghirs or revenue-free estates.

accounts from the Surbarcar [rent collector] of Surjapore and the farmers of the northern pergunnahs of the incursions of three separate parties of Fakeers who have killed six men and plundered to the amount of near 2000 Rs.....About 20 days since a banditti of Fakeers from Morung attacked one of the villages on the frontier in Pergunnah Futtypore Singeah wherein resided two principal ryots, or indeed Kutkeenadars,[1] attacked their houses, possessed themselves of the portable property with 1500 rupees in money and they tied the two men to bamboos set round with grass and other combustible matter and absolutely burnt them to death because there were no more money which the ryots concealed and they meant that to be an example to the other villages which they intended to visit. All this happened and the Fakeers were off in the course of one Ghurry or twenty minutes. I have had an estimate delivered me which I have reason to think tolerably accurate of the different sums plundered by the Fakirs in the course of the present Bengal years, it amounts to near 60,000 rupees." Mr. Burges ascribed these plunders entirely to the help and connivance of the Subah of Nepal in Morung.[2]

Government action.

At last in December, the Governor-General in Council in a Resolution agreed to the proposals of Mr. Mathew Leslie and passed stringent orders against the Fakirs. The Magistrates of Dinajpur, Purnea and Rangpur were directed to issue a written proclamation in all current languages and affix copies of them in thanas and kutcheries of zamindars notifying that all zamindars, talookdars and farmers of land and the inhabitants of the country at large in the event of their persons or property being attacked by armed Fakirs were at liberty to repel them by force and that if in repelling the attack they should kill any of the Fakeers they would not be held accountable for their death. It was further to be notified that all zamindars, talookdars and farmers of land and the Darogas of Police were authorised and directed to seize the arms of all armed Fakirs whether they committed depredations or not and all Fakirs apprehended and convicted of robbing, murdering and wounding or attempting to do any of the acts would be liable to be transported to the Andaman Islands and there confined and kept in hard labour.[3] The situation was considered serious for, in a General Letter to the Court of Directors dated the 29th December, the Governor-General in Council communicated the various measures adopted for the suppression of the Fakirs.

To the remonstrance of the Governor-General regarding the raids of Fakirs, the Raja of Nepal replied "that agreeably to his orders his sepoys attacked the Fakeers at the place where they reside and drove them out of the limits of Nepal....Kureem Shah went to his capital but

[1] Under-farmers.

[2] Judicial (Criminal), Original Consultation, No. 4, dated 16th January, 1795.

[3] Judicial (Criminal), Body Sheet, Resolution, dated 19th December, 1794.

as according to the laws of his religion he could not confine and put to death a Fakir he had sent him under charge of Mohussils (peons) to be turned out of the limits of his country." But Mr. Burges, Collector of Purnea, reported in January that "Kurreem Shah had been released by the Raja of Nepal and was at his favourite encampment at Mollunee a village belonging to Morung threatening to pay Raja Madoo Sing, the zemindar of Durrumpore, a visit unless he pays a sum of money and otherwise conforms to Kurrim Shah's demands."[1]

The following reply was given by the Governor-General categorically denying the effectiveness of the steps taken by the Raja: "Fakirs and Currim Shah who notwithstanding the orders which you have issued for their expulsion from your territories still find an asylum there and after committing depredations on the lands of this Government retire within the limits of your dominions. With respect to Currim Shah, I learn he resides in the village of Abur near Muthany in zillah Turriany where he has erected a small fort and has collected a body of armed followers....It is but lately and since your last letter was written that Curreem Shah has had the insolence to make a demand on the Raja of Tyrhoot and to threaten him with an attack in case of non-compliance." Mr. Burges further reported on the basis of reports received from an European Commercial Agent that "within last week Currim Shah is in force and plundering the country northward of Durbhanga from whence he retires occasionally to his village in Pergunnah Motiria (near Roopelah Ghurry) which the Nepal Raja lately gave him and where he has erected a small ghurry or mud fort and that Raja Mahdo Sing[2] [of Darbhanga] received a letter from Currim Shah desiring that he would give him two villages and two thousand rupees or else &c. The Raja immediately waited on Mr. Graham who ordered the Daroga to take the two hircarrahs into custody and the letter they brought, he carried with him to Mozaffarpur. At Mr. Graham's recommendation the Raja is entertaining a large body of Burkundazes to protect his country. Azeet Sing a zemindar on the borders of Tirhoot and not far from Purnia marched on Thursday last with two hundred armed Rajpoots to the Raja's assistance at his earnest appeal."[3]

Darbhanga.

1795-1796.

Malda.

Lieut. Thomas Darrah commanding a detachment at the Darga [at Pandua], reported in January, 1796, to the Adjutant and Quarter Master to the troops in the districts of Rangpore and Dinajpore: "The last trip I made through the district at the earnest request of the villagers I stationed a party of sepoys at Porsa consisting of a Havildar Naick and 12 sepoys. The Havildar writes me that agreeable to the orders I had given him to assist the ryots in whatever part of the district the

[1] Judicial (Criminal) Proceedings, dated 20th March, 1795, pp. 473-77.

[2] Raja of Darbhanga succeeded his brother Pratab Singh in 1776.

[3] Judicial (Criminal), Original Consultation, No. 1, dated 13 March, 1795.

Fakeers made their appearance he had marched at the requisition of one of the aumildars[1] to the relief of a number of people whom the Fakirs had taken from different villages with an intention of making them pay a heavy ransom. After two very long marches he had to arrive at the place they were laying just at daybreak. The Sonasees posted centinal over the villagers, (who) challenged, on which one of the sepoys presented his piece and shot him. The Havildar writes that nine others were also killed but that owing to their being close to a jungle the rest of the party made their escape carrying off their wounded along with them so that no prisoners were taken. The number of ryots and villagers released from these rascals amounted to a hundred. Everything had been settled and they were to have paid the rupees the very day the sepoys arrived and set them at liberty. A second party whom I had sent to the Puchley jungle near Maldah have taken three of Soobannyally Shaw's Fakeers with arms &c. I have also taken from other rascals near my post who were endeavouring to extort money from the villagers."[2] The two leaders of the parties, viz., Jowhurry Shah and Mutteeullah, were tried and convicted by the Court of Circuit; the former was sentenced to 18 years' imprisonment and the latter to 10 years' imprisonment. It appears Motteeullah was not a Fakir leader but "a famous imposter who assumed the title of Company's Jamadar of Burgandasses and with a forged Parwana and an armed force obliged the riots and villagers to pay him contribution as proved by affidavits before the Zillah Court of Dinajpur." The Fakirs had "a pukka magazine in the Puchely Jungle near Maldah in which the Fakirs deposited their arms and ammunitions."

The records are silent on the further activities of these banditti till December 1797, when Mr. Bird, the Collector of Dinajpore, reported to the Board of Revenue that a large body of plundering Fakirs had entered the district by different routes and that he was concerned about the safety of the treasury.[3] Nothing more was heard of those Fakirs. 1797-1798.

In March, 1798, two Fakir leaders Sobhan Ali Shah and Amudi Shah were on a marauding expedition in Dinajpur district. But about the middle of March the two leaders had some dispute about the division of the plunder which ended in a separation of their respective forces.[4] The Fakirs under Sobhan Ali Shah proceeded in a southerly direction and the Magistrate of Dinajpur reported that "Capt. Wroughton the officer commanding at Gajole marched immediately in pursuit of the Fakirs in Dinajpur.

[1]A revenue collector.

[2]Judicial (Criminal), Original Consultation, No. 5, dated 12th February, 1796.

[3]Revenue Department, Ori inal Consultation No. 32, dated 15th December, 1797.

[4]Judicial (Criminal) Proceedings, dated 4th May, 1798. Dinajpur Magistrate's letter, dated 28th April, 1798.

Banditti and after a harrassing march of upwards of ninety miles which he accomplished in four days, came up with and attacked them on the 30th March in the Moygunge jungle [Malda district] and after an engagement of about an hour completely defeated and dispersed them. Their number could not have been less than six hundred. About forty of these marauders are said to have been killed and between sixty and seventy wounded, while the loss on the side of Captain Wroughton amounted only to one sepoy who was shot on the first onset. The prisoners confessed to be accomplices of Sobhan Ali Shaw and have been committed to take their trial before the Court of Circuit." The Magistrate in the exuberance of his zeal suggested that the Court of Circuit should be instructed to sentence the prisoners to transportation for life.[1] But he met with a very peremptory reply from the Governor-General. "He must be sensible that the Government cannot dictate sentences to the Courts of Justice and as a specific rule is laid down in Section 10 of Regulation IV of 1797 regarding sentences of transportation, the Acting Governor-General is surprised that it should have escaped the Magistrate's notice."[2]

Weakened by the reverse Sobhan Ali rejoined Amudi who "carried off two Mundals from the Pargana of Dehutt with a view of extorting money but the ryots of the adjoining villages irritated at this circumstance and encouraged by the diminished number of Fakirs assembled in some hundreds and Captain Charron's detachment fortunately coming about the same time were enabled to secure a greater number of prisoners."[3] Capt. Charron gives the following account of the encounter : "Having received information on the 2nd instant that Soubanally Shaw with upwards of 300 well armed followers was trying to make good his retreat by the northwest road, directly got a party under arms of a zemedar, four Havildars and thirty-four sepoys total 39 men. They marched off directly and proceeded without stopping to Rannygunge. I ordered them to that place on account of having received information of the plunderers being at Tackoorgunge and altho' Tackoorgunge was on the high road to Rannygunge I did not march there by that route, but along the east bank of the river for four coss and then across country over paddy fields to Rannygunge. By this direction, the Fakirs knew nothing of my people, having marched from Dabeddooba much less of their being in front. The next morning my Jamadar placed himself along their line of march. Finding they could not get off, they fought bravely, the action commenced at day light, and continued till afternoon. Soubhanali Shah with a few of

Defeat of Fakirs.

---

[1] Judicial (Criminal), Original Consultation, No. 3, dated 13th April, 1798.

[2] Judicial (Criminal), Body Sheet, dated 13th April, 1798. Order on Original Consultation, No. 3.

[3] Judicial (Criminal) Proceedings, dated 4th May, 1798.

his best men moved to the W. N. West with the plunder the moment he saw my party across his road. My Jamadar and two sepoys are very badly wounded but not a sepoy killed....The road for eight miles was covered with the dead, the dying and the wounded the numbers must have been very great, few of the Fakeers having been able to get away. Of prisoners I have pleasure to send you seventy one. Amongst the prisoners is Undesa (Amudi Shah) a sirdar of note and next in rank to the Shah. The Havildar will deliver over to you besides 71 prisoners, 12 firelocks, 9 matchlocks, 14 tulwars, 4 shields, etc."[1] A list of hill people taken prisoner was sent which showed that 28 were subjects of the Nepal State—one of them appears from his name to be a Sannayasi.

It appears from a report by Mr. Parr, Magistrate of Dinajpore, to the Governor-General, dated 28th April, that "Subhan Ally and Amudi Shah in their last incursions were accompanied by about 300 Fakirs, Sannyasis and Nepaliahs armed with firelocks (of the Monghyer manufacture), matchlocks and swords besides a body of unarmed men, most of the arms were the property of the two ringleaders by whom they were distributed among their followers and the firelocks were in general found in the hands of Nepalis who received them from Amudi Shah."[2]

Owing to the swift movement of the Fakirs, who "one day had been 15 coss to the southward of Dinajpore and the next as far in an opposite direction," Mr. Parr recommended the suggestion of Capt. Wroughton for raising a corps of Native Cavalry to be stationed at Dinajpore and employed in the districts of Dinajpore, Rangpur, Purnea, and Cooch Behar against the Fakirs[3] and asked the proposal to be submitted to the Commander-in-Chief. The suggestion does not appear to have been carried out.

In a letter to the Governor-General from the Raja of Nepal, received in August, the Raja explained his inability to check the raids of Fakirs: "The case is this that I have frequently inflicted chastisement on them but as they have no fixed place of residence, whenever they are driven from this country they take refuge without opposition in the Company's territories, notwithstanding these people are well known there to be a banditti of robbers yet the Judge in conformity to the established regulations will not bring them to punishment unless they shall be detected in the act of plundering and even punish those people who at any time molest them." The Raja promised to "issue strict and private orders to his officers to expel these people, Sobhan Allie &c., so that they shall not have a place of refuge within his country."[4]

---

[1]Judicial (Criminal) Proceedings, dated 4th May, 1798.

[2]Judicial (Criminal) Proceedings, dated 4th May, 1798.

[3]Proceedings, Judicial (Criminal) Department, dated 11th May, 1798.

[4]Proceedings, Judicial (Criminal) Department, dated 31st December, 1798.

1798-1799. In spite of the assurance of the Raja of Nepal, the depredation of the Fakirs continued and became a menace to the collection of revenue. In March, 1799, Raja Radhanath of Dinajpore wrote to Mr. Bird, the Collector of Dinajpore: "The plundering Fakeers with a number of armed men are in the habit of annually committing depredations in the Pergannahs belonging to my zemindary, plundering the houses of ryots and taking away the revenue from the cutchery and also of murdering and wounding the inhabitants, burning their houses and carrying them to the hills. In this manner they carry on their oppression. My Pergunnahs are therefore depopulated and I am unable to collect the Revenue. I am therefore hopeful that you will forward this petition to the Huzzoor that necessary steps may be taken against the like depredations in future; the ryotts will then remain undisturbed and pay their revenue."[1] In forwarding the petition to the Board, Mr. Bird, the Collector stated that "although the subject more properly appertains to the Magistrate's department, the realisation of the revenue of Government depends so much on the personal security of the ryotts that he felt it incumbent to state to the Board that it is a fact of notoriety that from the month of November to the commencement of the rains, the whole of the zemindarry of Dinagepore is annually exposed to the incursions of this banditti, who plunder the ryotts of their property and by various means extort money from them. Hitherto every plan which had been adopted has proved ineffectual and the return of the dry season is invariably attended with a renewal of their depredations which evinces the necessity of some measures being adopted for the protection of the lives and properties of the inhabitants. Add to these reasons the exposed state of the mofussil treasuries now left to the mercy of this lawless banditti whose attack cannot be repelled by the few Burkandazes stationed by the zemindars at their cutcherries. Independent of the representation from the Raja of Dinagepore, many of the other landholders have represented the inconvenience to which their ryotts are exposed."[2] The Board of Revenue, however, directed the Collector to communicate any incident regarding the depredation of Fakirs to the Magistrate of the district leaving it to him to adopt necessary measures for preserving the peace.[3] At the same time, Government "offered a reward of Rs. 4,000 for the apprehension of Sobunally the leader of a numerous band of marauders inhabiting the Morang hills who have long infested Dinagepore

Fakirs in Dinajpur.

[1]Board of Revenue, Miscellaneous, Original Consultation, No. 11, dated 2nd April, 1799. This contributed to the breaking up of the Dinajpur Raj, which was sold off for arrears of revenue by the end of 1800.

[2]Board of Revenue, Miscellaneous, Original Consultation, No. 10, dated 2nd April, 1799.

[3]*Ibid.*

and the adjacent districts."[1] In their General Letter of the 31st October, 1799, Government informed the Court of Directors of the offer, adding that "the amount of this reward though undoubtedly large will not we trust appear to your Honourable Court extravagant when you consider that it is of great importance to the peace of the country that offenders of this description should be brought to punishment."

Late in the next season the followers of Sobhan Ali renewed their 1799-1800.
depredations and appeared in the heart of the district of Bogra. In February, 1800, Mr. Parr, the Magistrate of Dinajpore, reported "that the police Daroga of Keitnol [thana Khetlal now in Bogra district] about eighteen coss to the southeast of Dinajpore on the borders of Rajshahi, has informed him that a body of marauding Fakeers and dacoits have lately made their appearance in the vicinity of the thana and not satisfied with having their usual contributions on the inhabitants have been guilty of various atrocities. The above Bogra
gang consists of upwards of one thousand persons and is now become the terror of that part of the country which they keep in a constant state of alarm and emboldened by the natural timidity of the inhabitants and confident in their own strength have twice proceeded to attack the Thanah with a view of cutting off the Darogah and his officers who had fortunately such timely intimation of their intention as to enable them to be on guard and to collect a number of people together for their mutual defence. As, however, the threatening language held out to the Thanadar by three Sirdars named Newazoo Shaw, Buddoo Shaw and Emambari Shaw, originally accomplices of Subanally who has in so many occasions infested these districts, leaves little room to doubt of their intention of making another attempt on the thanah, I have considered it expedient to detach a party of sebandies as well as for the protection of that station as also to enable the Darogah in the event of a favourable opportunity occuring the more effectually to apprehend these offenders which it is not to be expected he will be able to accomplish without some resistence on their part."[2]

Mr. Parr suggested that the party of the Regulars stationed at Bogra should help the Daroga. He reported another atrocity committed by the the Fakirs. "A short time ago through the activity of a person named Jhapprah, six of the gang were apprehended and committed to trial by him. Of these two were then under sentence of imprisonment and two were about a month ago acquitted......One of the two named Butter Shaw subsequent to his release rejoined the gang and about ten days ago went to the house of Jhapprah accompanied by the persons mentioned

[1]Judicial General Letter to Court, dated 31st October, 1799.

[2]Judicial Department (Criminal), Original Consultation, No. 11, dated 20th February, 1800.

before (viz., the Fakir sardars) and carried off his property, in the evening they again returned and murdered him plundering his house of other effects and wounding his wife and son with Tulwars in a desperate manner." For the apprehension of Newaz Shah, Buddoo Shah and Emmumbux Shah the Magistrate requested the permission of Government to "offer a reward of Rs. 300 and Rs. 20 for each of their accomplices."[1]

In April, Mr. Parr gave the following particulars of the depredations of the Fakirs in thana Khetlal: "On the 28th of February, the Daroga of Khetlal having received intimation that Newaz Shah and Emam Bux Shah two of the sirdars of the gang with several of their accomplices were assembled in the village of Byrincha in zillah Rajshahi proceeded with a party of Sebandies to apprehend these daring offenders. The Daroga and sepoys surrounded the gang before daylight and would have apprehended the whole of it had not the escape of the greater part been facilitated by the opposition made to the police officers by the inhabitants of the village of Byrincha; the whole of whom armed with clubs attacked the Daroga's party wounded Abu a paik who accompanied him and carried off Soreefer another Paik of whom no intelligence have since been procured, and I have little doubt of his having been murdered, my suspicion being corroborated by the circumstance of a turban he wore having since been found stained with blood. In consequence of the opposition made by the inhabitants Imam Bux Shah, Newaz Shah and their principal accomplices made their escape, but....sixteen of the gang have been apprehended and committed for trial." Mr. Parr suggested the offer of a reward of Rs. 30 for the apprehension and conviction of each of the rioters and Rs. 50 for the apprehension of the accomplices of the murderer of Soreefa Paik. Government reported the facts to the Court of Directors, adding that "the numerous bodies of Fakeers and Sunnasies who formerly infested the northern districts of Bengal have of late been excluded from that part by the judicious position of the troops stationed in Purnea, Dinajpore and Rangpore."[2]

About a year later Government further reported "Since the date of the last dispatch the northern districts have remained entirely free from any incursions of Fakirs."[3] Again in January, 1802, the Vice-President in Council in a despatch to the Court of Directors observed that "acts of outrages have not been recently committed on that (Nepal) frontier."[4]

---

[1]Judicial Department (Criminal), Original Consultation, No. 11, dated 20th February, 1800.

[2]Judicial General Letter, para. 27, dated 5th September, 1800.

[3]Judicial General Letter, para. 6, dated 31st July, 1801.

[4]Judicial General Letter, dated 31st January, 1802.

Martin in his *History, Antiquities, Topography and Statistics of Eastern India* quotes Dr. Buchanan Hamilton (who surveyed some Bengal Districts from 1807—1813) regarding the Fakirs. "It was a number of adoptive Fakirs that some years ago assembled in great bodies in this (Rangpur) and the neighbouring districts which they plundered with the utmost barbarity and when pursued were wont to retire to Morung in the dominions of Nepal, where they found shelter and a sale of their booty ....Many still reside in Morung but their depredations have of late been on a small scale nor have they ventured for some years to enter this district in hostile array."[1]

Further on in his book, Buchanan Hamilton writes about the extermination of the Fakirs. "The horde of Fakirs which resided at Nidantara in the dominions of Gorkha and infested this district (Rangpur) and Dinajpur has of late entirely dispersed. The military guards placed on the frontiers prevented them from entering the Company's territory, so that when their ill-gotten wealth was expended, they began to pilfer in the neighbourhood. The Nepalese then set upon them, killed about forty and totally dispersed the remainder so that they retired to some more convenient station. This horde, I am told, besides Fakirs contained many Nagas[2] or snakes a description of rogues who from going quite naked close shaved and well rubbed with oil are so slippery that no one can seize them while they force their way with a dagger pointed at both ends and held by the middle."[3] It thus appears that by the early years of the Nineteenth Century raiding fakirs and sannyasis ceased to be a feature of the countryside of Northern Bengal.

[1] *History, Antiquities, Topography and Statistics of Eastern India* by Martin, Vol. II, p. 727.

[2] Dr. Buchanan Hamilton confuses "Naga" with "Nag," the latter meaning snake. The former is derived from "Nagna" which means "naked".

[3] Martin: *Op. cit.* Vol. III, p, 517.

CHAPTER XIII

Resident Sannyasis

THE Sannyasis from Upper India established monasteries in Bengal many years ago. The large and beautiful temple of Siva in charge of Sannyasis at Madhupur in Mymensingh district appears from its style of architecture and general condition of preservation to be more than 300 years old. The temple is on land dedicated to Siva and grants in support of it are dated between 1192 B.S. to 1200 B.S. [1785 to 1793 A.D.]. But the Sanads are renewed grants, given as usual on changes of succession. According to the author of *Gauriya Vaisnava Sects in Bengal*, the Vaisnava Naga Sannyasis of Upper India being hard pressed by the Saiva Nagas and Mundies came to settle in Bengal during the middle of the Sixteenth Century " like the wandering Jews." In a petition to the Governor-General in 1780, the zamindars of Parganas Alapsingh, Mymensingh, Jaffarshahi and Sherpur, stated: "Mohuntpory [Mohan Puri], Durnicunt Geer, Darby Geer, Bopaul Gery, Luchmungeery, Aumgery and other Sunnassis formerly entered our Pergannahs on the footing of mendicants and settled themselves by single persons at a time at the Rumnah where they behaved peaceably and carried on a little trade without disturbances to the ryots. The Sunnasses at the Rumnah in Coot behayer [Cooch Behar] who offending against Mr. Martin and other gentlemen having been put to rout by the mofassul Foujdary, it appears that part of them at different times joined Mohunpoory and the other Sunasses who had taken up their residence in our Purgunnahs. Several of the former are dead but 2500 of the latter are established in our Purgunnahs."[1] Ramna is a camping ground. In pargana Jaffarshahi there is one at Singjani now commonly known as Jamalpur. In Rennell's map (1766) it is shown as Sannyasigunj.[2] In another petition by them in 1783,[3] it is stated that Sannyasis who assembled in or about Behar [Cooch Behar] and created disturbances took up their residences in various places in this district and began to carry on business as Mahajans [money-lenders]. The Cooch Behar disturbances of the 1760's appear to be referred to.

---

[1]Proceedings of the Provincial Council of Revenue at Dacca, dated 12th May, 1780.

[2]A cantonment was established here in 1813 and a Battalion of Native Infantry (13th Regiment) appears to have been posted here in 1820.

[3]Proceedings of the Committee of Revenue, dated 17th April, 1783.

During the Muhammadan time, the zamindars were required to have guards on the frontiers of their zamindaries. In the *amalnamas* granted by the English Supervisor to the zamindars of Rangpur there is a stipulation for zamindars "to station guards and chowkidars upon the borders of their zamindaries." These guards were known as Barkandazes, and the posts were known as thanas, the frontier posts being called ' *Simanar thana* " implying a police contingent stationed on the frontier of a pargana. One such thana was at Chandrakona in the district of Mymensingh where up-country Burkandazes acted as guards. Posts of guards in thanas were " always filled up by up-country burkandazes under an idea of their possessing more bravery than the inhabitants of Bengal,"[1] and the " west country burkandazes who came to Bengal for employment had no other object in view than to get rich as fast as they can by lending money on usury and there were very general complaints against them for lending money at an exorbitant rate of interest and other violences."[2] So the nomadic Sannyasis found ready employment as Barkandazes under the zamindars of North and East Bengal. " The emmissaries of the predatory sannyasis that inhabit the province either hire themselves as Burkandazes or set up as petty merchants lending small sums to zamindars."[3] In Mr. Eliot's report of 1789, which will be referred to later on, mention is made of Domur Giri Sannyasi residing at Mathean as holding the appointment of Thanadar under the Raja of Dinajpur. The Sannyasis were also settled by the zamindars within their estates to fight with their rivals generally over possession of lands on the borders of their properties. In 1793 a large area of land was granted to one Chandan Giri Sannyasi in Subarner Char, an island in the Brahmaputra, by the zamindars of pargana Sherpur. This was probably to gain his support against the Raja of Putia, the proprietor of the neighbouring pargana Pukhuria, who later on in 1798 sent armed men to take forcible possession of the char. After the dismemberment of the Rajshahi zamindari of the Nattore family, pargana Pukhuria, appertaining to it was purchased by the zamindar of Putia. But the Nattore Raj claimed some villages known as Baje Taluk as having been granted as a taluk or tenure to Tara Devi, the daughter of Maharani Bhawani. The Sannyasis of Madhupur helped the Nattore Raj in maintaining possession of the taluk against the Raja of Putia.

The resident Sannyasis carried on business principally as money-lenders, and came into conflict with the Government for levying extortionate rates of interest and the atrocities committed to realise the loans.

With the establishment of Supervisors in the interior their oppressions were reported to the authorities at headquarters.

---

[1] *Further notes on the Rungpore Records* by Glazier.

[2] *Ibid.*

[3] Revenue Department, Original Consultation, No. 59, dated 20th January, 1790.

The Committee of Circuit framed the following rule in 1772 regarding adjustment of debts and rates of interest[1] which, however, was disregarded by the Sannyasis as will be seen later on.

" *Clause 18th.* That in adjusting the claims of old debts it shall be observed as a Rule that they bear no further interest after such adjustment but that the amount shall be payable by Kistibundee [instalment] according to the circumstances of the party, and as the rates of interest hitherto authorised by custom have amounted to the most exorbitant usury, the following rates are now established to be received and paid as well for past debts as on future loans of money; viz. on sums not exceeding 100 Rupees principal, an interest of 3 Rs. 2 ans. per cent. per mensem or ½ anna in the rupee. On sums above 100 Rupees Principal an interest of 2 Rupees P. Cent. P. Mensem. The Principal and Interest to be discharged according to the conditions of the bond and all compound interest arising from an intermediate adjustment of accounts to be deemed unlawful and prohibited; when a debt is sued for upon a bond which shall be found to specify a higher rate of interest than the established rates, the interest shall be wholly forfeited to the debtor and the principal only recoverable; and that all attempts to elude the law by deductions from the original loan under whatever denomination shall be punished by a forfeiture of one moiety of the amount of the bond to the Government and the other half to the debtor."

Hastings while taking vigorous measures against the itinerant Sannyasis proposed to take action against the resident Sannyasis as well. Writing to Laurence Sulivan on the 20th March, 1774, he says: "It is my intention to proceed more effectually against them by expelling them from their fixed abode which they have established on the north-eastern quarter of the province and by making severe examples of the zamindars who have afforded them protection or assistance."[2] In 1776, the Provincial Council of Revenue at Murshidabad deputed a Havildar, named Doolub Sing, in Pukhuria pargana to guard against the oppressions of the sannyasis. He reported to the Chief of the Council: "A sepoy was placed as sentry but a certain sunnassee regardless of the word was preparing to go to the Naib of the Pargunnah. An altercation arose between them and the sunnasse drew his sword and giving notice to the station (aukaurah), Lachmun Geer, Poorun Geer, Suckchain Geer and three or four hundred sunnassees entered the cutchery, illtreated Bulram and Jye Govind, Naibs of the Pergunnah, carried them to their station and confined them. As they were carrying them away, the sepoys endeavoured to prevent them but they beat the sepoys and carried off the Naibs for there are no orders for sheding the blood of the sunnassies. They will not obey the command of the Huzzoor and say that they

[1]Proceedings of the Committee of Circuit, dated 15th August, 1772.

[2]Gleig's *Memoirs of Warren Hastings*, Vol. I, p. 395.

are not under the orders of the Europeans. The sepoys will attend at the Huzzoor and give a particular account of the transaction."[1] Consequently, the Provincial Council complained to the Governor-General in Council forwarding a copy of the petition and adding that "upon receipt of which we immediately called upon the zemindar who further acquaints us that these Nagas or sunnassis who inhabit the Pergannah Pookereah, are of the same caste with those itinerants, who infest the country so frequently and receive and entertain them when they pass through the districts by the way of their habitation. These people who reside in Pookereah are money-changers and lend sums to the farmers and ryotts at a very exorbitant interest which the necessity of the inhabitants often obliges them to take at unreasonable rates. When the payment of these sums becomes due, it often happens that the borrower is unable to pay the debt owing to its being charged with so heavy a rate of interest. The consequence is that the Nagas all join and assist each other in compelling the inhabitants to pay their exorbitant demands and proceed to such extremities as are now complained of. We have taken this subject into our serious consideration and are but too sensible, Gentlemen, of the many evil consequences attending such a system. In the first place the practice of usury is expressly forbid by the regulations of the Governor and Council. In the second it is a most insolent disregard of the laws of Government to exercise force in support of a breach of its institutions. We have therefore come to a resolution to send a company of sepoys to demand the release of the Naib who is confined by the Nagas to prevent any loss arising to the revenue ; but as we are not acquainted with the force and strength of these Nagas or whether they will make any resistance, we have taken the precaution of directing the zemindar to send a responsible person on his part from Burnagore[2] under whose direction the sepoys are to be put; that this person be instructed, first of all, to make a formal demand of the confined naib and acquaint the Sunnasses that if they have any cause of complaint they must refer it to us and they shall receive ample justice ; but that we cannot or will not suffer any persons to be guilty of illegal violence or become judges in their own cause. That if they refuse to listen to these terms and to release the Naib to acquaint them he has directions to make use of the force which accompanies him. But that even if it should be necessary to proceed to this extremity he is first of all to inform himself as far as lies in his power of the strength of the sannasses ; and if he is in the least doubt of being able to cope with, to remain quiet till he can inform us of the circumstances and to obtain a reinforcement, for to attempt to

[1]Proceedings of the Provincial Council of Revenue at Murshidabad, dated 8th February, 1776.

[2]On the Bhagirathi in Murshidabad district, Maharani Bhawani of Nattore spent the last years of her life here and transacted the business of the great Zamindari of Rajshahi on behalf of her son Ramkrishna.

rescue the Naib without being equal to the attempt would make these people more insolent and expose the lives of sepoys. This resolution is confined merely to the circumstances that has given rise to it and is meant to procure the release of the Naib and so prevent any loss of revenue. But we are of opinion that the evils complained of by the zemindar extend much further than this act of confining the naib and that the remedy should be extended in proportion. The practice of usury is in itself ruinous to the inhabitants, the method of carrying it on by violence and in open defiance of Government and its laws is a great aggravation of the crime. Their connections with the sunnasses who are forbidden the country is another circumstance that makes them obnoxious to the laws of the Governor and Council, for which reason we think measures should be taken for extirpating these people out of the province. But as it is a matter of importance and may be attended with very serious consequences in the execution we have taken the liberty of addressing you on this subject and request to be honoured with your commands."[1]

In reply the Governor-General in Council sent the following orders: "We direct that you do immediately apply to the Naib Soubah for his warrant for the apprehension of the senassies who were guilty of the outrages complained of and to bring them to justice. If he shall require the assistance of a military force for this purpose, you will apply to the commanding officer at Burrampore for such a force as you shall judge necessary to be employed on this service under the orders of the Naib Soubah or such person as he shall appoint to execute his warrant, and upon every occassion of the like nature we desire you will observe the same rule without waiting for a reference to us. The rates of interest having been settled by the Public Regulations of Government must be enforced by the decrees of the Dewanny Adawalat which we hope will be always open to every complaint against such persons, as shall offend against this rule. We will not allow individuals to assume the right of attacking the persons of their creditors or exacting payment even of their just debts by violence and we direct that you refer every complaint against this species of oppression to the Fouzdary Courts that they may be tried and punished according to law of the same."[2]

In the meantime, the Chief of the Provincial Council received the following petition from Hustoory Sing, " the soubadar who was sent to apprehend the sunasses who had seized on the company's treasure" "Representing that he went from the Huzzoor and arrived on the 21st Faugon [about 1st week of March] in the Pergunnah Pukharia where we found that the sunnasses had before his arrival released Bulram Roy and Jye Govind Roy the naibs of that Pergunnah and fled. After the

[1]Proceedings of the Provincial Council of Revenue at Murshidabad, dated 8th February, 1776.

[2]*Ibid*, dated 1st April, 1776.

petitioner's arrival a man came on the part of the sunasses and promised that if they were assured of safety, Luchmeegeer, Poorungeer, Suckchingeer and the other sunnassies, would attend him. In consequence of this and the concurrence of the Naibs of the Pergunnah and Ody Chund Sircar who came from Burnagur on the part of the Maha Ranny Bowanny with the petitioner, he promised them safety and called them before him. The sunnasses accordingly two days after attended and after a great deal of dispute he caused them to refund the sum of 2000 rupees on account of the company's collections which they had taken by force." The Council sent directions to the Subedar "to oblige the three principal men to repair immediately to Moorshedabad that an enquiry may be made into their conduct regarding this affair."[1]

In November, 1776, Khawja Waun,[2] the dar-ijaradar [under-farmer] of parganas Mymensingh and Jaffarshahi, represented to the Provincial Council at Dacca that "on account of the disturbances from the Sennassies two guards of seapoys were sent as Negabans [guards] into the above Purgunnah. On the 22nd of the month of Cartic [about the first week of October] in the Bengal year 1183 [1776 A.D.], Mocheragcer and Roygeer Senassees belonging to Anundgeer and Koosilgeer Senasees residing in Pargana Pookryah [Pukhuria] and Budgerassoor came into the cutchery of the same Pargunnah beat Ram Persaud Vaqueel on the part of Kishenram Gomastah to the zemindar in danger of his life and carried him away by which means there is a deficiency of Revenue of Government. Ruttensing and Basoochan seapoys on guard opposed them whereupon the Senassees wounded the said Negabans with a sword, in consequence of this the seapoys who were wounded are come to Dacca."

The Provincial Council of Revenue at Dacca agreed to request the Chief "to give directions to the party in Momensing to keep themselves together and in case Mohungeer and Roygeer or indeed any other Sannassees who may come to make a disturbance at the Public Cutcherry they will endeavour to apprehend them and send them prisoners to Dacca." It was further resolved to issue the following proclamation in the Persian and Bengali languages to be affixed to the cutcherry in Mymensingh: "Whereas information has been laid before the Chief &c., Provincial Council of Dacca that sundry senassee merchants residing on the boundaries of Momensing and Jaffershy make a practice of lending money to the zemindars and ryotts and create disturbances by forcibly exacting payment of their loans with an exorbitant interest upon the same, this is, therefore, to give notice that such merchants as

---

[1]Proceedings of the Provincial Council of Revenue at Murshidabad, dated 1st April, 1776.

[2]An Armenian. The Armenians at Dacca who came to trade acquired large zamindaries in Mymensingh and Dacca districts.

lend money upon interest are prohibited from taking more than two P. Cent. P. Mensem and that any sums lent upon a higher rate of interest shall be forfeited to the Government. It is moreover declared that any Sonassy or other merchant, who shall attempt to use violence over the ryotts or the officers of collections for the recovery of his loans will be seized and sent a prisoner to Dacca."[1] The Provincial Council at Dacca also requested the Provincial Council at Murshidabad "to publish in Pookarah such orders as may be expedient for preserving the peace of the country and preventing an infringement of the Judicial regulations." The Council at Murshidabad replied—"we have issued a Perwanah to the persons complained of to appear before us to answer for their conduct and we shall take such measures as we hope will effectually prevent these merchants from transgressing the Regulations relative to the loan of money and from giving any further trouble on this account."[2]

The measures taken by Government against the Sannyasis checked the oppressions for some time. Moreover, the itinerant Sannyasis on whose help they counted so much received a check from the measures taken by Hastings and did not come to Bengal in large number for some years. A counter-effect was produced, and the zamindars sometimes tried to evade payment of loans to the Sannyasis. The Talukdars [tenure-holders] in Pargana Bungroolah under pargana Jahangirpur in Dacca district, named Mahamad Samun, Mahamad Monur and Mahamud Kawnul had taken a loan from Atabar Gir Sannyasi. In 1778 a decree was obtained from the Diwany Adalat ahd two peons deputed by the Adawalat "having seized the defendants they were rescued by their naibs with the assistance of the ryotts.......Representations were made to the Chief of the Provincial Council at Dacca who issued a Dustuk [warrant] accompained by two sepoys to seize the delinquents.......The sepoys (Moore Ram and Roop Sing) returned with the like success being treated ignominiously, the delinquents whom they also apprehended being wrested from their hands......." Thereupon the Provincial Council at Dacca issued a parwana on the zamindars of the Pargana "to produce the talukdars within 12 days and to pay the loans, in default the taluk will be sold by public outcry and made kauredge [separate] from the pargana."[3]

The oppressions of Sannyasis were renewed and the collection of revenue was threatened. Towards the end of 1778, a force of 32 sepoys under a Jamadar was deputed to pargana Alapsingh against "three Head Sanassies who for recovery of private loans and exorbitant interest

---

[1]Proceedings of the Provincial Council of Revenue at Dacca, dated 13th November, 1776.

[2]Proceedings of the Provincial Council of Revenue at Dacca, dated 13th November, 1776, and 2nd December, 1776.

[3]Proceedings of the Provincial Council of Revenue at Dacca, dated 9th April, 1778.

have promised to seize and confine the zemindars, naibs and agents and put an entire stop to revenue." In January, 1779, the Chief of the Council at Dacca recorded that "the cause of the balance of Rs. 2700 in Pargana Alapsingh was the disturbances raised by certain sannyasis, and that the party of sepoys sent against them have quieted them."[1] Revenue instalments being then monthly, arrears of revenue increased month after month. In a petition in June, Rudra Ram Sarma, the Zamindar of Alapsingh, represented to the Provincial Council that he has cleared the arrears of Government revenue by borrowing Rs. 40,000, "but part of the debt is due to Sennassies and Bheyleas whom being unable to repay, I have been necessitated to retire with my family and leave my Naib to manage in the Moffusil—but this he is unable to do from the oppressions of the sunassies."[2] The situation grew sufficiently serious for the Provincial Council of Revenue at Dacca to take action.

In 1780, a Regulation was passed lowering the rates of interest fixed by the rule of 1772. But the Regulation had no effect on the usurious Sannyasis. Some zamindars of Mymensingh complained to the Governor-General that "Sannyasis who immigrated latterly to their Parganas commit various acts of violence oppressing the ryots and taking improper interest in their concerns in trade by which they have unjustly brought many people into their debt not hearing our complaints, but arming themselves to the number of 5 to 700 people ready to fight and we being poor zamindars and unable to withstand such a body applied to the Council at Dacca in consequence of which forty or fifty sepoys have been sent at different times from thence to our assistance but these have also been disregarded by the Sunasses and several wounded, we can with difficulty live in the country from the above circumstances and have been obliged to remove our families to other parts." They prayed that "five companies of sepoys may be sent out to apprehend the said people and that two companies may be always stationed here in order to protect the country in future. That the Sunnasses may be also obliged to pay what debts they may appear to owe and we will discharge agreeable to kistbundy what may appear due to them." A list is given of 28 Sannyasi Sardars residing in various places of parganas Jaffarshahi, Mymensingh, Alapsingh and Pukhuria. Of these, twelve were residents of Singjani [Jamalpur] and its neighbourhood, Bazrapur.

The Chief of the Provincial Council at Dacca in placing the petition before the Council admitted that "some daring instances of violence were committed (in spite of stationing of sepoys) and even the zemindar of

---

[1]Proceedings of the Provincial Council of Revenue at Dacca, dated 6th and 12th January, 1779.

[2]Proceedings of the Provincial Council of Revenue at Dacca, dated 15th June, 1779.

a large portion of Alepsing was forcibly carried away without the limits of this [Dacca] Province into some perganna under Silberris nor was it till I applied to the Resident there and at the same time sent an additional number of sepoys and issued purwanas upon the neighbouring zemindars that his release could be obtained. The offenders could not be taken." But he argued that "the Sunnasses are not in open arms and must be esteemed more in the light of exorbitant money-lenders and oppressors of the people individually than as a body of marauders and though occasionally they may assemble, yet they do not continue in large bodies but are dispersed throughout the Purgunnahs. To send therefore an armed force would be of no avail. It might oblige them to retire for a short time but upon withdrawing the force they would doubtless return to a man, neither did he conceive there were sufficient accusation or at least proof to proceed against them as persons in rebellion to the Government." He suggested that "the mode which strikes him as most likely to restore order and good Government is to promulgate upon the spot the Regulations of Government for administering justice. They should in his opinion be each allowed an equitable hearing of every claim for debt he has to advance and all their dues faithfully discharged," adding that "this can only be done by deputing some person into the Purgunnahs who shall visit each and hear and decide all disputed claims of money lent. . . ."[1]

The Council gave further intimation of the action it had taken : "We now beg leave to lay before you in an Extract of our Proceedings the particulars of a commission we have thought it expedient to issue for suppressing the violent disturbances daily occasioned in the Purgunnahs of Momensing, Jaffirshahy, Alepsing and Shairpore [Sherpur] by the oppressions and extortion of the senassie money-lenders who are dispersed throughout those districts. . . . The growing evil required that somewhat should be immediately done to quiet the people and check the rapacity of the senassies, we have therefore ventured to depute Mr. Hatch into the Mofussil but as it will of course take sometime before that gentleman can reach the places of his destination and enter upon the enquiries, we hope to receive the sanction from your Honourable Board necessary to give validity to the decisions which he may pass during the commission before any Judicial process shall have been executed."[2]

The Board approved of the action. Mr. Hatch's minute detailed the various obstacles against adjustment of the loans and the arguments put forward by the parties. The Sannyasis claimed that " the bonds were executed by zemindars in the name of Head Sannyasis or Mohunts to obviate keeping a multiplicity of accounts, although the money

[1] Proceedings of the Provincial Council of Revenue at Dacca, dated 12th May, 1780.

[2] Revenue Department, Governor-General in Council, Original Consultation, No. 31, dated 30th June, 1780.

lent represented the joint property of themselves and their dependents. The payments made in part of the loans had ever been divided amongst the original bond proportionately to the share each had in the joint loans. Many of these people have received their whole dues and were deceased or living in distant part of the country, some who have still claims now lived with them. The difference arising from the mode of adjustment required by the zamindars will be a loss to the Headman, the Headman in many instances having actually paid their proportions to other sannyasis who joined in the ceremony who were absent and from whom money can not be recovered." The zamindars on their part claimed 'an adjustment of 12 years' accounts with the persons in whose favour the bonds were executed, the interest being calculated at rates prescribed by the Regulations'. Mr. Hatch concluded with the following remark: "The zemindars appeared to have wished another mode to have been established for the redress of the grievances. This delay in producing the accounts, the circumstances of their really being brought in as debtors to many of the Sannyasis even upon the mode of adjustment prescribed in the Purwanahs, together with their prayers of their original petition for an armed force to be sent after the Sannyasis and to remain in the lands to protect them, all conspire to form a conclusion that merely a civil prosecution was not their aim. The dues to the Sannyasis will, upon the adjustment I had adopted be the heaviest upon the Alapsingh and Sherpur Parganas." He, however, remarked on the contumacy of the Sannyasis. "Hitherto he had never been able to enforce the appearance of a single person residing in the Parganas to answer any complaint preferred to him. And many instances have arisen wherein they had practised various oppressions over the lands and persons of such who have entered their suit in the Adwalat and his officers put in fear of their lives whenever they have been deputed on business to their cutchery." He mentioned one instance when his attempt at an adjustment according to the then laws "occasioned a meeting of a body of Sannyasis, consisting of over 800 persons who declined giving any reply." He added that "persistence in this procedure would have ripened their present discontent into an open opposition and to take any coercive steps to oblige them to submit would not have been productive of any salutory effect against such numbers." He suggested as a remedy that "the Provincial Council should summon the Head Sannyasis to prefer any objection against this mode of adjustment, as taking any vigorous measures while the Sannyasis were in the Parganas would subject revenue and person of the zemindars to trouble."[1]

After Mr. Hatch's return, seven Head Sannyasis were summoned by the Provincial Council to Dacca. But they returned without leave of the Council and began to oppress the zamindars as before. On further

[1]Proceedings of the Provincial Council of Revenue at Dacca, dated 28th November, 1780.

complaints being made, Mr. Lodge was ordered by the Committee of Revenue to make an adjustment of accounts between the zamindars and the Sannyasis.

The trouble recurred later and in January, 1782, the zamindars of parganas Mymensingh and Alapsingh again petitioned "that the Senassies are at present assembled in such numbers in the parganas and are commiting such enormities that the zemindars, talookdars and officers of the collections are unable to stay to look after the Revenues. They have all been obliged to flee for safety, wherefore we request you will please issue orders to Mr. Holland to appoint 200 sepoys to quell these disturbances." The Committee of Revenue expressed its inability to supply a force as Mr. Holland, the Chief of Dacca, was unable to furnish a detachment and added that "the want of a military force to accompany Mr. Lodge has hitherto prevented him proceeding on the commission with which he has been invested by you nor can he venture to proceed in it without some force for his immediate protection as well as to give weight to his authority."[1] The Governor-General asked the Revenue Committee to direct Mr. Holland to furnish the sepoys required either from Dacca or "recalling from those places where they were least required." There was, however, still delay and another representation was received by the Committee from Ramjee Mull, the vakil on behalf of zamindars of pargana Mymensingh, stating that "the opposition and disturbances raised by the Sonassies in Purgannah Maimonsing and Zuffershahy are so considerable that if some steps are not immediately taken to check them, there will be great difficiency of Revenue." The Committee alarmed at this wrote to Mr. Lodge: "Having received repeated complaints of the disturbances committed by the Synasses in Momensingh and Juffershahy we must again repeat our directions to you to repair to those Purgunnahs without loss of time in order to effect the objects of your appointment."[2] In August, 1782 Mr. Lodge reported unfavourably on the conduct of the zamindars. "That the zemindars in their complaints have exaggerated matters I think cannot be doubted. How far they merit any indulgence, after it being proved they are considerably indebted to many of the Sannyasis even calculating the amounts at a rate of interest favourable to them and attempting to impose on Government in hopes of totally expelling their creditors from districts, I leave to your determination." He concluded—"I am confident the zemindars have ample means of discharging their present bond debts to the Sannyasis with a moderate interest thereon. Yet compel them to it they will purposely, I fear, fall into arrears of Revenue. Nothing but a strong military force residing here [Begunbari] constantly will prevent the Sannyasis committing acts of violence. And should even this force at any period be withdrawn, they will adopt measures to enforce payment

[1] Revenue Department, Original Consultation, No. 10, dated 5th February, 1782.

[2] Proceedings of the Committee of Revenue, dated 3rd June, 1782.

of what they deem themselves justly entitled to." The Committee of Revenue ordered him to follow the instructions given to Mr. Hatch and the general Regulations of the Adalat in making adjustments.

Mr. Lodge reported from his camp at Begunbari in October that "numerous obstacles were put forward on the part of the zemindars whose object from the commencement has been to prevent any investigation whatever ; it is evident they are using every stratagem to delay it as long as possible, their last resource will be purposely falling in arrears to Government." Mr. Lodge added that "the hopes of speedy payment will alone induce the Sannaysis quietly to acquiesce with a low rate of interest," and enquired "if the bonds and kistbundis now held by the Sunassies not forcibly obtained but voluntarily granted them by the zemindars are not to be the grounds on which a decision should pass." He concluded by saying that "the cold season being near at hand when these people [Sannyasis] are most likely to be troublesome and can easily be assisted with others of their own caste from the neighbouring districts as likewise from the Gonnessur and Gurraw mountains."[1] He wrote to the Committee of Revenue again in November submitting some statements regarding the debts of zamindars to Sannyasis and the nature of adjustments made by him. He gave the alarming news that "the following Munts [Mohunts] Maan Geer, Baabud Geer, Anund Gheer, and Bowanney Gheer, etc. of Dewangunge have now with them a force of 1200 Sannassies, report says 2000, distinguished by the name of Ramtaah and who I believe have no particular fixed place of abode, whether they mean to attempt any act of violence and oppression I have not been able to ascertain but it is unusual I am told for so large a body of these Sennasies being at this time of the year together. The demands of the above Munts are mostly on Alepsing. They paid no attention to my last summons but ill-treated the peons I sent." The Supreme Board in reply asked him to pay particular attention to the motions of the Sannyasies and if possible to discover the object they had in view.[2]

On Mr. Lodge's report the Committee in December, 1782, summarised the claims of both parties and asked for information regarding the number of Sannyasis and the force that would be necessary to enforce obedience to the adjustments arrived at by him.

The incident of the meeting of Sannyasis referred to by Mr. Hatch and the subsequent events during Mr. Lodge's residence at Begunbari are described vividly in a petition by the zamindars of parganas Mymensingh, Jaffarshahi, Alapsingh and Sherpur, sent in March, 1783, by Mr. Lodge to the Provincial Council at Dacca. "Mohunpooree [Mohan

---

[1] Proceedings of the Committee of Revenue, dated 29th October, 1782.

[2] Proceedings of the Committee of Revenue, dated 25th November, 1782.

Puri] and Hannooman Gueer [Hanuman Giri] resided in the Purgunnah Zuffershay where they carried on the business of Mahjens [mahajans, i.e., money-lenders] in a fair and peaceable manner. You are well acquainted with the circumstances of the disturbances created by the senassies formerly assembled in and about Behar [Cooch Behar]. The same body of Senassies some time after they came to Pinjerahpore [Piarpur], Bowaly, Muddoopore, Shearpor, Sungjay [Singjani], Bokainagar, Beerahdangah, Dewangunge, Cabulpore, &c[1] where they took up their residence and began to carry on the business of Majens. They exacted an interest from Rs. 6 annas 4 to Rs. 12 annas 8 per cent. per month, and if the interest was not paid regularly, they practised flogging and other violent means of which we complained to the Governor General in Council and the Council at Dacca was directed to do us justice. Mr. Hatch was in consequence deputed for that purpose to Baigonbary. Upon his arrival he sent the Sannyasis his orders and they appeared at the katchary. Mr. Hatch called for their accounts and told them they must calculate their interest after the rate established in the Regulations of the Adawlat and settle their account accordingly. Upon this they assembled in a body to the number of seven or eight hundred armed men and surrounding us, began to revile us with abusive language and Govinda Chand Choudhuri brother of Shyam Chand Choudhuri making some reply, one of the Sannyasis by name Mangueer seizing him by his commerband [belt] drew his cutter and threatened to stab him, but a number of people interposing he was prevented. Complaining of this violence to Mr. Hatch, he sent for the Sannyasis and they assembled before him with their arms and in a tumultuous manner said they were determined to force us to pay them the full amount of their demands and that he should not prevent them. Upon this declaration Mr. Hatch returned to Dacca. Some days after we also went to Dacca to complain to the chief and at our request he was pleased to summon the sannyasis before him where they submitted to a fallacious enquiry, but after a while returned into the Mofasil without leave and immediately began to exercise their oppressions upon us by confining and extorting from us bonds and Kistbondies for such sum as they choose to charge us with. Sometime after this transaction they came to demand upon the Kistbondies and upon their being very pressing on Roodur chand, he observed that as he was unable to pay his Malgoozari [land revenue] how could they expect to be paid just then. Upon this reply Bhootgeer of the Sannyasis drew his cutter and threatened to stab him but he was fortunately rescued by a number of people who interposed. We complained likewise of this violence and in consequence Mr. Lodge was deputed to investigate and settle our accounts. Upon his arrival at Baigonbary, he sent a Hookamnama [summons] to the Sannyasis and few of the lower sort made their appearance.

[1]All these places are in Mymensingh district.

Mr. Lodge settled our accounts with these by which it appears that they are considerably indebted to us. As none of the principal men appeared, Mr. Lodge sent a sepoy to summon Bowany geer one of them before him, but he would not obey. He likewise sent a party to bring Jagurnautgueer of Madhupur and Purungueer, Diryagueer, Dommergueer and Bonackgueer of Bowaly but not one of them would admit them. He likewise sent Bijinaut Amildar [Havildar ?] and 4 sepoys with a summons to bring Bhootgeer of Pinjirpur to whom they made known their commission and upon his declaring that he would not obey summons, they told him that they would not return without him unless he tore the paper or beat them. The said Sannyassee, being offended at this, took 40 of his companions with him and went with the said Amildar to the Katchary of Sinjony to Shyam Chand Choudhuri to whom he said 'You are indebted to us and therefore have been the cause of a gentleman's being sent and of the coming of these sepoys to summon us' and the said Chowdhuri answered that the gentleman was sent to enquire into the validity of their debts and he was about to return and that they would receive whatever should appear justly due to them according to that gentleman's investigation. The Sanassee then replied that he would not pay any regard to that gentleman's orders and that they would not obey a summons. After they began to abuse the sepoys who would have prevented their going away and drew Talwar upon them. Upon seeing this the said Choudhuri endeavouring to make his escape from his house was presently pursued by three Sannassees by name Ram Krishan Geer, Punjib Geer and Neelur Geer with drawn swords who overtaking him took from him his clothes and would have carried him off but they were prevented by a number of people who opposed them. The Sannassees after this went back to their camp and presently returned with 300 more and they are now collecting from all quarters so that their body will not shortly consist of less than two or three thousand armed men. We now understand that they have determined to sieze and confine us amongst the hills and deserts, on which account we have quitted our habitations and the care of our lands and revenue and are fled for refuge to Baigunbari. All the officers of the collections together with the taluqdars, farmers and ryots are alarmed and daily quitting their lands and houses, so that the collections are almost at a stand. We hope you will please to take this matter into consideration and punish the offenders that we may return to our house and attend to the collections and payment of our revenue and for this purpose that you will please to issue orders to Mr. Lodge and to the several chiefs and collectors of Jahanghirnagar [Dacca], Rangpur, Dinajpur, Purnia and Shilbaris [Bogra] to apprehend every Sannasie in their respective districts and send them to the Huzzoor and whence they form encampment, to disperse them to prevent their coming into the country in future; that you will order 200 sepoys for the protection of these Parganas; that you will direct the several zemindars not to permit any Sannassee to settle in their respective districts; that you will take from each of the zemindars a moochulka [surety bond] to that effect."[1]

Mr. Lodge gave the following account of the incident regarding Bhoot Giri: "Serving a summons on Boput (Bhoot) Geer Munt [Mohant], the Sennassies asembled to the number of 150, beat the peons and sepoys after which they and others surrounded the habitation of Samchurn Chowdry in Zuffershahy and became very turbulent. I have in consequence addressed the chief of Dacca for a reinforcement of 50 men but shall wait enforcing obedience to the summons as ordered, till favoured with your further commands. In the interim, however, no support which Sam Churn may require that I can afford him, shall be wanting for his protection. Boput Gheer by the accounts which the zemindars have tendered and in conformity to the mode of adjustment prescribed will have to receive from Alapsing near 9000 Rupees and from Momensingh &c between 5 and 6000. The general character of this Munt gave me reason to believe he would prove less refractory than many others from whence I entertained a hope of prevailing on him to accept 12 or 18 months' Kistbundee for such balance as should appear due to him upon a settlement of accounts, conceiving it would tend to induce the residue to acquiesce with similar terms; the opposition he has shown renders me apprehensive that the attendance of these people can be affected by no other mode than compulsion alone. I could therefore wish to be favoured with your orders as speedily as possible both in regard to this point and to the terms of payment the zemindars are to abide by." In another letter from Begunbari, dated 8th March, 1783, Mr. Lodge further stated that "the zamindars of these pergunnahs having been under the necessity of quitting their habitations and repairing to Bygonbarry for a refuge I have thought it expedient to apply to the Chief of Dacca for 100 sepoys."

In reply the Committee of Revenue wrote: "In consequence of the resistance of Boput Gueer to the summons you issued we should not hesitate to direct you to apprehend him if we were not apprehensive that the force you have with you is insufficient to enforce your orders. But as this appears to be the case and as the Chief of Dacca cannot furnish you with any force in addition to what you have, we must leave it to your own judgment to act in such a manner as your situation allows. If you deem the force you have with you sufficient you will in that case apprehend Boput Gueer and the others concerned with him in resisting the authority you are invested with; if not you will not attempt a measure which by proving ineffectual might tend to lessen the authority of Government but wait till the chief of Dacca can supply

[1] Committee of Revenue Proceedings, dated 17th April, 1783.

you with an additional force. We see neither hardship nor injustice in settling the mode of payment to the Senasseys by a Kistbandy of 12 or 18 months and direct you to adopt this measure where the amount of the demand requires it.... You will give every assistance and support to the zemindars against any attempt made by the Sennassies to oppress or injure them."[1] Mr. Lodge remained at Begunbari till 1784 and no other incidents of violence by the resident Sannyasis were reported for some years.

The resident Sannyasis, however, continued their exactions in other districts. Mr. Hatch, Collector of Dinajpur, wrote to Mr. McDowall, Magistrate of Rangpur, in December, 1788 : "In order to put a stop to any further coercion by the Sannyasis with committing outrages, as also to guard against the necessity for detaching of an armed force to disperse or apprehend them, I am of opinion that Durrum Gheer of Kisshenagar in the nine annas of Goraghat [known as Edrackpur] should be forthwith apprehended as being the person by whose directions, it at present appears the disturbance and illegal conduct of the Sannyasis assembled in Pergunnah Apole has been occasioned. In the interim I shall send a Peace Officer to endeavour and bring them to obedience, but eventually should lenient measures fail, I shall direct the detachment stationed at Silberris to march to Appole."[2]

Mr. McDowall replied : "Immediately on the receipt of your letter of the 3rd instant, I despatched two peons with a summons for Dussun Gheer and a perwanah to the public officers requiring them to apprehend him in case of his refusing to obey the summons." But when the Guru [preceptor] of Dharam Giri appeared, Mr. McDowall was favourably impressed and wrote recommending that he should be leniently dealt with and his loan realised. "This will be delivered to you by Soodisein Gheer Groo [Guru] to Dusur Gheer whom you requested me to apprehend but who I find has made his escape. This seems to be a respectable looking man and he has acknowledged his fault and throws himself upon your clemency, I hope you will let him off as easily as possible and endeavour to recover his money for him. He promises to behave better in future."[3]

Other accounts of the oppressions of the Sannyasis in Mymensingh and Bogra districts appear from the reports of Mr. Eliot who was deputed in 1788 as a Commissioner to settle the disputed boundaries between parganas Pooladosy and Jaffarshahi.

"Application having been made to me to release some persons confined by Domer Gheer Sannyasi residing on the attached land of

---

[1]Committee of Revenue Proceedings, dated 17th April, 1783.

[2]*Dinajpur District Records*, Vol. I, p. 176.

[3]*Dinajpur District Records*, Vol. I, pp. 179 and 187.

Muthean,[1] I am under the necessity of representing the conduct of this man for your orders.

"Sometimes before my journey to Muthean, the Vakeels of Sherpur submitted a petition to me, the purport of which was—Manugheer and Domergheer Sannyasis had threatened to seize and confine the sons of some respectable merchants residing at Sherpur if they were not paid some money said to be owing to them by the choudhuries of Sherpur and that these people were then on their way to perform some religious ceremony on the Ganges; they requested that I would send for Manugheer who resided at Bazrapur[2] within a quarter of a mile of the place I was at, and threatened him, otherwise the people would be confined and maltreated, which I refused and referred them to the proper Collector.

"At Muttean, the vakils of Sherpur made a second application and having undoubted proof of the people being seized by Domergheer and concealed in some part of the district, I then thought it my duty to afford the redress required, and in consequence sent for Domergheer, who excused himself saying he was ill and sent his chellas. But as I know too well how chellas were employed, in the evening I walked out and passed the Akrah where they were building a large Lutcha[3] of about 100 hauts, this I made them destroy first cutting up the string myself and then Domergheer came out of his house, but did not appear to be ill, and promised to come to the catchery the next day, but not appearing for 4 days under the same pretence of illness, I thought it time to see into the truth of his excuse.

"Returning from surveying the ground in dispute, I called at the Akrah with the guard of 6 sepoys I then had with me, with a determination to make him come to catchery if he was not ill. On returning to the Akrah I was surprised to see about 200 Sannyasis some

---

[1]Muthean was a village on the Manash. It is in Bogra district and on the border of the two parganas. The lands were attached by Mr. Eliot on the complaint of the zamindars of Mymensingh pargana that the Raja of Dinajpur "has dispossessed them of some lands belonging to Muthean in Zuffershahy and annexed to Pooladussay." Letter from Mr. Eliot to the Collector of Dinajpur, dated 27th November, 1788.

[2]A village near Jamalpur on the Brahmaputra. The site of the Akhara [monastery] has been partially washed away by the river.

[3]Long narrow dacoity boats prohibited by the Regulations in force at the time. Compare section XX of Regulation XXV of 1793, which re-enacted the previous Regulations. The section is as follows—

> "The Darogahs are to seize all boats built, used or transferred in opposition to the rules contained in this section.
>
> *First*—All persons are prohibited from building or making use of boats of the following denomination and dimensions without previously obtaining from the Magistrate the written authority hereafter directed. Luchas—Covids [cubits] length 40 to 90 covids; breadth, 2½ to 4."

armed, others with their spears stuck to the ground before them. On going towards the house where Domergheer was, they began to call out in a clamourous manner which made me give up all hopes of taking him by force at this time. As I was well aware from such conduct I should be opposed, I therefore desired to see Domergheer. He was then brought out and appeared ill, but not so bad as to be unable to come to the catcharry. To keep up appearance, I fell into conversation with them and by way of arrangement that they might not leave the place I made them to give my amla protection in the Akrah during my absence.

" The Jamadar guard I had with me might have seized him, though I am confident it could not have been effected without the loss of lives, on which account I have thought it most prudent to address your Board. At the same time I beg leave to inform you that this man is said to be a murderer and dacoit. Indeed this is the general character of all the Head Sannyasis residing in this country; their mode of murder is not immediate but produced by long confinement and maltreatment to extort payment of money they pretended to be owing to them. Domergheer holds the appointment of Jamadar (Thanadar) under the Raja of Dinajpur. There is besides another man on the attached land of Muthean called Omergheer, who by report is said to be as bad as Domergheer. I got intelligence of a Lutcha belonging to him which I fished up measuring 80 hauts and as there is an enmity between these two men, I made over charge of this boat to Domergheer as Tannadar, in hopes that Omergheer from his stigma would inform me where Domergheer keeps his boats which I dare say will be the case when I seized his boat." Mr. Eliot added—"Your justice and equity would adopt with the first convenient opportunity some measures to correct and suppress these flagrant extortions, oppressions and malpractices."[1]

The Revenue Board forwarded Mr. Eliot's report to the Governor-General and asked for " instructions in case a zemindar or landlord be carried off by Sannyasis as in the instance of Attia."[2] The Government orders suggested that the aggrieved party might obtain redress regarding usury, extortion and other malpractices by an application to the Court of Adalat. Regarding the Luchas, it was ordered that the Magistrates of districts should be communicated with.[3] In 1787 by the plan of Sir John Shore, rearrangements of districts were made and Mymensingh was formed into a separate district but the Collector lived at Dacca. The Collector was directed by the Revenue Board to live within his district, instead of at Dacca, to prevent the oppressions of the Sannyasis.

---

[1]Letter from Mr. Eliot to the Revenue Board, dated 29th July, 1789.

[2]Board of Revenue, Original Consultation, No. 21, dated 8th July, 1789.

[3]Revenue Department, Governor-General in Council, Original Consultation, No. 21, dated 6th July, 1789.

Mr. Eliot has left on record an interesting account of these Sannyasi money-lenders : "They call themselves fakeers, merchants, ryots but their real profession is that of usury and having the command of cash, they let it out at interest some in the most artful manner to escape the law. They give a sum, suppose 40 rupees which is put into the borrower's hands in the presence of witnesses and a note taken at the rate of 12 per cent. per annum payable in a month, but prior to this the party wanting the money agrees to give a douceur for lending the money. This is generally one-quarter of the sum viz 10 rupees, he is also to keep in pay a peon or Burkandaz at the rate of 8 or 6 rupees per month to see that he does not run away, so that in the end, the man gets only one half of the sum he borrows. Others let out their money from one to six and a half per cent per mensem, but this is a mere trifle considering the consequences ; the man shortly after may go to pay the money borrowed, and when behold he has a further charge for the drawing of the note, douceur to the moharar,[1] short weight,[2] batta,[3] shroffing[4] and takoorbary[5] charges ;[6] a new note is drawn up for all these additional charges, so that it becomes a debt of eternity from father to son. At the stated times the interest is demanded. If he has no cash, his child is confined to oblige him to pay the money and sometimes sold ; and as delay in payment is made, so is torture executed on the child though not so as to leave the mark on the skin, but by keeping the child from food, putting it out in the rain, or in the cold season in the dew all night or putting it in the stocks or in irons. I never went into a Sannyasi's house but I saw in the middle of the compound a large pair of stocks.

"The petty Sannyasis who cannot oppose a zemindar or a Gomastah assemble a party and take an opportunity to carry him or both on water and then confine them till payment is made in part and security is given for the rest and also until the expenses of the people assisting in their confinement is defrayed. Some zemindars on these occasions give up a part of their zemindaree to these usurers in the following manner. The Sannyasi agrees to pay a fixed revenue[7] yearly upon having the village for a certain number of years and to cancel his own debt from supposed profits but in reality by mulcting the ryots and seizing their grain.

---

[1]Fees to the scribe.

[2]Clipping of coins was common in those days.

[3]There was at that time a very large variety of current coins, viz., Arcot, sicca and Narayani rupees which differed in value and a discount was charged for exchange.

[4]Charge paid to the shroff.

[5]Payment towards the maintenance of temples.

[6]All these charges excepting for short weight and batta are still charged by money-lenders in Bengal districts.

[7]This was probably the origin of the taluks held by the Sannyasis.

"Others again have Akrahs, where they keep up a force of two or three hundreds of their sect, who go boldly to the cutchary and demand the money but seize whatever Revenue may be at hand and if not sufficient to discharge their demands, carry off the naib or zemindar or some of the Amlas by way of security till they are satisfied.

"Complaints of the daring acts and cruelties of these Sannyasis must have frequently reached the Collectors of these districts if these people had not contrived by acts of threatenings and severities to suppress them. The complainants themselves told me in excuse for not applying for justice and relief that the Collector's distance was too great for them to bear expenses ; that the Sannyasis if they learnt that they were absent with an intention of complaining would seize and maltreat their family from whom besides they cannot remain so long absent as to give time for summoning witnesses. In short, they always added 'I am a poor man, it was a debt of my fathers and though I have paid in twice or thrice over, yet I cannot go so far from my family for justice.' "[1]

In May, 1790, the Revenue Board submitted to the Governor-General a " letter and enclosures from the Collector of Rajshahy communicating a daring robbery perpetrated by the Sannassies in Pergunnah Pokarreah," and the Board drew the attention of the Governor-General to Mr. Eliot's letter regarding the conduct of the Sannyasis and suggested "the expediency of stationing a detachment in the parts of the country inhabited by them to prevent as far as possible, a continuance of the audacious acts of violence so often practised by them."[2] The Board in a further letter of 7th June, gave its opinion that "it would be most advisable to station the military force at or near Bygunbary in the Mymensingh Collectorship as the best station for the troops to be employed against the Sonassies."[3]

Complaints of exactions continued to come from Mymensingh. In September, 1790, Mr. Stephen Bayard, the Collector, wrote to Lord Cornwallis : " A sinassie sirdar one Ageet Geer with about 150 adherants established himself in a village called Bowally [near Madhupur] in the Purgunnah of Caugmarry in defiance of the authority of the zemindar, where he has for sometime past committed every species of violence and oppression upon the inhabitants, I have found it necessary in consequence of a complaint of a most daring murder sworn against him and from his resistance of the civil authority to apply to Captain Mackenzie for a detachment of 30 sepoys and a native officer to apprehend him and the other accomplices in his crimes.......The long impunity with which the Sinassies have committed their depredations in this district, has rendered them outrageously turbulent and so intimidated the zemindars that most of them rather passively bear their injuries, than risk their

[1]Appendix No. 14 to *The District of Rangpur* by Glazier.

[2]Revenue Department, Original Consultation, No. 58, dated 2nd June, 1790.

[3]Board of Revenue, Original Consultation, No. 29, dated 7th June, 1790.

resentment by complaint. I, therefore, consider it an indispensible duty to make the earliest examples of these disturbers of the peace and a favourable opportunity now offers to surprise Ageet Geer by the absence of part of his followers."[1] In the following month the detachment apprehended the Sannyasi Sardar, Ajit Giri and his accomplices without bloodshed. Some time later another detachment apprehended Joy Singh Giri, a Sannyasi Sardar "in consequence of several depredations being committed in a village called Rusgong near Parganah Torroff [Sylhet District]." In 1791, Mr. Stephen Bayard removed from Dacca to the present station of Mymensingh where he could exercise more direct control. In 1792, the Magistrate of Mymensingh reported that "the Sanassee merchants inhabiting the mountains bordering on the Pargannah Sherpur [Garo Hills] had not long since carried off the zemindars and had it not been for the vigilance and exertions of the Collector they would not have escaped with their lives."

The Collectorate records furnish further accounts of Ajit Giri. He acquired an estate (estate No. 4229 of the Mymensingh Collectorate) with a land revenue of over Rs. 1,000, which was named after him as Ajit Giri Sannyasi at the time of the Permanent Settlement of 1793. Ajit Giri, was acquitted of the charge of murder. Rup Giri was the most powerful ally of the Nattore Raj in the dispute with the Raja of Putia over the possession of Baje Taluk. He was removed from his chellaship by Ajit Giri Sannyasi for being unmindful of his religious duties and accepting service under the zamindar. Even to-day, people of those parts speak of "Rup Gir's lathi" symbolical of terror and power. He acquired considerable properties, and established the worship of a god, named Radha Govinda at Boali, which he endowed with considerable property. Numbers of rent-free Sibottars were also granted to him by zamindars. Rup Giri built buildings for his residence at Boali, known as Rup Giri's *bari* situated in the Madhupur Jungles. The following description of it is given in his *Sikar Kahini* by the late Maharaja Suryya Kanta Acharya, who visited the place during one of his hunting expeditions. "The place is a fortified one according to the then idea of fortification, viz, it is surrounded by double walls. There are four tanks—two in the inner appartment and two in the outer. Of the two tanks in the inner appartment, one was called Mathaghasa [head scrubbing]." The Maharaja remarks that this is a euphemistic name to denote the pleasure resort of the mistresses of the head Sannyasis. He added that " of the two other tanks one was used for drinking purposes by the Sannyasis and the other for bathing and they were closely guarded." Even to-day although it is in ruins there are sufficient indications of its being well-fortified, with one two-storied building for the residence of the Head Monk, and the other two-storied building for the accommodation of the Sannyasis. The

[1]Revenue (Judicial) Department, Original Consultation, No. 11, dated 8th October, 1790.

former building has no doors or windows facing the latter, which confirms the supposition of the Maharaja that it was also used as a Zenana for the mistresses. The one-storied building with one hall on the bank of the Mathaghasa tank is pointed out by the people of the locality as the summer resort of the Mohunt. In 1809, Rup Giri, Ram Krishna Giri and Gurudayal of Boali were implicated in a case of murder and the estate Ajit Giri Sannaysi was attached by order of the Collector. They were so daring that in 1811, according to the tahsildar, they murdered the two peons who were carrying the collections to the Mymensingh Treasury.

The resident Sannyasis in other districts also participated in criminal acts. Writing in 1808, Mr. Strachey, the third Judge of Circuit, refers to one Domeen Giri Gosain having lands in Bogra district and harbouring dacoits.[1]

The resident Sannyasis acquired considerable properties principally in the districts of Mymensingh, Rangpur, Bogra, Malda and Dinajpur. Instances have been given of oppressions and exactions practised by some of them in most of these districts. With the establishment of a more settled form of Government under British rule, their activities were checked. Legislation was passed against usurious rates of interest and other malpractices and the administration improved, consequently the number of resident Sannyasis declined and monasteries were deserted. Two revenue-free estates granted in 1759 and 1764 near Sherpur in Mymensingh district were resumed by Government as there were no heirs, the last owners having relinquished the religion of Sannyasis and gone away from the country leaving no information about their whereabouts or making arrangements for the worship of the gods established on the lands. In 1801 the Lakheraj land of Bhoopal Giri Sannyasi in mouza Nurrackpara [probably Barapara] in Pargana Sherpur was sold in liquidation of dues. Whatever properties now remain to the monasteries are only some of the rent-free lands dedicated to the gods established on them. Most of the revenue paying taluks have passed away to other persons either by private sale or by auction for arrears of revenue.

The oppression of the Sannyasis has left its mark in the land revenue of Mymensingh district. In 1788, in the proposal for the Decennial Settlement, the Collector of Mymensingh allowed deductions in revenue to the zamindars of pargana Alapsingh owing to "hardship suffered from the Sannyasis," and this deduction remains unalterable by the Permanent Settlement of 1793.[2]

---

[1] Appendix to the *Fifth Report of the Select Committee on the affairs of the East India Company* (1812).

[2] This chapter is mainly based on author's *Sannyasis in Mymensingh*.

The institution and practices gradually died away but we find to this day, in Eastern and Northern Bengal, relics of these earlier times in delapidated monasteries where Sannyasis still live on the produce of the endowed lands.

An endeavour has been made in these pages to give an idea of the life led by the Sannyasi and Fakir raiders in Bengal in the Eighteenth and in the early years of the last Century. Their incursions and depredations and the great havoc they committed in terrorising the people present only a chapter of the history of the period of which so little is known. It should not, however, be supposed for a moment that these Sannyasi and Fakir raiders, although belonging to the same sect, by any means represent that glorious band of real ascetics who will always be held in reverence and worship. There may be a falling off in attainments from their great predecessors but the ideals remain the same to this day.

APPENDIX.

মজনুর কবিতা।

শুন সভে এক ভাবে নৌতুন রচনা।
বাঙ্গলা নাশের হেতু মজনু বারনা॥
কালান্তক যম বেটাক্‌কে বলে ফকির।
যার ভয়ে রাজা কাঁপে প্রজা নহে স্থির॥
সাহেব সুভার মত চলন সুঠাম।
আগে চলে ঝাণ্ডা বাণ ঝাউল নিশান॥
উঠ্‌ গাধা ঘোড়া হাতী কত বোগদা সঙ্গতি।
জোগান তেলেঙ্গা সাজ দেখিতে ভয় অতি॥
চৌদিকে ঘোড়ার সাজ তীর বরকন্দাজি।
মজনু তাজির পর যেন মরদ গাজি॥
দল বল দেখিয়া সব আক্কেল হৈল গুম।
থাকিতে এক রোজের পথ পড়্যা গেল ধুম॥
বড়ই দুঃখিত হৈল পলাইব কোথা।
মন দিয়া শুন সভে লোকের অবস্থা॥
যে দিন যেখানে যা'য়া করেন আখড়া।
একেবারে শতাধিক বন্দুকের দেহড়া॥
সহজে বাঙ্গালী লোক অবশ্য ভাগুয়া।
আসামী ধরিতে ফকির যায় পাড়া পাড়া॥
ফকির আইল বলি গ্রামে পৈল হুড়।
গাছুয়া বেপারী পলায় গাছে ছাড়্যা গুর॥
নারী লোক না বান্দে চুল না পরে কাপড়।
সর্ব্বস্ব ঘরে থুয়া পাথারে দেয় নড়॥
হালুয়া ছাড়িয়া পলায় লাঙ্গল জোয়াল।
পোয়াতি পলায় ছাড়ি কোলের ছাওাল॥
বড় মনুষ্যের নারী পলায় সঙ্গে লয়া দাসী।
জটার মধ্যে ধন লয়া পলায় সন্ন্যাসী॥
থাল, লোটা লইল না পাইল উদ্দিশ।
টাকায় নালচে চিরে শিওরের বালিশ॥
আল্‌দা মাটী দেখি ফকির করে পোচ পেচ।
টাকার লাগি যে মারে বাক্সর খোট॥

মহাজনের সিন্দুক কাড়ি টাকা লইল ঝাড়া।
আগে লুটে বাড়ী ঘর পাছে আড়াপাড়া॥
ভাল মানুষের কুলবধূ জঙ্গলে পলায়।
লুটুরা ফকির যত পাছে পাছে ধায়॥
যদি আসি লাগ পায় জঙ্গল ভিতর।
বাজে আসি ধরে যেন লোটন কৈতর॥
বসন কাড়িয়া লয় চাহে আলিঙ্গন।
যুবতি কাকুতি করি কি বলে বচন॥
দন্তে কুটা করি বাপু ধরি হাত পাও।
অতিথ ফকির তোমরা দুনিয়ার বাপ মাও॥
ফকির হইয়া কর ছাগলের কাজ।
পরিণামে দুঃখ পাবা ঈশ্বর সমাঝ॥
সুজন ফকির হয়ে শুনি হস্ত দেয় কাণে।
অধম ফকির হাত বাড়ায় যৌবনে॥
পরিণাম নাহি শুনে করয়ে শিঙ্গার।
দৌড়িয়া যাইতে কাড়ি লয় বস্ত্র অলঙ্কার॥
লাজে নাহি কহে কথা রাখে গুপ্তভাবে।
ধর্ম্ম সাক্ষী করি তারা মজনুকে শাপে॥
তারা বলে ঈশ্বর এহি করুক।
মজনু গোলামের বেটা শীঘ্র মরুক॥
কোন্ দেশ হৈতে আইল অধম।
ইহাকে ভারথে থুয়া পাশরিছে যম॥

ইতি মজনুর কবিতা সমাপ্ত।
সন ১২২০ সালের ১৪ই কার্ত্তিক।

শ্রীপঞ্চানন দাসস্য।*

Rangpur Sahitya Parishad Patrika, 1317 B. S., Vol. V. Special number—*History of Sherpur*, pp. 79-80. The reference was kindly supplied by Mr. P. C. Sen, Pleader, Bogra.

For "Sannyasi and Fakir Raiders in Bengal"

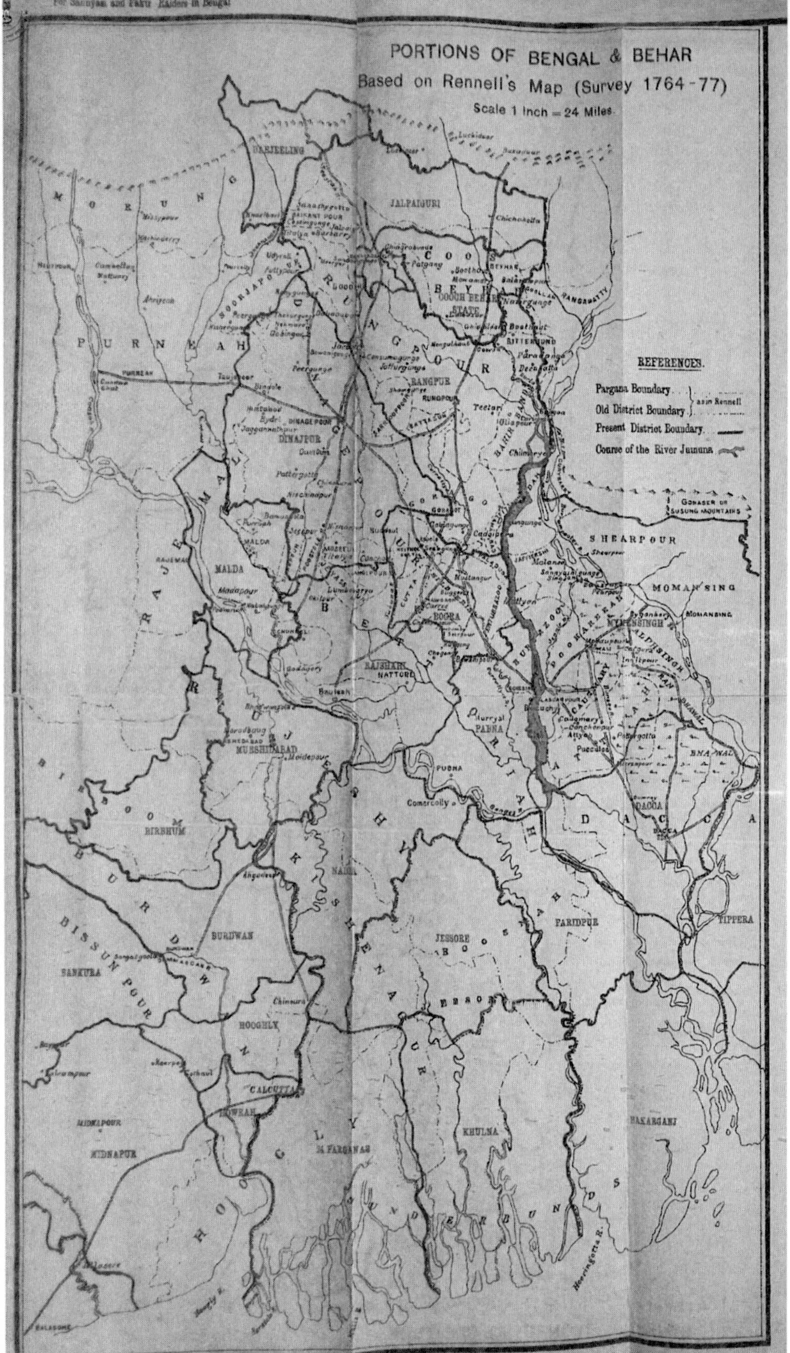